Predicting Hotspots

Predicting Hotspots

Using Machine Learning to Understand Civil Conflict

Atin Basuchoudhary
James T. Bang
Tinni Sen
John David

LEXINGTON BOOKS
Lanham • Boulder • New York • London

Published by Lexington Books
An imprint of The Rowman & Littlefield Publishing Group, Inc.
4501 Forbes Boulevard, Suite 200, Lanham, Maryland 20706
www.rowman.com

Unit A, Whitacre Mews, 26-34 Stannary Street, London SE11 4AB

British Library Cataloguing in Publication Information Available

Library of Congress Cataloging-in-Publication Data Available

LCCN 2018945966 | ISBN 9781498520676 (hardback : alk. paper) |
ISBN 9781498587006 (electronic)

∞™ The paper used in this publication meets the minimum requirements of American National Standard for Information Sciences—Permanence of Paper for Printed Library Materials, ANSI/NISO Z39.48-1992.

Printed in the United States of America

Contents

List of Figures

Acknowledgments

My father was a captain in the Indian merchant marine who exercised his privilege to carry his family on board ships he commanded for the Scindia Steamship Company. My travels broadened my horizons even as both my parents participated in my home (ship?) schooling. These experiences were not universally happy though. One of my earlier memories was of visiting Chalna port in newly liberated Bangladesh. Bangladesh had just seen tumultuous civil conflict. Prisoners of war were still being repatriated, postwar aid was trickling in, and trade was beginning to restart. My father's command was presumably part of all this. Those details were beyond me at the time. In my memory, we had taken the boat from the anchorage to shore. We were walking down a path along a football field. I don't remember why. But I do remember a mother carrying the lifeless body of a boy my age and screaming, "why?" That scream still reverberates with me. This book is dedicated to those mothers who scream, "why?" in the hope that it can help eliminate some of this pain in the future.

Acknowledgments:

1. My parents Mrs. Jayashree Basu Choudhary and Capt. Ashim Kumar Basu Choudhary.
2. My philosopher guide Partha Sengupta.
3. My history teacher, Ms. Raktima Dutta, who understood my passions and opened up the possibility of economics as a field of study.
4. The two people who taught me economics—Professor John Conlon and Professor William F. Shughart II.

5. My children, Oishani Basuchoudhary and Saara Sen Basuchoudhary, who will be part of a better future and have inspired me to strive to be worthy of that promise.
6. My wife and co-author, Tinni Sen, who encouraged me to quit whining about what cannot be and go for what can.

Atin Basuchoudhary

James T. Bang thanks and dedicates this book to his family: Ryan, Evan, Dilan, and Jane.

To Jenny from John.

Tinni Sen dedicates this book to her parents Professor D.K. Sen and Mrs. Subhadra Sen.

Preface

Steven Pinker in his masterful *The Better Angels of Our Nature* makes the compelling argument that we may be living through some of the most peaceful times in human history and possibly prehistory. So, why this book? Let us ignore the incessant and depressing notifications of violence from various news media outlets and "friends" on our wired devices for a moment and look at some stylized facts. The Center for Systemic Peace, a nonpartisan think tank, has an informative chart on its website (Center for Systemic Peace, 2016) that shows global trends in armed conflicts from 1946 to 2015. Over this period, interstate war declined steadily but societal warfare (civil war) increased steadily until the 1990s, then declined. We report a similar trend in our dataset in Figure 1. Further, the incidence of civil war throughout this time was much higher than that of interstate war. At the same time, the most recent data on the website shows that at least 10% of all states are in some kind of conflict. The number of terrorist attacks also appears to be increasing since 2010, after showing steady declines since 1980 (Bang, Basuchoudhary, David, and Mitra, 2016). Moreover, the proportion of noncombatant deaths to combatant deaths remains quite high. Possibly, as a consequence, close to 65.3 million people have been displaced from their homes. To put this in perspective, that's almost double the population of Canada. Thus civil conflict, Dr. Pinker's optimism notwithstanding, remains a peculiarly human tragedy.

In this book, we set out to *predict* civil conflict so policy makers can reduce human suffering. We do not care to be caught in the many controversies over the precise definition of civil conflict: the finer distinctions between what constitutes a guerilla war and an insurrection, for example. Therefore, we adopt a broad definition of conflict, one that includes (conflict-related) deaths from political wars, ethnic wars, regime change, genocides, and politicides, based on data from the Political Instability Task Force (PITF). If any one

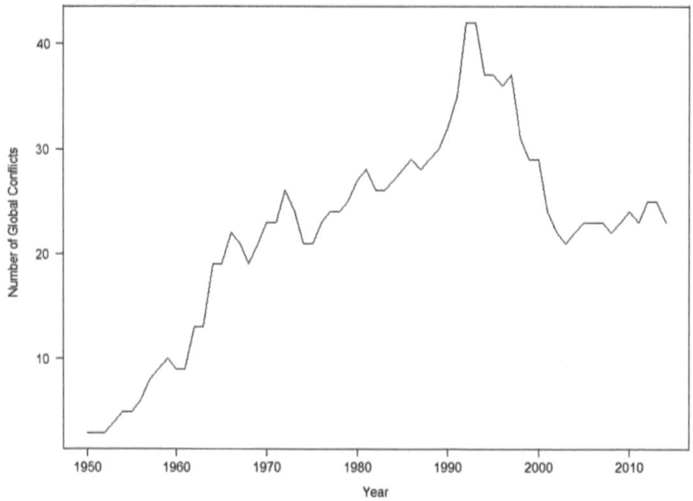

Figure 1 The Number of Conflicts Over Time.

of these events happens in a country in any given year, PITF considers that country to be in conflict. The PITF uses certain death thresholds to categorize whether a country is in conflict, but they make no distinctions on whether, for example, those deaths were the result of an insurrection or a terrorist attack. In addition, PITF considers a country to be in conflict if there was an adverse regime change, or if the state targeted a group because of its communal or political characteristics. Thus, our definition of civil conflict includes almost all aspects of conflict, short of interstate war.

We need to understand the driving forces behind conflict to prevent or mitigate it. To this end, we assemble a dataset that includes a wide range of economic, political, social, demographic, and geographic variables comprising the usual suspects in the conflict literature. We then use Machine Learning techniques to find links within these data that gives us the best predictions. Machine Learning algorithms leverage this dataset to predict the likelihood of any conflict over a five-year period. For example, we use data from 1990 to predict whether conflict occurs in the period 1991–1995. These give us the material to begin shaping a predictive theory of conflict.

There is a varied literature devoted to conflict. This literature, though vast, does not yield a unique theory of conflict. Of course, it is possible that different conflicts happen for different reasons, so that there can be no one theory of conflict. Nevertheless, so far, no one has asked whether there is a unifying theory of conflict, or even if there are a few "umbrella" theories. We write this book to address this question. We introduce Machine Learning to help understand whether there can even be a unified theory of conflict. Thus, one of our book's themes is to show how Machine Learning can help choose between competing models of conflict. Of course, if no choice is possible then we are left with the conclusion that conflict may not have unifying principles. On the other hand, if we can identify some unifying principles of conflict by identifying a particular class of theoretical models as having greater predictive power than others, we can develop the basis for a causal and predictive theory of conflict. This is not just an academic issue: Policy makers can benefit from predictive models of conflict. They are, above all, concerned about the effect of a policy change on the likelihood of conflict. It makes sense that they would like to choose a policy lever that has the biggest impact on conflict.

This brings us to our focus on prediction: We want to identify variables that best predict conflict. We do not use the word prediction lightly. Most statistical models of conflict try to identify the correlates of conflict and, in some cases, try to tease out causal patterns. However, none truly predict conflict by asking the following question—how well do the identified correlates of conflict perform in identifying conflicts that *have not yet happened*? A reasonable answer to this question would identify factors that ought to be part of a unified theory of conflict. Such an answer could therefore jumpstart investigations into the causal patterns among these factors. After all, a theory is no good unless it can predict, that is, *have some generalizability*: A theory of gravity that cannot predict how gravity on the moon is different from gravity on earth is no theory at all. A theory of conflict that cannot predict what factors will lead to conflict as a matter of course is not a theory either. Moreover, as we have noted earlier, policy makers want to know the impact of their policies. At worst, they would like to eliminate policy levers—variables—that do harm, and at best they would like to implement policies that have the biggest impact on reducing death and dislocation from conflict. Obviously, the effect of a policy is felt in the future. Thus, from a policy-making perspective, predictability is a key feature. We therefore argue that prediction should be at the heart of any scientific investigation into identifying underlying principles of conflict. Predictability remains the true scientific test of a theoretical model and it is the key to good policy as well.

How do we get a sense of a good predictive model? After all, it is impossible to test for the validity of a model by comparing it with something that has not yet happened. We can however simulate the comparison by dividing any dataset into two parts. We build an empirical model by training it to perform well in one part of the data. Then we see how well this trained model performs in the other dataset. If the trained model does not perform well out of sample, then clearly it is not generalizable at all. And, if it is not generalizable, it cannot be predictive. At that point, the variables used to build the empirical model are suspect, as are the theoretical models that suggest these variables matter. In short, this approach can help eliminate non-predictive variables and therefore potentially non-predictive theoretical models. The predictive variables that remain after this process should then be explored for causal links rooted in theoretical models.

To summarize, if there is indeed any general theory of conflict, building theoretical model structures and empirically testing those structures should be a comparative process where predictability is the margin of comparison. This process can identify the best predictive theoretical models. These validated "best" models predict well out of sample, that is, they are generalizable.[1] Only the most validated and therefore generalizable theoretical models can wear the mantle of "theory." We suggest that this process of cross-validation should become a scientific standard in the literature on conflict in particular, but more generally, in all data-based social sciences.

The approach we suggest leaves us open to the charge of data mining. If the charge is that we let cross-validated evidence guide us toward a theory of conflict, we are guilty. So are Galileo and Copernicus. They started with an Aristotelian theoretical model of the universe. However, that model did not predict the observed movement of the planets. Those observations changed the theory of earth's place in the universe—and history. We do not claim the hubris of changing history. We merely suggest that scientific validation should guide conflict theory. In any case as scientists, Galileo and Copernicus are good company. Indeed Ostrom (2000) makes a similar case for developing a theory of collective action from experimental results and real-world observation.

Our goal, then, is to identify the viable and consistent predictors of conflict. In the process, we hope to identify a unified theory of conflict that policy makers can use to understand and predict conflict. In short, we want to predict conflict in order to prevent it. We use Machine Learning technology to meet these goals.

Existing cross-country analyses of conflict often provide conflicting results, even as the literature appears to converge on a few consistent correlates of war. These conflicting results are rooted in inconsistencies in the way variables are interpreted, in coding and measurement problems, as well as ad hoc specifications developed from competing theoretical models. Further, most of these empirical studies do not provide any evidence on which of these competing theories best explain conflict. Thus, clear theoretical causal links supported by evidence remain elusive. We use *theoretically agnostic* Machine Learning techniques to identify predictive patterns. Machine Learning identifies these predictive patterns by first identifying modeling technologies that are best at out-of-sample prediction. Some of these technologies can also identify the variables with the most predictive powers. In the process, they eliminate those that have weak or low predictive powers.

If we are to use a theoretically agnostic framework, how do we decide which variables to include? We choose an inclusionary method: we use all the variables that are in competing theoretical models. This has an added benefit: since Machine Learning techniques consistently eliminate some variables as being not very predictive, we should also eliminate the theoretical approaches that suggest those variables matter for conflict. To reiterate, in our telling, non-predictive theoretical models cannot really be theories of conflict.

Conflict is rare. This may bias estimated marginal effects from traditional parametric estimation techniques. It may also make it difficult to interpret the meaning of the marginal effects when the explanatory variables are correlated with one another. For example, parametric models may be over-fitted and still return significant marginal effects for explaining conflict. Moreover, parametric estimates are also misleading because of the tangled causality between conflict and its correlates. This tangling happens for a couple of reasons. Often causality may run both ways: Low GDP may cause conflict but conflict may also result in low GDP. Further, there may be an omitted variable that affects both GDP and conflict.

The conflict literature is particularly rife with such endogeneity problems, leading to biased and inconsistent parametric estimates of the marginal effects of explanatory variable on the likelihood of conflict. In fact, as we will allude to later, even advanced econometric techniques designed to mitigate these problems fail to solve them largely because the parametric estimates generated in these models are sensitive to model specifications. These parametric estimates therefore do not provide clear guidelines for deciding which variables matter for conflict. However, efforts to identify the marginal effect of the change in one variable or another have spawned a veritable small cottage industry in academic papers. While this may be part of the "sausage making" process in science, it offers scant comfort to the policy maker. Policy makers cannot be confident of the effect of a policy change in one or the other variable on the likelihood of conflict. All this suggests the need for a mechanism to search for a more parsimonious list of explanatory variables.

As noted earlier, Machine Learning techniques can develop parsimonious cross-validated lists of predictive variables. We delve into this variable-winnowing process at two levels. First, we use factor analysis methods to extract the variation from different, correlated variables, to identify specific classes of institutional variables. For example, contract enforcing economic institutions and democratic accountability share the characteristic that together they make state institutions inclusive and credible. Factor analysis can extract these elements of commonality. At the second level, we use various Machine Learning technologies to identify the most predictive among these factors and other variables, and winnow out the non-predictive variables. Together, these address some of the over-fitting problems and help policy makers identify *predictive* policy levers. At the same time, to the extent that we do not estimate parameters, the issue of biased or inconsistent parameters does not arise freeing us from some of the econometric problems raised by endogeneity and the rarity of conflict. Therefore, to the extent that these techniques develop a parsimonious list of *predictive* variables, we can offer the academic a cross-validated sense of which theoretical models predict well, and therefore light a path toward a potential unified theory of conflict. Moreover, we can also offer the policy maker some science by giving them a validated way to distinguish between the impacts of different variables on the likelihood of conflict.

We do not estimate traditional marginal effect parameters in this book. The lack of marginal effects would be a problem for the policy maker since she needs to know not only if a policy lever has any impact on the likelihood of conflict, but also the direction of impact. Parametric estimates are valuable precisely because they can give the policy a sense of both the magnitude and the direction of the policy effect. Not all is lost though. Machine Learning algorithms can also generate partial dependence plots (PDPs) that relate how changes in any single variable affect the likelihood of conflict. In fact, these PDPs are more informative than point parametric estimates. PDPs also trace out how the likelihood of conflict can change with changes in one of the covariates of conflict. Thus, they give a detailed trace of a "marginal effect" and can identify nonlinear relationships between the changes in a covariate and the likelihood of conflict. This too is useful to a policy maker.

Spotty data, particularly from conflict-torn regions, plague the conflict literature. Further, much of the data have subjective roots and may suffer from measurement errors. The predictive element of Machine Learning techniques helps address some of these concerns as well. We use sophisticated and *validated* data imputation techniques to plug data gaps. This process allows us to retain much of the "good" information we would have thrown out because of missing observations. Moreover, poorly measured variables should not be able to predict well. Therefore, if variables predict well, we should be confident about the lack of measurement errors.

Our discussion here may read like a breathless love affair with Machine Learning. We are very aware of the limitations of Machine Learning. Foremost, predictive models are not the same as causal models. Our models say absolutely nothing about causation. What use, then, are our predictions? Even though we cannot identify or establish causality, our results help the investigator identify potential pathways for causality through *further* theoretical modeling and traditional econometrics. We suggest that Machine Learning ought to be part of an *iterative* process toward a unified predictive theory of conflict. Nevertheless, it is only one part of the process. Therefore, the process needs theoretical modeling and traditional econometrics. We describe a first step in this iterative process in what follows. We hope others will see this book as a first step, a useful beginning, of a process leading toward a unique predictive theory of conflict.

The book proceeds as follows: chapter 1 presents an overview of the literature on conflict, chapter 2 describes the Machine Learning techniques we use, chapter 3 lists and describes all our variables, chapter 4 talks about our data; the tools we used to prepare the data and the reasons behind such preparation, chapter 5 includes details on how to use *R* to predict conflict, chapter 6 discusses our methodology and results, chapters 7 and 8 discuss how our results fit with the seminal models of conflict and the drilled-down microeconomic models of conflict theory respectively, chapter 9 uses Partial Dependence Plots (PDPs) to sort the variables that predict conflict, and to reconcile them with the models of bargaining failure arising from commitment problems, and, finally, in chapter 10, we attempt to bring it all together by developing a framework for a predictive theory of conflict. Those who wish to pursue a nontechnical reading may safely skip chapters 2, 4, and 5.

NOTE

1. Indeed, validation by definition means that the model predicts well out of sample.

Chapter 1

A Brief Overview of the Literature on Conflict

Internal wars have not only become more persistent, but also more commonplace (Blattman and Miguel, 2010). It is not surprising, therefore, that there have been numerous studies and analyses of conflict across both the political science and economics disciplines that try to understand conflict. Such studies are more *models* of conflict than *theories* of conflict since there is a piecemeal aspect to them. This becomes apparent when one reads some of the comprehensive and definitive works on conflict—Sambanis (2000), Blattman and Miguel (2010), and Coyne and Mathers (2011)—among others. All of these works are organized in ways that make it evident that there is not one, or even a few, theories of conflict under whose umbrella one can organize the existing theoretical and empirical works, whether it be predation versus production, greed versus grievance, or rational versus Irrational models of conflict. Each of these demarcations speaks more to the modeling framework adopted than the theories they present. The task, then, of presenting a comprehensive account of the existing models for predicting conflict is at best unwieldy and at worst challenging. We take it on in this chapter.

First-generation models of conflict focus their studies on understanding ethnic conflict insofar as it occurred in response to economic modernization, that is, on the way social groups responded to changes in the structure of the economy and to growth (Sambanis, 2002). Newman (1991) and Congleton (1995), among others, study how rapid growth can cause or intensify social conflict. If society organizes along ethnic lines, it can save on information and enforcement costs in business and other endeavors. This 'ethnic network' idea that appears beneficial to society by providing a way to increase trust and cooperation can become exclusionary mechanism in times of growth when competition for resources may intensify. In such situations, minorities can be left out, thus increasing resentment, and perhaps pushing them to violence as the only way to redress the situation. However, although these models of conflict do present one possible explanation for conflict, they cannot account for incidents of ethnic conflict when there is no rapid economic growth, or when there is growth in a homogenous society.

Second-generation models of conflict can be categorized variously, but perhaps the best way to understand their evolution is to think of them as models of rational choice. The motivation behind such models is to think of why war ever occurs when it is so risky and expensive. What is the rationality behind choosing war when bargaining is cheaper? How is it ever a rational choice? Fearon (1995) presents three scenarios for a rational war: asymmetric information, commitment problems, and indivisibility issues (Blattman and Miguel, 2010). To this, we add the models that explore the continuation of conflict as a rational choice, the choice between models of greed versus grievance, and finally 'irrational' models.

ASYMMETRIC INFORMATION

The presence of asymmetric or incomplete information on preferences or strategies could be one way to account for a rational party choosing war over peace. In other words, conflict ensues as a direct result of asymmetric information. The simplest stories are ones where each party lacks the information about, say, the military strength of its opponent. However, this kind of lack of information is not likely to lead to conflict since the warring factions could find out that information, or it could be revealed on the battlefield. So, the existence of asymmetric information is not as likely to increase conflict as the presence of a mechanism that deliberately impedes the flow of such information would.

Such a mechanism could be informational asymmetry because of deliberate misrepresentation (Fearon, 1995). Bargains cannot be reached because there exists information that is misrepresented. For example, if party one to a conflict lets party two know its true military strength, it will be at a disadvantage. So, it misrepresents that information.

Esteban and Ray (2001) develop a model with multiple players. They show that when there are as few as four parties, pareto improving social decisions are not possible when each player has imperfect information about the other's cost of conflict, even if this lack of information is very minimal. In their model, information asymmetry among multiple agents is the direct cause of conflict rather than a force exacerbating the chances of war.

According to Hirshleifer (1995) conflict is the result of "three interacting determinants: *preferences*, *opportunities*, and *perceptions*" (Hirshleifer, 1995, p. 172, *Emphasis original*). Conflict is the rational choice when the parties involved have different preferences resulting in differing perceptions about the expected benefits of violence versus the costs. This makes it difficult to bargain for peace. In his model, two agents are presented with the decision to acquire or share a scarce resource. They can do so through a peaceful exchange or through war. Conflict is expensive, requiring the expenditure of resources, while bargaining is not. Clearly, this modeling approach makes war less desirable. However, if, because of asymmetric information, the agents incorrectly estimate each other's costs of war, bargaining becomes harder, and conflict may ensue.

Chassang and Padro-i-Miquel (2009) look at the effects of temporary exogenous shocks on conflict in the presence of incomplete information in a poor country. Their model suggests where the 'pie' is small, negative income shocks increase the likelihood of conflict. The shock reduces the current opportunity cost of fighting not only because the pie is now smaller, but also because the pie may become bigger in the future, and that's what the players care about. Such a shock, for instance a drought, in a nation where the players have incomplete and differing information about the state, exacerbates fears. In fact, players in this model who attack first obtain the entire spoils. Therefore, conflict is the most likely outcome. This model explains the possible mechanism behind two robust empirical findings: that conflict mostly occurs in poorer countries, and that negative income shocks are correlated with conflict.

The political science literature studies the mechanism by which the spoils of war are shared between a government and a rebel force as a way to understand conflict. The lack of transparency in the workings of the government, and therefore an accurate knowledge of the size of the spoils of war, introduces asymmetry into the story.

Dal Bo and Powell (2009) propose a model of asymmetric information wherein the government offers a portion of the existing resources to the opposition. Although the opposition has an idea about the average size of the pie, (i.e., whether times are good or bad), it does not know the actual size. Therefore, it will occasionally refuse the offer and engage in conflict to deter the government from lowballing the offer. In this situation, conflict hurts both players by reducing the spoils of war. Knowing this, if the government signals the true value of the spoils to the opposition to avoid an inefficient war, (say by giving them positions in the cabinet), this becomes a commitment problem, since the now more powerful opposition my renege and ask for a higher share.

COMMITMENT PROBLEMS

Dal Bo and Powell (2009) model incomplete information in the context of a commitment problem. However, conflict occurs even when there is complete information, as long as there are commitment problems. Let us now turn to those models that study the mechanisms by which commitment problems increase conflict. We could think of those as ones that model commitment problems under three different circumstances. First, when parties to a conflict agree to a transfer as a condition of peace. In such cases, there is an incentive to renege on the transfer. Second, when the long-term benefits of war outweigh the short-run costs. And, finally, when conflict is over a limited resource the acquisition of which would increase military or strategic strength.

Fearon (1995) posits a rational choice theory of war in the Political Science literature where commitment problems cause civil conflict. In his model, commitment problems lead to civil conflict under three scenarios: if there is a first-strike advantage, if preemptive war prevents losses in the future, and if the bargaining is over actual resources that can increase military power. In all these situations, the benefits from reneging on the commitment outweigh the costs. An advantage from the first offensive, such as the situation with two gunslingers and no sheriff, occurs when states can gain further power by being the first to attack. In such cases, the gains from defecting outweigh the benefits of a bargained peace. Second, in cases of a dynamic interaction, if the post-war situation puts one state at a further disadvantage if it loses, it has an incentive to engage in preemptive war, as long as the costs of war are less than the expected costs of further decline. Finally, when parties bargain over resources that increase military capability, neither state can credibly commit to using those resources for only peaceful purposes; it might use them to increase its military power. Thus, the zero-sum nature of resources lowers the probability of successfully bargaining over them.

In Garfinkel and Skaperdas (2000), despite there being short-term incentives to settle a war, conflict can continue if the long-term benefits outweigh the short-run costs. In other words, because of time-dependence, conflict will continue if one party feels that even though they will get a slice of the pie today if they settle, they will get a permanently larger slice in the future if they don't settle today. This is because today's performance will determine tomorrow's gain. For example, Columbian warlords or tribal lords could appear weak in the eyes of their rivals if they settled today, and so would be cut off from future gains. In such cases, the expected gains from fighting today are that your rival will be weakened enough to ensure victory in the future. The cost is the possibility of defeat and weakened power today. Garfinkel and Skaperdas (2000) also find that the more parties to a conflict value the future, the more the likelihood of conflict today. This conclusion contradicts Fudenberg and Tirole (1991) who say that the "long shadow of the future" fosters cooperation; Adversaries who interact repeatedly over time will develop strategies to avoid conflict.

Acemoglu and Robinson (2001) develop a model in which coups may follow democracy because of the lack commitment of the displaced elites to the bargained outcome. In the model, the poor and elites compete for control.

The poor can revolt in bad times since the opportunity cost of war is low. But once the elite-rich concede to them by allowing them to vote, the redistribution of wealth that takes place once democracy is established causes the elite to renege and go back to a nondemocratic regime.

Fearon (2004) looks at wars that have a long duration. He finds that coups or anticolonial wars are on average short-lived, but 'peripheral insurgencies' last a long time. When guerillas who live in the periphery of the state repeatedly attack the central government, and when these conflicts are over natural resources such as land, the conflict is long-lived. This is also true when the guerillas are an ethnic minority and are funded by contraband such as opium.

Ray (2009) uses a multi-player model to show that conflict is difficult to prevent when the frissons in an economy are along several lines, even when all parties have complete information and are committed to accepting their share. In this framework, the divisions along ethnic, geographic and religious lines are so many so that it is not possible to arrange transfers that satisfy all parties simultaneously.

Civil conflict from lack of commitment highlights the need for Fearon's (1995) 'sheriff': if existing political and legal institutions are weak or nonexistent, or if the government is not subject to checks and balances, reneging on deals becomes more beneficial (Fearon and Laitin 2003, La Ferrara and Bates, 2001, Skaperdas, 2008). Poverty, rough terrain, and large populations can cause such weak institutions, or at the very least, weaken the reach of such institutions (Fearon and Laitin 2003).

INDIVISIBILITY ISSUES

Fearon (1995) raises the issues of those resources that cannot be bargained over simply because they are indivisible. For instance, as put elegantly in Ray (2009) "What would be the compensating price that a fundamentalist Hindu might accept for the conversion of the Indian state to a Muslim rashthra? (Or vice versa?)." In such situations, conflict becomes a rational choice. Powell (2006) has argued that indivisibilities are really commitment problems (Blattman and Miguel, 2010). He postulates that a lottery with the same odds as that of war would be preferable to the destruction of war, where the winner of the lottery would be awarded the indivisible prize.

ROLE OF RATIONAL CHOICE IN CONTINUING CONFLICT

There is one class of models in which the state is at war, and the continuation of that war is a rational choice. In these models, conflict becomes a rational choice when the opportunity cost of predation or appropriation is less than that of production. These models of armed conflict depart from the assumptions of standard economic theory in at least three ways: property rights are neither well defined nor automatically protected, contracts between parties cannot be enforced and rulers can be replaced by means other than the ballot box. In this lawless setting, predation and defense are alternatives to directly productive activities.

One of the empirical regularities of conflict is that income levels are strongly and persistently related to civil war. Several theoretical models attempt to explain this, with causality running both ways. First, poverty lowers the opportunity cost of war, making it a rational choice. Second, the richer the state, the higher is the payoff from capturing the state. And, finally, revenue-rich states can successfully put down or buy off an insurrection, so richer countries have a lower likelihood of war.

Contest models are typically used to model these three channels of interaction of poverty and conflict. Political scientists usually look at the contest as something that happens when bargaining fails (Fearon, 1995). Economists model the decision process through which two parties to a contest (usually a government and a rebel group) allocate their resources between production and predation. In these models, production is modeled in the standard neoclassical way, and predation is modeled as a 'contest success function' where the inputs, such as guns, determine the probability of one side winning and getting the loser's production, as well as its own.

Grossman (1991) extends the standard contest framework by modeling one ruler and many citizens, yielding the additional insight that more individuals will fight as the opportunity cost of fighting falls. He treats insurrection as an economic activity that competes with that of soldiering—deterrence of conflict—and production. Therefore, the 'peasant' has to choose among three activities: predation, production and soldiering. His general equilibrium model yields the result that the choice of optimal allocation of time among these three activities, and the probabilistic income of the peasants and the ruler's cohorts, depend on the technology of insurrection. One key result is that even though allocating more time to conflict lowers production, it can yield higher expected income for the peasants, making conflict a rational choice for them. If the state is poor, wages are low so the return to production is low (Basuchoudhary and Dutheil de la Rochere, 2016, Basuchoudhary and Hentz, 2016). Therefore, citizens turn to war.

An alternative explanation for the link between income levels and conflict is that if the state is poor, the returns from conflict are low since the appropriations from insurrection are small. In other words, the richer the state, the higher the payoff, a bigger slice of the pie, from conflict. Therefore, there is a greater incentive to put more effort toward fighting than producing:

Insurrection rises with increases in the wealth of the country. Therefore, countries with higher per capita income could see more conflict (Garfinkel and Skaperdas, 2007, Grossman, 1999). Dal Bo and Dal Bo (2011) theorize that shocks that make a country richer may increase conflict as long as conflict is more labor intensive than the economy. Therefore, the relative factor intensity of productive and conflict activities matter.

Therefore, in a nutshell, currently, there is no compelling theoretical argument for deciding the direction of the interaction: In poor countries, although the size of the resources seized through conflict is small, so is the opportunity cost of conflict. Therefore, poor countries may choose war. Conversely, in rich countries, a lot more wealth can be extracted through conflict even though the opportunity cost of that conflict, forgone income, is also high. Therefore, rich countries may choose war. Net incentives will decide whether people choose war or peace. Fearon's (2007) model demonstrates this logic.

Blattman and Miguel (2010) provide the insight that the likelihood of the capture of the state, whether it is poor or rich, depends largely on structural reasons. For instance, as we have mentioned in the section on commitment problems, according to Fearon and Laitin (2003) and Fearon (2007), the state itself could be weak because of insufficient institutions. Poorer countries tend to have weaker institutions, making them more vulnerable to capture. Also, countries with rougher terrains, or with large populations, can be captured relatively easily since the existing institutions cannot establish their jurisdiction effectively. Further, if the state's wealth derives largely from its primary sector, that sector can be captured by war. However, if the wealth of a rich country comes from human capital, appropriation of that wealth through conflict is not possible. Therefore, that sort of a rich country is not prone to conflict.

So, does poverty increase the incentive for war or reduce it? Empirical forays into this question are largely inconclusive. One relatively robust result is that the probability of winning increases with an increase in fighting technology, where technology can be many things: skillful leaders, rough terrain, foreign help etc. The challenge, of course, is that studies of the link between low income and conflict are plagued by endogeneity problems. Further, the exogenous variables (instruments) used to address the bias are often subject to weaknesses.

Climate shock is one common way to isolate the variations in income (Burke et al., 2009, Hsiang et al., 2011, Miguel et al., 2004). The problem with this approach is that states affected by severe weather can experience conflict through three different channels. First, the subsequent loss of crops in areas affected by the intense weather could reduce the opportunity cost of conflict in those localities. Second, extreme weather could hamper the state's ability to maintain peace in those regions, as well as reduce its revenues.

Any combinations of these factors could increase the incentive for conflict. Therefore, these approaches do not allow us to identify a single causal channel linking poverty to conflict. Moreover, such shocks are localized in rural areas. Therefore, the conclusions cannot be applied, for instance, to the effect of shocks to industrial production on income, or even generalized to the country level (Miguel and Blattman, 2010).

Other studies have looked at exogenous trade shocks as a way to isolate the income variation (Besley and Persson, 2008, Bazzi and Blattman, 2014). Besley and Persson (2008) find theoretically and empirically that an increase in the terms of trade can increase the within-country incidence of civil war[1]. Bazzi and Blattman (2014) use export prices and conclude that though when states get richer the capability of rebellion increases, this does not increase the individual's incentive to participate in conflict. So, states with rising revenues are not more prone to capture. However, whether the trade shock is a change in commodity prices (experienced by farmers), or in primary goods such as minerals and energy (affecting the government) or in the aggregate, they are neither consistent nor robust predictors of conflict (Miguel and Blattman, 2010).

GREED VERSUS GRIEVANCE

A discussion of models that study conflict is incomplete without a discussion of the Greed versus Grievance issue. Starting with Collier and Hoeffler (1998) and followed by a storm of research on either side, these models distinguish between economic reasons for conflict and political reasons for war. Unlike the frameworks we have discussed so far, grievance theories focus on civil war, or rebellion, as a way to redress grievance. One can think of grievance as arising from impediments to a good life such as lack of opportunity, political oppression, weak institutions, collapsing institutions, painful transition of systems, or informational problems (Sambanis, 2002). The best way perhaps to understand this debate is to look at the empirical and theoretical evidence on each side. Theoretical and empirical models that favor grievance are Gurr (2000), Elbadawi and Sambanis (2000, 2002), Reynal-Querol (2002), and Hegre et al. (2001).

Gurr (2000) uses political regime as the measure of motives for grievance. He argues that those ("ethnopolitical" groups) who live in democracies are more likely to resort to peaceful protests rather than rebellion. On the other hand, those who live in nondemocratic society, such as autocracies, choose conflict to redress their grievances. He also looks at regimes in transition, and concludes that established democracies are less likely to experience insurrections.

Elbadawi and Sambanis (2002, 2000b) provide econometric support of Gurr's conclusions (Sambanis, 2002). Using data from 150 countries during 1960–1999, they find a lower likelihood of the prevalence of civil war in those countries that are democratic. In African countries especially, where there are high levels of ethnic fragmentation, Elbadawi and Sambanis (2000b) find that in particular, in countries with ethnic polarization, democracy plays the role of defusing conflict. Their findings agree with Sambanis (2000) who finds that the onset of war is significantly reduced in democratic regimes.

These models use a democratic index to measure the level and extent of the regime. Reynal–Querol (2002) extends this work by incorporating different types of democratic systems such as proportional representation versus presidential systems. She finds that religious polarization, rather that linguistic divisions or religious fractionalization, is more likely to cause conflict. Also, she finds that civil unrest is less likely the more political rights people have, as proxied by the level of representation in the election. Therefore, the kind of democracy matters for conflict.

Hegre et al. (2001) use data from 1816–1992 data on 152 countries. They separate the effects of the level of democracy from the effects of changes in regime. They find that regime transitions are risky, and that there is an inverted U-shaped relationship between the level of democracy and the risk of conflict. Even though democracy is beneficial since it reduces conflict, transitions away from autocracies towards democracy can increase the risk of conflict. Although this is an important contribution, their conclusions are not robust since the variables in their models are not fully specified (Sambanis, 2002).

On the other side of the debate are Collier and Hoeffler (1998, 2004) and Fearon and Laitin (2003). Collier and Hoeffler (2004) find strong evidence in favor of opportunity ("greed") as the cause of conflict, whereas their proxies for grievance add little explanatory power to their model. In a nutshell, a group's ability to organize and finance is the strongest reason for conflict. So those economic factors that create an opportunity for groups to arm and attack are the strongest correlates of conflict. For instance, secondary school education is significantly related to conflict—presumably, education spears organizational capabilities—while democracy (a proxy for grievance) is not. Fearon and Laitin (2001) largely agree with these findings, though they find a correlation between political instability and civil war (Sambanis, 2002).

The greed versus grievance is far from settled. As Miguel and Blattman (2010) aptly put it "Scores of papers have followed in their (Collier and Hoeffler, 1998, 2004 and Fearon and Laitin, 2003) footsteps, most sharing a handful of traits: a dependent variable that indicates war onset or incidence, proxy variables representing possible causes of conflict, and a regression-based test of these competing determinants. In other words, it is impossible to compare conclusions when the models cannot be compared."

IRRATIONAL MODELS OF CONFLICT

Our reading of the literature thus far seems to imply that many of the causes of civil conflict are simple to understand but difficult to measure. Further, some of the reasons for war can be outside what we consider the rational decision making process. Let us now turn to those 'irrational' models of conflict.

How do we model a situation where the leader of a revolution has biases, such as a when the leader's return from war is different from the groups (Fearon, 2004)? Or, what if the leader miscalculates, or makes systematic errors? To understand such behavioral issues, we turn to the literature on the psychology of war.

Hardie et al. (2011) outline the various psychological biases that affect decision making in situations of war. People often go to war because of non-material, symbolic reasons, such as glory, reputation, honor, or because they are overconfident (Hardie et al) etc. Such biases are rooted in several factors:

Often when assessing threat, people view their own opinions or behavior as objective, based on situational causes such as environmental constraints. They attribute the behavior of others to "dispositional" causes like personality or intentions (Darley and Cooper, 1998). Such Fundamental Attribution Error (FAE) in threat assessment biases people against others, and justifies their belief that other people are in a conspiracy against them.

Prospect theory says that when outcomes are uncertain, people are risk averse when choosing between potential gains, but risk loving when choosing among potential losses (Darley and Cooper, 1998). Thus, a leader may incorrectly underestimate the discounted future losses from war and overestimate the benefits of war. This makes war more likely.

Social identity theory (Turner, 1987) says that people rapidly identify with in-groups (even strangers assigned to arbitrary groups), overvalue their own-group's performance and virtues, and devalue the performance and values of out-groups. This contributes to racism, prejudice, xenophobia, violence and war.

An interaction of these factors can lead to conflict. Prospect theory may lead someone to overvalue war, and FAE and Social Identity theory may lead to the creation of enemies. Overconfidence then combines these to push nations into war.

What kind of broad conclusions can we draw from our survey of the literature on conflict? The first obvious one is that it seems to be "all over the place." We cannot trace one or even two strands of definitive conclusions. We believe that the reason for this, with particular reference to empirical conclusions, is that the kind of econometric tools used to understand conflict are inadequate. They do not allow a holistic or comprehensive view of conflict.

After presenting our model and results in the next few chapters, in Chapter 7, we attempt to present a breakdown of the literature in a way that allows us to draw broad conclusion using Machine Learning techniques. We sort models into whether they are a) greed or grievance models, b) rational choice models, wherein agents maximize utility (roughly like the contest models), c) models involving strategic interaction between rational agents, d) models of indivisibility issues, e) behavioral models based on psychological biases, and, finally, f) models that look at state capacity (weak versus strong states).

NOTE

1. These price effects are present in countries with weak or non-existent political institution.ns (proxied by parliamentary democracy and existence of strong checks and balances).

Chapter 2

Machine Learning Methods

Data analysis has three goals: explaining, predicting, and describing. Shmueli (2010) defines explaining as using statistics to find causal effects, predicting as applying statistical models to predict new observations, and describing as the process of concisely summarizing the distributions of the variables in the data. Although these goals are distinct, studies commonly conclude that a model that explains causal effects well will necessarily predict new observations well. However, some techniques predict well, but do poorly at inferring causal effects, other techniques may infer causal effects using valid and sophisticated tests, but yield inaccurate predictions. In fact, as noted by Hagerty and Srinivasan (1991), a "less true model can have a higher predictive validity than a truer but less parsimonious model." Moreover, models that describe existing distributions well may be over-fitted, and may therefore predict poorly out of sample.

Machine Learning refers to a wide range of techniques used to recognize patterns in data. Some of these techniques are designed to predict, such as linear discriminant analysis (LDA), classification and regression trees (CART), and artificial neural networks (ANNs), while others describe patterns of correlation among variables, such as principle component analysis (PCA) and factor analysis (FA). Some of these techniques identify and explain causal effects, such as least angle regression and shrinkage (LARS), and least absolute shrinkage and selection operator (LASSO).

One familiar Machine Learning technique is actually regression analysis, which in the case of a categorical outcome variable (such as our conflict variable) usually takes the form of a Logit or Probit regression. Many studies use this methodology for explaining, and presume that this means it will be good for predicting as well. However, as we will see in later chapters, other methods have superior predictive power. Many of these methods are nonparametric and involve trees. Later in this chapter, we summarize the various predictive models we evaluate for predicting conflict. Before doing so, however, we outline some of the goals and advantages of Machine Learning.

GOALS AND ADVANTAGES OF MACHINE LEARNING FOR PREDICTION

The Machine Learning models we focus on in our empirical analysis are those that excel at predicting new outcomes. We compare those models (and a "super learner" combination of models) to the more traditional approaches for predicting discrete outcomes such as Logit regression and LDA.

The goal of a good predictor is to minimize the prediction error of the learning algorithm when it encounters new observations. To do this, the first step in the algorithm's "learning" process is to divide the existing dataset into a learning sample and a test sample. The algorithm uses the learning sample to define its parameters and construct its decision rule for classifying observations. It then uses the test sample to evaluate the out-of-sample predictive power of the algorithm.

Note that this step of the learning process can offer a useful addition to any empirical study. Many studies using time series or panel data use all of the available data to estimate the parameters of their models. This might be acceptable if the only goal is to *explain*. However, if the number of variables included as controls is "large," estimating a model using all available data risks over-fitting the model. If that is the case, the predictive power of the model, and even the causal effects of the individual variables, may not apply to new data. This presents a dilemma for extrapolating policy implications from these types of studies: How does one gauge the impact of a particular policy if the validity of the results advocating those policies is confined to the peculiarities of the data used to estimate the model? Any study seeking to predict future policy implications should test the predictive power of its model using observations that the method did not "see" when estimating its parameters. Machine Learning techniques allow us to do that.

Another advantage of Machine Learning methods is that many of its techniques estimate parameters and predict new outcomes without making strong assumptions about the distribution of the outcomes or the errors, or placing unrealistic restrictions on the functional form of the relationship between the inputs and the outcomes. This means that Machine Learning methods can empirically determine an appropriate functional form for the relationships when theory is either silent, or when the functional form predicted by an applied theoretical model is predicated on strong assumptions about agents' preferences, technology, or behavior.

A third advantage to using certain Machine Learning methods is that they make use of all information available, instead of only information from complete cases. In other words, the method does not throw out an observation simply because a particular variable in the model has missing observations. In particular, for cases where a variable has missing values, nonparametric tree algorithms make use of "surrogate" information from other variables to predict the direction of the split. This leads to an effective method for imputing the missing values, one that is based on information from those variables that are closely related to the one that has missing observations. Averaging these imputations over hundreds of random trees (as in a Random Forest model described later in this chapter) yields highly accurate imputed values for the missing values for a variable. The ability to impute missing values is particularly important in the case of predicting conflict because it is precisely the countries that are most at risk for conflict that are also most likely to have spotty data availability. While imputing the values may lead to some bias, the selection bias from omitting hundreds of observations, or omitted variable bias from omitting important variables, is likely to be at least as serious.

Finally, some Machine Learning methods can easily estimate both very large and very small datasets. For larger datasets, such as our conflict dataset, tree algorithms can effectively whittle out less predictive variables when there are many potential explanatory variables, especially when those variables are correlated with one another, or include a mixture of data types and scales of measurement.

PARAMETRIC METHODS

Linear Discriminant Analysis

Linear Discriminant Analyis (LDA) classifies observations by finding a linear combination of the inputs that creates the greatest amount of separation between the outcomes. Specifically, LDA determines the maximum separation between groups by solving for the eigenvector, ω, associated with the largest eigenvalue of the matrix, $W^{-1}B$, where B is the matrix of between-group sums of squares and cross products,

$$B = \begin{pmatrix} \sum_{j=1}^{J} N_j (\bar{x}_{j1} - \bar{x}_1)^2 & \cdots & \sum_{j=1}^{J} N_j (\bar{x}_{j1} - \bar{x}_1)(\bar{x}_{jK} - \bar{x}_K) \\ \vdots & \ddots & \vdots \\ \sum_{j=1}^{J} N_j (\bar{x}_{jK} - \bar{x}_K)(\bar{x}_{j1} - \bar{x}_1) & \cdots & \sum_{j=1}^{J} N_j (\bar{x}_{jK} - \bar{x}_K)^2 \end{pmatrix} \quad (2.1)$$

Where j indexes the class groups (conflict or no conflict), $\bar{x}_{jk}$ is the mean of variable k for group j, and $\bar{x}_k$ is the grand mean for variable k. W is the corresponding within-group matrix.

$$W = \begin{pmatrix} \sum_{j=1}^{J}\sum_{i=1}^{N_j}\left(x_{ij1}-\bar{x}_{j1}\right)^2 & \cdots & \sum_{j=1}^{J}\sum_{i=1}^{N_j}\left(x_{ij1}-\bar{x}_{j1}\right)\left(x_{ijK}-\bar{x}_{jK}\right) \\ \vdots & \ddots & \vdots \\ \sum_{j=1}^{J}\sum_{i=1}^{N_j}\left(x_{ijK}-\bar{x}_{jK}\right)\left(x_{ij1}-\bar{x}_{j1}\right) & \cdots & \sum_{j=1}^{J}\sum_{i=1}^{N_j}\left(x_{ijK1}-\bar{x}_{jK}\right)^2 \end{pmatrix} \tag{2.2}$$

Given the hyperplane generated by this eigenvector, $\omega x = 0$, determines the decision rule for LDA. LDA assigns each "side" of the hyperplane with an outcome based on the outcome of the majority of the observations on that "side." Then, the predicted outcomes can be used to generate a confusion matrix of correctly and incorrectly classified outcomes, and to calculate an overall misclassification rate for the predictions. The *misclassification rate*,

$$\hat{R}(d) = \frac{1}{n}\sum_{i=1}^{n} I\left(d\left(\mathbf{x}_i\right) \neq y_i\right) \tag{2.3}$$

is simply the proportion of the observations that the decision rule misclassifies.

Logistic Regression

Logistic regression (Logit) is perhaps the most familiar prediction method for models looking to estimate the probabilities of a binary (or multinomial) variable. In the binary Logit model, the probability that the outcome variable is equal to one can be expressed in terms of a nonlinear transformation of a linear function of the inputs and an error using the logistic cumulative distribution function,

$$P\left(y_i = 1\right) = \frac{e^{x_i'\beta+\varepsilon_i}}{1+e^{x_i'\beta+\varepsilon_i}} \tag{2.4}$$

Alternatively, the model can be expressed in terms of the natural log of the odds ratio as

$$\frac{P\left(y_i = 1\right)}{1-P\left(y_i = 1\right)} = x_i'\beta + \varepsilon_i \tag{2.5}$$

The Logit model estimates the parameters, ω, using maximum likelihood estimation. In Logit regression, an observation for a binary outcome variable is classified according to whether the predicted probability is greater than 0.5.[1] Once again, we calculate the misclassification rate of the Logit model using the misclassification rate, which is the proportion of the total number of cases that the model predicts incorrectly.

Artificial Neural Networks

An Artifical Neural Network (ANN) is a generalization of the simple linear (or transformed linear) predictors that we derive using LDA and Logit models. However, in contrast to LDA, which bases its prediction on a purely linear function of the inputs to separate and classify the outcomes, and the Logit model which only considers a logistic transformation of a linear function of the inputs, ANNs can consider an arbitrary number of functions, interactions, and relationships among the input variables (including simple linear and Logit functions) to obtain the best prediction of the learning sample.

A simple, single-layer ANN has two components: a matrix of weights, W, and a *link function*, $h_i(\mathrm{w}_i \mathrm{x})$, that transforms the linear combination of the inputs and weights to separate and predict the data. The simplest ANN—the *perceptron*—is simply a single-layer ANN with a *sign* link function. Specifically, given an initial set of weights for each input, $w_1, \ldots, w_{k,}$ the perceptron calculates the predicted value of y (the "neuron") to be: $\hat{y} = \mathrm{w}'\mathrm{x} + b$, where b is a constant referred to as "bias." The classification rule identifies an observation as "active" (state failure) whenever $\hat{y} > 0$, and "inactive" if $\hat{y} < 0$.

Starting from an initial value for **w**, the perceptron uses an "error-driven" updating rule, which means that as it considers each outcome it only makes changes to **w** if it stumbles across an observation for which the prediction differs from the actual outcome. In that case, the perceptron increases **w** by yx and increases the bias by y. If the prediction is incorrect for some observation with $y = 1$, the new neuron will be:

$$
\begin{aligned}
\hat{y}'^{*} &= w'^{*} x + b'^{*} \\
&= (w+x)' x + (b+1) \\
&= \hat{y} + x' x + 1.
\end{aligned}
$$

Since $\mathrm{x}'\,\mathrm{x}$ is the sum of the squared values of the inputs, it is positive, and hence this increases a so that the perceptron will be more likely to correctly predict a positive value of y the next time it encounters the same case.[2]

One problem with the *sign* link function is that it is non-differentiable, and therefore makes minimizing a given loss function (mean squared errors, for example) difficult. To eliminate this problem, more common link functions for ANNs tend to come from the family of sigmoid functions. The most common link function is the *tanh* function (which can closely approximate the *sign* function for some parameters) and any differentiable cumulative distribution function, including the logistic function. In fact, a single-layer ANN with a logistic link function yields exactly the same prediction as the logistic regression model.

In addition to the observed input weights, **w**, a two-layer network adds additional an additional "hidden" layer with corresponding weights, *v*, that can function to generate "interactions" (such as "or" or "and" operators) between the inputs. The hidden layer may have multiple nodes, with each node permuting the inputs in different ways. In general, the hidden prediction can be expressed as:

$$\hat{y}'^{*} = \mathrm{v} \cdot f(\mathbf{wx}) = \sum_{j=1}^{J} \mathrm{v}_j \sum_{k=1}^{K} f(w_{j,k} x_k), \tag{2.6}$$

Using a *tanh* link function, we can define the predicted outcome, $\hat{y}$, to be:

$$\hat{y}'^{*} = \mathrm{v} \cdot tanh(\mathbf{wx}) = \sum_{j=1}^{J} \mathrm{v}_j \sum_{k=1}^{K} tanh(w_{j,k} x_k), \tag{2.7}$$

where v is a vector of weights assigned in the hidden layer; $j = 1, \ldots, J$ indexes the nodes in the hidden layer; and $k = 1, \ldots, K$ indexes the inputs (variables) in x. To find the input weights, **w**, and output weights, *v*, the ANN algorithm will minimize some loss function, such as the sum of squared errors:

$$\min_{\boldsymbol{v},\mathbf{w}} \sum_{i=1}^{N_{LS}} \left(y_i - \boldsymbol{v} \cdot f(\mathbf{wx})\right)^2 \tag{2.8}$$

The first-order conditions of this optimization problem are:

$$\sum_{i=1}^{N_{LS}} -2f(\mathbf{wx})\left(y_i - \boldsymbol{v} \cdot f(\mathbf{wx})\right) = 0; \tag{2.9}$$

$$\sum_{i=1}^{N_{LS}} -2\mathbf{x}\boldsymbol{v} f'(\mathbf{wx})\left(y_i - \boldsymbol{v} \cdot f(\mathbf{wx})\right) = 0. \tag{2.10}$$

Computationally, we can solve these FOCs using the gradient function as a step function that adjusts the weights from user-defined initial values until the functions converge toward zero. While this may seem simple enough, note that, since the objective function is non-convex (because of *f* and because of the interactions induced by v) the solution to these conditions is not necessarily unique. Hence, the solution to the ANN algorithm will depend on the initial values chosen for **w** and v. A common initialization method is to choose the initial values for **w** and v randomly. Random initialization helps to avoid trivial solutions.[3]

In ANNs, an observation will be predicted to be "on" (a country in conflict) if the predicted value, $\hat{y}'^{*}= v\ tanh(\text{wx})$, is greater than zero. We can then evaluate the predictive quality of the model using the misclassification rates described in the previous sections.

NONPARAMETRIC METHODS

k-Nearest Neighbors Algorithm

The *k*-nearest neighbors (KNN) algorithm is widely regarded as the simplest classification algorithm. The KNN algorithm predicts the outcome for each observation based on the observations with the most similarly observed values over the inputs. To classify observation i, the KNN algorithm first computes the distance between observation i and all other observations, $j \neq i$. For continuous variables, the KNN algorithm typically defines the "similarity," or "closeness" of two observations' inputs using the Euclidian distance[4],

$$\delta_{i,j\neq i} = \left[\sum_{k=1}^{K}\left(x_{ik} - x_{jk}\right)^2\right]^{\frac{1}{2}} \tag{2.11}$$

After calculating these distances, the algorithm selects the KNN to i as the observations with the smallest distance measures to i. The predicted class for that observation, then, is the result of a vote among those k neighbors to observation i.

The most important decision for the researcher, when implementing the KNN algorithm is, how to select an appropriate value of k. With too small of a k, there is likely to be a lot of noise in the classification (e.g., for $k = 1$, we would be classifying based on only a single point). However, with too large of a k, it may be difficult to define clear boundaries between sets of observations predicted to be in one class or the other. The choice of k is often somewhat *ad hoc* by the researcher, although it is common practice to choose an odd number for k in order to avoid ties in the voting.

Although KNN is simple to implement, it suffers from a number of problems. First, the accuracy can sometimes be very sensitive to the scaling of the variables relative to one another. Therefore, it is common to rescale the input variables by using a z-transformation of each observed value of the inputs so that each variable has zero mean and unit variance. A second issue is that the KNN algorithm is more prone to the problem of the "curse of dimensionality" than some of the other nonparametric techniques we discuss. This is because, with an increasing number of inputs, there will be an increasing number of observations that are included in many more other observations' sets of nearest neighbors of than average. Finally, in order to calculate the distance between *i* and *j*, the algorithm requires that both observations be fully observed for all of the elements of the training sample.

Tree-Based Classifiers

CART[5] diagnose and predict outcomes by using data from a learning sample, $L = \{(y_1,x_1), \ldots(y_N,x_N)\}$ to find binary splits in the input variables, $(x_1, \ldots, x_K)$, to optimally divide the sample into subsamples with successively higher levels of purity in the outcome variable, y . More specifically, a tree, T, has four main parts:

1. Binary splits to splits in the inputs that divide the subsample at each node, t;
2. Criteria for splitting each node into additional "child" nodes, or including it in the set of terminal nodes, T^*
3. A decision rule, $d(x)$, for assigning a predicted outcome to each terminal node
4. An estimate of the predictive quality of the decision rule, d.

The first step is achieved at each node by minimizing a measure of impurity. The most common measure of node impurity, and the one we use for our tree algorithms, is the Gini impurity index, $g(y) = 1-\sum_c \in_C p^2(y_c \mid t)$, where $p(\cdot)$ is the probability of observing outcome j conditional on having reached node t.[6] Intuitively, this method first searches for the "best" cutoff in each of the inputs, that is, one that minimizes the chosen measure of impurity. Then, it selects the inputs that yield the greatest improvement in node impurity using its optimal splitting point.

Next, a node is declared to be terminal in the second step if one of the following conditions is met: (1) that the best split determined by the application of step one fails to improve the node impurity by more than a predetermined minimum improvement criterion; or (2) the split creates a "child" node that contains fewer observations than the minimum allowed.[7] At each terminal node, the decision rule typically assigns observations with a predicted outcome based on the outcome that is most frequent (more than one-half of the observations in that node for binary outcomes, for example).[8]

Finally, we can calculate the tree predictor's misclassification rate, $\hat{R}(d)$. Tree misclassification rates are often cross-validated by splitting the sample several times and re-estimating the misclassification rate each time to get an average misclassification of all of the cross-validated trees.

Adaptive Boosting Algorithm (Adaboost)

Combining ensembles of trees can often improve the predictive accuracy of a CART classifier. The bootstrap aggregating (Bagging) predictor, adaptive Boosting (Adaboost) algorithm, and Random Forest predictors all predict outcomes using ensembles of classification trees. The basic idea of these predictors is to improve the predictive strength of a "weak learner" by iterating the tree algorithm many times by either modifying the distribution (Boosting) or randomly resampling the distribution (Bagging). Then, they either classify the outcomes according to the outcome of the "strongest" learner once the algorithm achieves the desired error rate (Boosting), or according to the outcome of a vote by the many trees (Bagging).

Boosting is a way proposed by Freund and Schapire (1996) to augment the strength of a "weak learner" (a learning algorithm that predicts poorly) and making it a "strong learner." More specifically, for a given distribution D of importance values assigned to each observation in L, and for a given desired error rate $\hat{R}$, and failure probability, φ, a *strong learner* is an algorithm with a sufficiently high probability (at least 1-φ) or achieving an error rate no higher than $\hat{R}$, a weak learner has a lower probability (less than 1-φ) of achieving the desired error rate. Adaboost creates a set of M classifiers, $F = (f_1, \ldots, f_M)$ that progressively re-weight the importance of each observation based on whether the previous classifier predicted it correctly or incorrectly.

Starting with a $D_I = (1/N, \ldots, 1/N)$, suppose that our initial classifier, $f_1 = T$ (the single-tree CART predictor), is a "weak learner" in that the misclassification rate, $\hat{R}(d)$is greater than the desired maximum desired misclassification rate, $\hat{R}$. Next, for all observations in the learning sample, recalculate the distribution weights for the observations as:

$$\mathcal{D}_2 = \frac{\mathcal{D}_1(i)}{Z_2} \times \begin{cases} \dfrac{\hat{R}_1(d)}{1-\hat{R}_1(d)} & \mathit{if}\ d_1(\mathbf{x}_i) = y_i \\ 1 & \mathit{otherwise} \end{cases}, \tag{2.12}$$

where Z_m is a scaling constant that forces the weights to sum to one.

The final decision rule for Adaboost is

$$d(x) = \arg\max_{y \in Y} \sum_{m:d_m(\mathbf{x})=y} \log\left(\frac{1-\hat{R}_m(d)}{\hat{R}_m(d)}\right) \tag{2.13}$$

Using this decision rule and its corresponding predictions, we calculate the estimate of the misclassification rate in the same way as in step (4) of the single-tree algorithm.

Bootstrap Aggregating Predictor (Bagging)

The Bagging predictor proposed by Breiman (1996) takes random resamples $\{L^{(M)}\}$ from the learning sample *with replacement* to create M samples using only the observations from the learning sample. Each of these samples will contain N observations—the same as the number of observations in the full training sample. However, in any one bootstrapped sample, some observations may appear twice or more, others not at all.[9] The Bagging predictor then builds M classification trees using those rules for splitting and declaring nodes to be terminal that we described in the previous section.

To complete steps (3) and (4), the Bagging predictor needs a way of aggregating the information of the predictions from each of the trees. The way that Bagging predictors (and other ensemble methods) do this for class variables is through *voting*. To obtain an observation's predicted class for each tree, the voting processes that observation[10] that was constructed from each of the bootstrapped samples through each of the M trees. The predicted class for the entire model, then, is equal to the mode prediction of all of the trees. The predictor then calculates the redistribution estimate in the same way as it did for the single classification tree using the predicted class based on the voting outcome for each predictor.

Random Forests

Like the Bagging predictor, the Random Forest predictor is a tree-based algorithm that uses a voting rule to determine the predicted class of each observation. However, whereas the Bagging predictor randomizes the selection of the observations into the sample for each tree and then builds the tree using the same procedure as CART, the Random Forest predictor may randomize over multiple dimensions of the classifier (Breiman, 2001). The most common dimensions for randomizing the trees are the selection of the inputs for node of each tree and the observations included for constructing each of the trees. We briefly describe the construction of the trees for the Random Forest ensemble below.

A Random Forest is a collection of tree decision rules, $\{d(x, \Theta_m), m = 1, \ldots, M\}$, where Θ_m is a random vector specifying the observations and inputs that are included at each step of the construction of the decision rule for that tree. To construct a tree, the Random Forest algorithm takes the following steps:

1. Randomly select $n \leq N$ observations from the learning sample;[11]
2. At the "root" node of the tree, select $k \in K$ inputs from x;

3. Find the split in each variable selected in (ii) that minimizes the Gini impurity index[12] at that node and select the variable/split that achieves the minimal impurity;
4. Repeat the random selection of inputs and optimal splits in (ii) and (iii) until some stopping criteria (minimum improvement, minimum number of observations, or maximum number of levels) is met.

The Bagging predictor in the previous section is, in fact, a special case of the Random Forest estimator where, for each tree, Θ_m consists of a random selection of $n = N$ observations from the learning sample with replacement (and each observation having a probability of being selected in each draw equal to $1/N$) and sets the number of inputs to select at each node, k, equal to the full length of the input vector, K so that all of the variables are considered at each node.

VARIABLE IMPORTANCE AND "MARGINAL EFFECTS"

Variable Importance

Traditional methods consider the issue of variable *importance* as being synonymous with statistical *significance*. While statistical significance measures the likelihood that a particular variable "*causes*" the outcome at the desired degree of precision, it is not a good proxy of that variable's *importance* relative to others. For example, in a dataset with thousands (or tens of thousands) of observations, one can reasonably expect that many of the variables included in the model will be highly "statistically significant." This is because the consistency of the estimators ensures that their standard errors converge to zero. With such large sample sizes, it may sometimes be difficult to measure how well a variable predicts the outcome variable. Ziliak and McCloskey (2006) have noted that in these cases statistical significance is a very blunt tool for deciding which variables really *matter*.

Machine Learning models approach the question of how important each variable is a little differently. Statistical significance answers the question, "Can we reject, to a certain degree of precision, the hypothesis that a particular variable has no marginal effect on the outcome variable?" Instead, Machine Learning models answer the question, "by how much would the predictive accuracy deteriorate if that variable were excluded from the model?" Alternatively, "when a variable is added to the model, by how much does it *improve* the predictive accuracy of the model?" The first question starts from the full model with all of the possible variables under consideration, and iteratively *removes* one variable at a time (starting with the weakest predictor). The second question starts with the null model and adds one variable at a time (starting with the strongest predictor). The answers to these questions will lead to similar rankings of the variables, but not identical ones.

Marginal Effects and Partial Dependence Plots

Partial Dependence Plots (PDPs) help visualize how, all else equal, a change in a covariate affects the probability of conflict in the learning sample. Thus, these PDPs give us a sense of how each input variable affects the outcome variable at the various levels of the distribution of that input. More specifically, partial dependence plots display the marginal effect of variable x_k conditional on the observed values of all of the other variables, $(x_{1,-k}, x_{2,-k}, \ldots x_{n,-k})$. Specifically, it plots the graph of the function:

$$\hat{f}(x)=\frac{1}{n}\sum_{i=1}^{n}\left\{ln\left[\hat{p}_1\left(x_k \mid x_{i,-k}\right)\right]-\frac{1}{C}\sum_{s=1}^{C} ln\left[\hat{p}_s\left(x_k \mid x_{i,-k}\right)\right]\right\}. \quad (2.14)$$

Here, s indexes the classes of the target variable and C is the total number of classes. So, if an increase in a given factor, x_k, increases the probability of state failure ($s = 1$), then the value of the function plotted by the PDP also increases. For two outcomes (such as predicting conflict versus no conflict as in our dataset), this reduces to:

$$\hat{f}(x)=\frac{1}{n}\sum_{i=1}^{n}\left\{ln\left[\frac{\hat{p}\left(y=1 \mid x_k ; x_{i,-k}\right)}{\hat{p}\left(y=0 \mid x_k ; x_{i,-k}\right)}\right]^{1/2}\right\} \quad (2.15)$$

This is essentially the (square root) of the logged odds ratio, and also corresponds to the interpretation for the linear coefficients for the Logit regression model.

NOTES

1. For a multinomial outcome variable, each observation is classified according to the class that has the highest probability compared with all of the other classes.
2. If the prediction is incorrect for some observation with $y = -1$, the new neuron will be: $\hat{y}'^{*}=\hat{y} - x' x - 1$, which always negative, and therefore decreases $\hat{y}$ and trains the perceptron to predict similar observations negatively.
3. One example of poorly chosen initial weights would be the choice of setting both sets of weights equal to zero. However, doing so makes the first order conditions trivially equal to zero, and so the algorithm never updates from its initial value of zero for either set of weights.

4. This distance measure can also be used for categorical variables that have been converted into a set of binary variables. A common distance measure for variables that are strictly categorical is the hamming distance, which counts the number of points at which the two vectors of categorical observations differ. For example, $dh(\{0,1,1,0,0\},\{0,0,1,0,1\}) = 2$.

5. We provide only a brief summary of tree construction as it pertains to our objectives. For a full description of the CART algorithm, see Breiman et al. (1984).

6. Another common measure is the "information" measure, $h(y) = -\ulcorner c \in C\ p(yc\ |t) \log[p(yc\ |t)]$.

7. Note that there is a tradeoff here: setting lower values for the minimum acceptable margin of improvement or the minimum number of observations in a child node will lead to a more accurate predictor (at least within the sample the model uses to learn). However, improving the accuracy of the predictor within the sample will also lead to a more complex (and therefore less easily-interpreted) tree, and may lead to over-fitting in the sense that the model will perform more poorly out-of-sample.

8. It is possible, however to consider decision rules that assign one class of a binary outcome anytime the proportion of observations exceeds one-third of the total observations in that node, especially if one type of misclassification error is more costly than the other.

9. Note that the probability that a single observation is selected in each draw from the learning set is $1/N$ Hence, sampling with replacement, the probability that it is completely left out of any given bootstrap sample is $(1–1/N)N$. For large samples, this tends to $1/e$. The probability that an observation will be completely left out of all M bootstrap samples, then, is $(1\text{-}1/N)NM$.

10. Note that the observations under consideration could be from either the in-sample learning set or from outside the sample (the test set).

11. In Bagging, the number of observations selected for each tree exactly equals the total number of observations in the learning sample, and the draws are always sampled with replacement. In contrast, the number of observations selected for each tree of the Forest can be set to be less than the total size of the learning sample, and can therefore be sampled with *or without* replacement. This also allows for slightly greater flexibility with respect to stratified or clustered sampling from the learning sample.

12. Or information index, if so desired.

Chapter 3

The Variables

In this chapter, we present and describe the variables in our model. Our variables are from six databases, the 2014 Cross-National Time-Series (CNTS) data archives, the 2012 Database of Political Institutions (DPI), the International Country Risk Guide (ICRG), the Political Instability (formerly, State Failure) Task Force (PITF), the Polity IV, the Standardized World Income Inequality Database (SWIID) and the World Development Index (WDI).

It is useful to sort our fifty-eight independent variables into broad categories. In order not to preempt our findings, we sort them mostly according to their sources, but also according to certain broad cohesive categories. These categories are ones that capture civil conflict, those that speak to the quality of political institutions, and those that portray the stage of economic development of the country. Please note that our conclusions are not dependent on the way we categorize these variables. Neither re-sorting the variables across the categories nor choosing other categories changes our conclusions.

Our dependent or target variable is Conflict. We use data on political and ethnic war, adverse regime changes, and genocide and politicide from the PITF database. In our model, Conflict = 'conflict' if there is conflict in the period (t+1) to (t+5), when the corresponding predictor variables are from year t. So, for example, if GDP per capita et al is from 1990, Conflict = 'conflict' if there was conflict in the period 1991–1995.

CIVIL CONFLICT VARIABLES

Next, let us look at our independent variables, starting with what we call 'domestic conflict variables.' These are events where entire or subsets of the populace express a systematic discontent with a government or government policy. An extreme form of this could be riots that break out or (attempts at) assassinations of government officials. There could be less violent expressions by way of general strikes and anti-government demonstrations. The ruling government itself could also initiate conflict: for instance, if the government begins a systematic attack on the civil liberties, or even lives, of those individuals who oppose it. To capture such civil conflict, we use seven variables. We draw these variables from the CNTS database unless either wise noted:

1. LagConflict: This is conflict lagged by one year from the start of the five-year period for which Conflict = 'conflict'. To continue the example from the definition of Conflict, if Conflict = 'conflict' because there was conflict in the period 1991–1995 (with the predictor variables such as GDP per capita et al from 1990), then LagConflict = 1 if there was conflict in 1990. Data is from the PITF database.
2. Assassinations: This counts the number of times there is an attempt to murder, or an actual murder of, any important government official or politician.
3. Purges: This counts the number of times political opponents, whether part of the regime, or outside it, were systematically eliminated.
4. Strikes: This counts the number of times there were mass strikes by 1,000 or more industrial or service workers, across more than one employer, protesting a government policy.
5. Government crises: This counts the number of times there was a crisis that threatened the downfall of the government, other than a revolt specifically to that end.
6. Demonstrations: This counts the number of times there was peaceful protestations of government domestic policy by 100 or more people.
7. Riots: This counts the number of times there was a violent protest by 100 or more people.

To these we add two variables that are from Hendrix and Salehyan (2002):

8. EthnicPolariz: This is the Reynal-Querol index of ethnic polarization. What matters for this index is not the number of different ethnic groups but their relative size.
9. ReligPolariz: This is the Reynal-Querol index of religious polarization and measures the extent of religious diversity. What matters for this index is how threatened one group feels by the presence of another group, not the number of different religious groups, where the size of the other group is the measure of the threat. So, for example, it reaches the maximum value when there are two groups of equal size.

QUALITY OF POLITICAL INSTITUTIONS

Next, we turn to those variables that speak to the quality of the existing political institutions. These variables capture the transparency, inclusiveness and stability of political institutions. Some of these look at the quality of the legislature and the legislative process while others look at the government as a whole.

We include five variables from the ICRG that measure political stability:

1. Government stability (0 to 12) assesses "the government's ability to carry out its declared programs and ability to stay in office." The risk rating is the sum of ratings on three subcomponents, Government Unity, Legislative Strength and Popular Support, each with a maximum score of 4 points (very low risk) and a minimum score of 0 points (very high risk).
2. Democratic accountability index (0 to 6); on the assumption that a government that is less responsive to its people is more likely to fall ("peacefully in a democratic society, but possibly violently in a non-democratic one"), the index considers how responsive a government is to its people. The measure of such responsiveness is the system of government: one subject to elections with political opponents is more accountable, more responsive, and therefore less risky. For example, a system wherein the government does not serve more than two successive terms is more accountable than one where the government can/has served more than two consecutive terms, and therefore, the former is assigned higher points. Similarly, a system with a varied and active opposition is assigned a higher score than one where such opposition is limited or restricted. This index also takes into account evidence of checks and balances between the three branches of government, how independent the judiciary is, and evidence of the protection of personal liberties.[1]
3. The investment profile index (0 to 12) assesses the risk to private investment according to how effectively contractual agreements are enforced, ease of expropriation, how easy it is to repatriate profits and the whether there are payment delays. Countries with lower risk are higher in the index.
4. The index of bureaucratic quality (0 to 4) assesses the efficiency of the bureaucracy. Countries with bureaucracies that are efficient and relatively autonomous tend to maintain stable policies and services even when governments change. They therefore are assigned higher points.
5. Corruption; The corruption index (0 to 6) focuses on the kinds of corruption, such as nepotism, bribes, etc. that, if revealed, may lead to political instability such as the overthrow of the government or the breakdown of law and order. Countries with less corruption receive higher scores.

Next, we look at those variables from the CNTS that evaluate the legislative process:

6. Legislative effectiveness (0 to 3): This is ordinal scaled and measures how independent the legislative is of the executive, and, therefore, how effective it is. It is coded 0 if no legislature exists, 1 if the legislature is ineffective, 2 if it is partially effective, and 3 if the legislature is considered effective. A legislature may be considered ineffective under three different circumstances: if the legislature is in effect a "rubber stamp", if, because of domestic unrest, legislation cannot be implemented, and finally, if the executive prevents or impedes the working of the legislature. The legislature is considered Partially Effective when the executive has considerable power over the legislature but cannot outweigh it completely. Finally, an effective legislature is one that has significant autonomy, especially in matters of taxation, disbursement and the power to override executive vetoes of the legislature.
7. Cabinet changes: This measures how many times either a new premier was named and/or the number of times new ministers replaced 50% of the cabinet positions. The fewer changes, the more stable the government;
8. Executive (0 to 3): This is the chief executive selection index. It codes the way in which control of executive power went to a new independent chief executive. If there were direct elections, the index is coded to 1, 2 if the election is indirect, and 3 if it is considered nonelective. Direct election is when the election of the effective executive is by popular vote or by delegates committed to executive selection. When the chief executive is elected by an elected assembly or by an elected but uncommitted electoral college, this is considered an indirect election. This coding is also used when a legislature is called upon to make the selection in a plurality situation. Finally, if the chief executive is chosen neither by a direct or indirect mandate, it is coded as Nonelective.
9. ParliamentResp (0 to 3): Parliamentary Responsibility. This measures the degree to which a premier must depend on the support of a majority in the lower house of a legislature to remain in office. It is coded 0, irrelevant, when the office of premier or legislature does not exist, 1, absent, when the office of premier exists, but has no responsibility to the parliament, 2, incomplete, when the premier's constitutionally responsibility to the legislature exists but is limited, and finally, 3, complete, when the premier is constitutionally and effectively dependent on a legislative majority for continuance in office.
10. PartyCoalitions (0 to 3) measures the number of parties in a system, and whether there are coalitions. It is coded 3 when there exists more than one party with no coalitions, 2 when there is more than one party, a

government coalition, and an opposition, 1 when there is more than one party, government coalition, but no opposition, and 0 if there is only one party, or no parties.

11. PartyExclusion (0 to 3): This looks at how inclusive the political system is by coding whether and how political parties may be excluded from the political process. It is coded in the following way: (3) if no parties excluded, (2) if one or more minor or "extremist" parties are excluded, (1) if there is 'Significant' exclusion of parties, and (0) if all but dominant parties and satellites are excluded.
12. Change in executive: Changes in the effective chief executive measures the number of times in a year that effective control of executive power went to a new independent chief executive.

To capture a sense of the transparency, stability, and inclusivity of the political and election process, we include ten variables from the DPI dataset. They are:

13. Executive electoral competition measured by the executive index of electoral competitiveness, EIEC (1 to 7). The EIEC measures the degree to which the selection of the executive is decided by free and fair elections. In cases where the executive is elected directly by the people, or by an electoral college which itself is elected by the people with the sole purpose of electing an executive, the score is a 7 or 6, whereas if an executive unilaterally declares a second term, the system is awarded a 2 in the second term. This index is similar to the LIEC[2].
14. Legislative electoral competition measured by the legislative index of electoral competitiveness, LIEC (1 to 7). The LIEC measures the degree to which the selection of the legislature is decided by elections. For example, an unelected legislature gets a 2 (no legislature is 1), while a system with multiple party elections where the largest party got less than 75% of the votes gets a 7[3].
15. Legislative fractionalization captures how politically diverse a system is by looking at the number of parties participating in a regime. It is measured by the likelihood that two deputies picked randomly from the legislature will be from different political parties. In cases where there is no parliament or no parties in the legislature, it is recorded as NA, and is blank if any government or opposition seats are blank
16. Government polarization takes values between 0 and 2 depending on the ideological distance between the legislative and the executive branches;
17. Executive years in office measures the number of years the current chief executive has served;

18. The government Herfindahl index measures the degree to which different parties share in the operation of the government. It is measured by the sum of the squared seat shares of all parties in the government;
19. Fraud, or allegations of fraud in the last election, is measured by whether claims of fraud, boycott of the elections by important opposition parties, or candidate intimidation were recorded during the election process. For example, FRAUD is 0 in countries where the opposition is banned. Less fraudulent elections are ranked higher in the measure;
20. System (0 to 3): This depicts the system of government. Systems of government that are elected are rated higher than those that are not. A parliamentary system is rated 2, an assembly-elected president is rated 1, while a presidential system is rated 0. For instance, a system with unelected executives get a 0, while systems with presidents who are elected directly, or by an electoral college (whose only function is to elect the president) is rated 4. In systems that have both a prime minister and a president, the power of the president versus that of the parliament and prime minister is considered in the rating. For example, in such a system, if the president has sufficient veto powers, or can appoint a prime minister, or can dissolve parliament, the system is rated higher.
21. Checks: Checks on power is a categorical variable that increases incrementally by 1 the more checks there are in the government system. For example, a presidential system with two chambers of the legislature has a higher rating by one than a system wherein the president's party has a majority in one of the houses.
22. Changes in veto power measures: This measures the percent drop in the number of players who have veto powers. The fewer the number of veto players within the government, the less open the government. For example, a presidential system with two houses will have a veto number of 3—the president and each house. If the president gains control of the legislature, veto power drops to 1
    a. Finally, we include two variables from the Polity IV project:
23. Polity index is the polity 2 democracy-autocracy index that measures the institutional regime in state. It ranges from –10, institutional autocracy to +10, institutional democracy; and
24. Regime durability: This is the number of years since the most recent change in regime or the end of a period of politically unstable institutions. The more stable the region, the higher the number

VARIABLES THAT PORTRAY ECONOMIC DEVELOPMENT

Finally, we include variables that give us a sense of the level of economic development. This list includes not only the usual measures of growth and wealth, but also the degree to which the country engages in trade, and the distribution of its population and level of education. These are mostly from the CNTS database, unless noted otherwise.

1. GDP per capita: This is a nation's Annual Gross Domestic Product Per Capita at factor cost.
2. Changes in GDP per capita: This is the change in per capita GDP.
3. Exchange: This is a nation's official exchange rate, at the end of the year in local currency per US dollar. If the official rate is inoperative after 1971, the effective rate (usually the IMF market or principal rate) is used.
4. Trade: This is from the World Bank's WDI database. Trade is the annual sum of exports and imports of goods and services measured as a share of GDP, with gaps filled in using Random Forest imputation.
5. Terms of trade: This is from the World Bank's WDI database. The terms of trade effect is the capacity to import minus exports of goods and services in constant prices. Data are in constant local currency.
6. Changes in imports per capita: This is the percentage change in per capita imports, measured in US dollars.
7. Changes in exports per capita: This is the percentage change in per capita imports, measured in US dollars.
8. PrimCommodityExports: This is from the World Bank's WDI database. It is a measure of the exports of primary commodities as a percent of merchandise exports. It is calculated using fuel exports, agricultural exports, and ores and metals exports.
9. AidAssist: This is from the World Bank's WDI database and is measured as aid assistance as percentage of GDP.
10. Area: This is from the World Bank's WDI database. Measured in square kilometers, it is a country's total area, excluding area under inland water bodies, national claims to continental shelf, and exclusive economic zones. In most cases the definition of inland water bodies includes major rivers and lakes.
11. DroughtIndex: The Palmer Drought Severity Index (PDSI) uses available precipitation and temperature data to estimate relative dryness. It is standardized to zero, and spans the range from –10 (relative dryness) to +10, (relative wetness).
12. DroughtIndexRange: This is the difference between the maximum and minimum values spatially for the PDSI.
13. ElectricPC: This gives a country's per capita gross generation of electricity. The data include production for both public and private purposes, and cover both thermal and hydroelectric output.
14. Gini: This is the SWIID Gini index measure of income inequality.

15. Inflation: Inflation as measured by the annual growth rate of the GDP deflator. This is from the World Bank's WDI database.
16. Investment: This is from the World Bank's WDI database. It is a country's gross capital formation as a percentage of GDP.

Variables that capture the total population, as well as where they reside are:

17. PopDensity: Also from the World Bank's WDI database, it is the number of people per sq. km of land area.
18. Populationgrowth: This measures the annual population growth rate. For year t is the exponential rate of growth of midyear population from year $t - 1$ to t, expressed as a percentage.
19. Urban population: This is from the World Bank's WDI database. Urban population refers to people living in urban areas as defined by national statistical offices. It is calculated using World Bank population estimates and urban ratios from the United Nations World Urbanization Prospects.
20. Urban population growth: This is the annual percentage change in the urban population.
21. RuralPop: This is from the World Bank's WDI database. Rural population refers to people living in rural areas as defined by national statistical offices. It is calculated as the difference between total population and urban population.
22. RuralPopGrowth: This is the annual percentage growth in rural population.
23. FemalePop: This is from the World Bank's WDI database. It is the percentage of the population that is female.

We capture communication with:

24. PhonesPC: This is the number of telephones per capita, including Cellular. It is largely drawn from telephone directory listings.

We have two variables that portray education rates:

25. SecEnrollPC: Secondary School Enrollment Per Capita is CNTS data on the number of students enrolled in secondary school per 10,000 people.
26. ChangesSecEnrollPC: This is the annual percentage change in per capita secondary school enrollment.

There is a varied literature on conflict that includes many of the institutional variables we include. However, many of these variables are correlated, and therefore may together capture a unique institutional dimension. Isolating these dimensions of institutional quality may not be entirely straightforward, and, in fact, each dimension may depend on multiple structural characteristics of a country's institutional structure. Yet even when this is not the case, the fact that these measures often capture elements of multiple concepts of institutions exposes them to considerable measurement error.

To address this issue, following Jong-A-Pin (2009) and Bang and Mitra (2011), we combine our measures of institutional quality and stability into an exploratory factor analysis (EFA) to develop a general view of institutions. Like these two studies, the EFA yields six dimensions of institutional

Table 3.1 EFA Table

<table>
<tr><th>Dimension</th><th>Democracy</th><th>Transparency</th><th>Protest</th><th>Credibility</th><th>Within Instability</th><th>Regime Instability</th></tr>
<tr><td>Assassinations</td><td></td><td></td><td></td><td></td><td></td><td></td></tr>
<tr><td>Bureaucratic Quality</td><td></td><td style="background:#ccc"></td><td></td><td></td><td></td><td></td></tr>
<tr><td>Cabinet Changes</td><td></td><td></td><td></td><td></td><td></td><td style="background:#ccc"></td></tr>
<tr><td>Changes in Vetoes</td><td></td><td></td><td></td><td></td><td></td><td></td></tr>
<tr><td>Checks on Power</td><td style="background:#ccc"></td><td></td><td></td><td></td><td></td><td></td></tr>
<tr><td>Corruption</td><td></td><td style="background:#ccc"></td><td></td><td></td><td></td><td></td></tr>
<tr><td>Dem. Accountability</td><td style="background:#ccc"></td><td style="background:#ccc"></td><td></td><td></td><td></td><td></td></tr>
<tr><td>Demonstrations</td><td></td><td></td><td style="background:#ccc"></td><td></td><td></td><td></td></tr>
<tr><td>Electoral Fraud</td><td></td><td style="background:#ccc"></td><td></td><td></td><td></td><td></td></tr>
<tr><td>Exec Electoral Competition</td><td style="background:#ccc"></td><td></td><td></td><td></td><td></td><td></td></tr>
<tr><td>Exec Years in Office</td><td style="background:#ccc"></td><td></td><td></td><td></td><td></td><td></td></tr>
<tr><td>Executive Changes</td><td></td><td></td><td></td><td></td><td></td><td style="background:#ccc"></td></tr>
<tr><td>Government Crises</td><td></td><td></td><td></td><td></td><td></td><td style="background:#ccc"></td></tr>
<tr><td>Government Herfindahl Index</td><td></td><td></td><td></td><td></td><td style="background:#ccc"></td><td></td></tr>
<tr><td>Government Polarization</td><td style="background:#ccc"></td><td style="background:#ccc"></td><td></td><td></td><td style="background:#ccc"></td><td></td></tr>
<tr><td>Government Stability</td><td></td><td></td><td></td><td style="background:#ccc"></td><td></td><td></td></tr>
<tr><td>Investment Prof</td><td></td><td style="background:#ccc"></td><td></td><td style="background:#ccc"></td><td></td><td></td></tr>
<tr><td>Legislative Fractionalization</td><td style="background:#ccc"></td><td></td><td></td><td></td><td style="background:#ccc"></td><td></td></tr>
<tr><td>Legislative Effectiveness</td><td style="background:#ccc"></td><td></td><td></td><td></td><td></td><td></td></tr>
<tr><td>Legislative Electoral Competition</td><td style="background:#ccc"></td><td></td><td></td><td></td><td></td><td></td></tr>
<tr><td>Polity2</td><td style="background:#ccc"></td><td></td><td></td><td></td><td></td><td></td></tr>
<tr><td>Purges</td><td></td><td></td><td></td><td></td><td></td><td></td></tr>
<tr><td>Regime Durability</td><td></td><td style="background:#ccc"></td><td></td><td></td><td></td><td></td></tr>
<tr><td>Riots</td><td></td><td></td><td style="background:#ccc"></td><td></td><td></td><td></td></tr>
<tr><td>Strikes</td><td></td><td></td><td style="background:#ccc"></td><td></td><td></td><td></td></tr>
</table>

quality and stability (Table 3.1). We use these dimensions instead of the actual institutional measures. These dimensions and their components follow. A cell is shaded if it is a dimension for the factor. For example, government crises, cabinet changes, and executive changes are dimensions of the factor for Regime Instability.

NOTES

1. For the specific definitions of the types of governance, please see the ICRG codebook, page 6.
2. For details, please see page 13 of the DPI codebook.
3. From DPI codebook, page 13: "Legislative and Executive Indices of Electoral Competitiveness (criteria modified from the scale created by Ferree and Singh, 1999) LIEC Legislative IEC.

Scale: No legislature: 1, Unelected legislature: 2, Elected: 1, Candidate: 3, 1 party, multiple candidates: 4, multiple parties are legal but only one party won seats: 5, multiple parties DID win seats but the largest party received more than 75% of the seats: 6, largest party got less than 75%: 7."

Chapter 4

Preparing the Data

In any attempt at data-driven mathematical modeling, there are key decisions about how the data should be prepared. These decisions can have important consequences on the exact nature of the phenomenon being modeled, on what sort of prediction algorithms can be used, on how effectively these algorithms will perform, and on how the model can be used both inferentially and predictively. In this chapter, we outline the various decisions we make in the data preparation process, and discuss how they relate to these issues.

There are two more issues that we have to consider. First, the choice of computational language is important. Currently, there is a wide variety to choose from R, C, Stata, SAS, Excel, MATLAB, Octave, Python, Julia, to name just a few. In choosing one, we weigh the strengths and weaknesses of these languages: their computational speed, cost, ease of use, availability of domain-specific toolboxes, documentation, support, and so on. We will not attempt to discuss all of these tradeoffs here but rather direct the reader to the following sources: Piatetsky (2014), Jordan and Mitchell (2015), and Brownlee (2014) articles. Second, we must consider whether to use a single language that allows a single unified group of code, or whether to use a variety of languages that allows the use of the strongest language for a particular task. In this book, we use a variety of language for data preparation and prediction. We list the language used for each task and the code where appropriate.

MERGING THE DATA

Our data are from the Political Instability Task Force (PITF), Standardized World Income Inequality Database (SWIID), World Development Indicators (WDI), Cross-National Time-Series (CNTS), International Country

Risk Guide (ICRG), Database of Political Institutions (DPI), and the Polity IV project. We merge these into a single database using STATA. Please see chapter 3 for a description of the variables.

Next, we make our first critical decision, we choose the target, or predicted variable. There are several potential choices. First, we could choose current conflict as our target variable. This would mean that we would be looking at the relationship between conflict in the current year and its predictor variables. There is merit in this choice, but, ultimately, it is a study of the social, economic, and political conditions that arise alongside conflict. Choosing current conflict as the target variable may be more useful in understanding the conditions of countries as they experience conflict.

Second, the target variable could be conflict in the upcoming year. The value of this choice would be that it could act as an 'early warning system' for conflict, much in the way a tornado siren works. Unfortunately, as with a tornado siren, such a model would allow time to escape or hide from a conflict, but not necessarily do anything to avert it.

Our third choice is to build separate models for the various types of conflicts: revolutionary war, ethnic war, regime change, or genocide. These models could potentially provide valuable information about the relationship of various economic, social, and political factors to these particular strains of conflicts. They could give insight into the predictors of each strain, as well as how these predictors relate to each other and differ from each other. However, a major drawback to this approach is that each individual type of conflict is rare and the relationships the models uncover may be tenuous based on the rarity of these events.

We construct LagConflict as our target variable. We explain our reasons for this choice below. We use the PITF's definition of conflict as the occurrence of any event of revolutionary war, ethnic war, regime change, or genocide as recorded by the PITF database. LagConflict is a binary variable that takes on the value 'conflict' if there is conflict in the next five years, excluding the current year, and 'not conflict,' if not. So, for example, if $t = 1990$, we consider LagConflict to be 'conflict' if there is conflict in the period 1991 to 1995. In this case, the predictor variables are from 1990.

This means that whatever inferences we draw regarding variable importance, we make about all of these types of conflict (revolutions, genocides, etc.) lumped as a single concept we call 'conflict.' That is, when we say a certain variable is important in predicting conflict, this does not tell us anything specifically about revolutions or genocides, but about conflict in general.

There are several consequences of this choice. First, including all the events in the dataset increases the total number of occurrences of conflict, that is, increases the number of observations in the dataset, which is an advantage.

However, this renders us unable to draw any conclusions about the relationship between the predictors and a particular kind of conflict. For example, we cannot say what predicts revolutionary wars, or what predicts regime changes. We can only draw conclusions about characteristics common to each of these types of conflicts.

Further, this choice makes the model entirely forward looking, that is, although the output of the model yields no information about the current conflict in a country, it provides information on the likelihood of conflict in the future. Thus, using 'conflict in the next five years' allows the model to track the factors that perhaps move a state toward conflict. In addition, this five-year forward window potentially provides the opportunity for strategic intervention, whereas the one-year forward window likely would not. Finally, this binary choice makes the target variable a 'class'—conflict or no conflict—so that most of the prediction algorithms will report a probability of conflict in the coming years. This is a prediction useful for policy makers.

HANDLING MISSING DATA

The second critical issue in this project is how to deal with missing observations in the dataset. Certain standard Machine Learning techniques, particularly the logistic regression and neural networks, do not have natural ways of doing this. Tree-based techniques tend to handle this issue easily, but, since a major goal of our work is to compare various techniques, we cannot restrict ourselves to using only one technique. A common way that prediction algorithms handle this problem is by ignoring observations with missing entries. However, conflict is a rare event, and, further, many of the countries that experience conflict have incomplete data. Therefore, ignoring missing observations would mean losing a large portion of our data.

We solve this problem by replacing the missing data with Random Forest imputation using the 'rfimpute/' function in R. This imputation method follows a two-step process. First, the missing entries are replaced with medians of the continuous variables and the most frequent value for categorical variables. Then, a Random Forest is grown relative to a target. The target we choose is the first principle component of the number of assassinations, strikes, demonstrations, crises, purges and riots in the year the data was missing. This principle component accounted for 70.67% of the variance in these variables. This was computed in MATLAB. This code is:

$$[\text{coeff,score,latent,tsquared,explained,mu}] = \text{pca}(X),$$

where X is the matrix containing columns with the number of assassinations, strikes, demonstrations, crises, purges, and riots, 'coeff' contains the loadings, 'score' contains the principle component analysis (PCA) scores, 'latent' returns the PCA variances, 'tsquared' returns the Hotelling's *T*-squared statistic for each observation, 'explained' is the percentage of total variance explained by each component, and 'mu' is the estimated mean of each variable in X.

The PCA is a common technique used in multivariate data analysis, particularly when one wants to reduce the number of variables in a mathematically rigorous way so as to capture as much of the variance in the original data as possible. Each principal component is a linear combination of the original variables, and each is orthogonal to all others, so that none contains any redundant information. When each observation is projected along each component, the new variable has the maximum amount of variance among all possible choices of axis, not including previous components (MATLAB PCA documentation).

In the final step, "The proximity matrix from the randomForest is used to update the imputation of the NAs (missing values). For continuous predictors, the imputed value is the weighted average of the non-missing observations, where the weights are the proximities. For categorical predictors, the imputed value is the category with the largest average proximity" (rfimpute documentation). This process is repeated for the number of iterations given in the function call. Note that the proximity matrix is the matrix whose entries describe the proportion of times an observation ends in the same leaf node for different trees in the Forest. The specific call of rfimpute is below. We used 500 trees, 10 iterations, a node size of 10, and the maximum number of nodes is 127.

RfImpute code

keeps.rfImpute <- rfImpute(DomesticPCA ~ Year + GDPpc + Trade + Investment + Area + AidAssist + Gini + Dependency + PopDensity + PopGrowth + FemalePop + RuralPop + RuralPopGrowth + UrbanPopGrowth + ChangeImportsPC + ChangeExportsPC + ChangePhonesPC + ChangeSecEnrollPC + ChangeGDPpc + ExchangeRate + ElectricPC + PhonesPC + SecEnrollPC + Inflation + TermsOfTrade + EthnicPolariz + ReligPolariz + PrimCommodityExports + DroughtIndex + DroughtIndexRange + System + LegCompetitiveness + PartyExclusion + Executive + ExecSelection + Regime + LegEffectiveness + PartyCoalitions + ParliamentRespons + GovStability + InvestmentProf + Corruption + DemAcct + BureaucraticQual + Polity2 + RegDurability + ExecYrsOffice + LIEC + EIEC + Fraud + GovHerfindahl + LegFrac + Checks + ChangeInVetoes + GovPolarization + Assassinations + Strikes + GovCrises + Purges + Riots + Demonstrations + EffectiveLeg + CabinetChgs + ExecutiveChgs + LagConflict +

YearsSinceConflict + Rubicon, data = ConflictData, ntree = 500, iter = 10, maxnodes = 127, nodesize = 10, localImp = TRUE)

One critical consequence of using this sort of imputation may not be readily apparent. This sort of imputation uses future values of predictor variables to impute missing values of predictor variables in the past. Note however that the imputation does not use the target variable, future conflict, in any way. This means that this study will function with the overarching assumption that conflict in this period is a relatively consistent phenomenon. This assumption attempts to compromise on potential tradeoffs. A benefit is that it gives us more data to find substantial relationships between social, political, and economic factors and future conflict. Its drawback is that it assumes these relationships are similar in 2009 (the last year we have five years of forward data to define our target) and 1955 (the first year).

VARIABLE REDUCTION

The next step is to reduce the size of the dataset in an interpretable way. Using exploratory factor analysis (EFA) in STATA, we create groups of more traditional metrics. This allows us to find a smaller number of unobserved or latent factors that can describe a larger number of observed variables. A more mathematically rigorous description of the technique is in Murphy (2012). Following Jong-A-Pin (2009) and Basuchoudhary et al. (2016), we use this technique to identify the underlying determinants of institutional quality. The five variables from the ICRG that we include in our EFA are (a) government stability, (b) the democratic accountability index, (c) the investment profile index, which captures the enforcement of contractual agreements and expropriation risk, (d) the corruption index, which measures the *absence* of corruption, and (e) the index of bureaucratic quality, which assesses the efficiency of the bureaucracy (Table 4.1).

An important note about several of the techniques used so far, PCA, EFA, and Random Forest imputation, is that these are all unsupervised data analysis techniques. In other words, none of these uses the target of interest in our model. They are all useful in understanding various factors about the predictor variables, but they ultimately tell us nothing about how these predictors relate to future conflict. We have not presented any lessons learned from these particular approaches to this data since the purpose of this book is to understand their relationship to conflict. However, one could potentially do so. Since we are focusing on the relationships of these techniques to future conflict, the focus of the primary algorithms and results will be in the context of supervised learning, where these algorithms learn the relationships between current social, political, and social conditions and future conflict.

Table 4.1 Exploratory Factor Analysis (EFA)

Variable	*Democracy*	*Transparency*	*Protest*	*Credibility*	*Within Instability*	*Regime Instability*
Gov. Stability	0.0038	0.1713	−0.1728	0.6894	0.0029	−0.0907
Investment Prof	0.1750	0.4171	−0.0656	0.6859	0.0225	−0.0407
Corruption	0.1773	0.7423	−0.0840	0.0259	0.0240	−0.0273
Dem Accountability	0.5419	0.5586	0.0051	0.1307	0.0685	0.0221
Bureaucratic Quality	0.2607	0.7813	0.0169	0.2429	0.0435	−0.0080
Polity2	0.7312	0.1463	0.0542	−0.0178	0.0322	0.0780
Regime Durability	0.1527	0.4118	0.1334	0.0470	−0.0427	−0.1325
Exec Years in Office	−0.3882	−0.0780	−0.0079	0.1056	−0.0932	−0.0514
Leg. Electoral Competition	0.8735	−0.0201	0.0236	0.0603	−0.0586	−0.0171
Exec Electoral Competition	0.9258	0.0148	−0.0018	0.0218	−0.0675	−0.0127
Electoral Fraud	−0.0194	−0.3141	−0.0138	−0.0049	−0.0099	0.0006
Gov. Herfindahl Index	−0.2905	−0.0981	0.0733	−0.0207	−0.6944	−0.0189
Leg. Fractionalization	0.6651	0.0254	0.0233	0.0301	0.5507	0.0378
Checks on Power	0.7687	0.1746	0.0126	−0.0725	0.1931	0.0122
Changes in Vetoes	0.1015	−0.0058	0.0317	−0.0775	0.0435	0.0710
Gov. Polarization	0.5059	0.3097	−0.0074	−0.0738	0.3628	0.0031
Assassinations	0.0685	−0.0979	0.1580	−0.1345	0.0050	0.0737
Strikes	0.1002	−0.0230	0.3793	−0.2023	0.0093	0.1050
Government Crises	0.1009	−0.0592	0.1858	−0.2407	0.0494	0.3666
Purges	−0.0429	−0.0438	0.1521	−0.0728	0.0003	0.1135
Riots	0.0614	−0.0396	0.7189	−0.1067	−0.0352	0.0529
Demonstrations	0.0630	−0.0110	0.7134	−0.0777	−0.0228	0.0153
Effectiveness of Leg.	0.5818	0.2206	0.0232	0.1032	−0.0664	0.0023
Cabinet Changes	0.0316	−0.0764	0.0547	−0.0988	0.0337	0.6186
Executive Changes	0.0860	−0.0064	0.0475	−0.0562	0.0099	0.6239

SPLITTING THE DATA INTO TESTING AND TRAINING SETS

A final issue in assessing the accuracy of various predictive algorithms, particularly those with a large number of internal parameters such as decision forests or neural network, is the splitting of the data. The dataset is split into a training set and a testing set. The former is the data on which the optimal parameters for each algorithm are found through a variety of optimization routines. The latter is the set of data to which the algorithms have never been exposed. It is this set that allows us to assess the generalizability of each algorithm to capture the phenomenon we are trying to model. This also gives some measure of the models' ability to assess future conflicts, and its effectiveness as a policy decision tool. Note that techniques that require a validation set, such as ANNs, use the training set for that purpose.

For this particular model, we used a stratified approach to splitting the data into the training and testing sets. In early testing, we found that those models that saw part of a particular country's conflicts were particular adept at predicting other conflicts. So our first criterion for splitting was that all observations for a particular country went in either the testing set or the training set. Second, as conflict is a rare event, the accuracy metrics for each predictive algorithm were sensitive to the number of conflicts in the test set. So, first we split the countries into two groups, one in which no conflict events were observed in the entire time period, and the second in which at least one conflict event was observed. After this split, 70% of the countries from each group were assigned to the training set, and 30% were assigned to the testing set.

Now that we have our data ready, we are ready to use Machine Learning techniques to rank variables according to how well they predict conflict. In the next chapter, we present some technical details on how to implement Machine Learning using R. Those wishing to jump to the results can move on to chapter 6.

SPLITTING CODE

```
# Cluster by Conflict History
ConflictData.Rubicon <- subset(ConflictData, Rubicon == “Conflict”)
ConflictData.NoRubicon <- subset(ConflictData, Rubicon == “No Conflict”)
# Randomly Subset “Rubicon” and “NoRubicon” sets by country into learning (“in”) sample and test (“out”) sample
## Rubicon
set.seed(8976)
```

1. Generate Random Number for Each Observation
ConflictData.Rubicon$rand <- runif(nrow(ConflictData.Rubicon))
2. Average Random Number by Country
ConflictData.Rubicon$randbar <- with(ConflictData.Rubicon, ave(rand, Country,FUN = mean))
3. Re-Scale the Averaged Random Numbers by Rank (so that they are again uniformly distributed)
ConflictData.Rubicon$randbarp <- rank(ConflictData.Rubicon$randbar)/ length(ConflictData.Rubicon$randbar)
4. Create Rubicon Learning and Test Subsets based on whether the re-scaled averaged randoms are less/greater than 0.7
ConflictData.Rubicon.LS <- subset(ConflictData.Rubicon, randbarp <= 0.70)
ConflictData.Rubicon.TS <- subset(ConflictData.Rubicon, randbarp > 0.70)
5. Drop the Random Number Variables rands <- c("rand", "randbar", "randbarp") ConflictData.Rubicon.LS <- ConflictData.Rubicon.LS[,!(names (ConflictData.Rubicon.LS) %in% rands)] ConflictData.Rubicon.TS <- ConflictData.Rubicon.TS[,!(names(ConflictData.Rubicon.TS) %in% rands)]
Repeat 1–5 for NoRubicon Subset set.seed(8976) ConflictData. NoRubicon$rand <- runif(nrow(ConflictData.NoRubicon)) ConflictData. NoRubicon$randbar <- with(ConflictData.NoRubicon, ave(rand,Country, FUN = mean))
ConflictData.NoRubicon$randbarp <- rank(ConflictData.NoRubicon $randbar)/length(ConflictData.NoRubicon$randbar) ConflictData.NoRubicon.LS <- subset(ConflictData.NoRubicon, randbarp <= 0.70)

Chapter 5

Implementing Machine Learning to Predict Conflict

Using R

In this chapter, we will lead readers through some of the code used in R to produce the learning results we discuss in the book. We hope that in doing so, readers will become sufficiently familiar with the technical details of how to use these commands in R so that it will not be too hard to apply these algorithms to a wide range of economic topics. To get started, you will need to download and install the following packages from one of the Comprehensive R Archive Networks (CRAN):

1. *foreign*	Loading STATA "*.dta" files
2. *rpart*	Recursive partitioning for classification and regression trees
3. *randomForest*	Classification and regression using random inputs
4. *adabag*	Gradient Boosting and bootstrap aggregating classification
5. *nnet*	Classification and regression using neural networks
6. *pROC*	Receiver operating characteristic curves
7. *rworldmap*	Drawing heat maps of predictions

In the interests of space, we limit our description of the packages and commands to the bare essentials that a researcher needs to replicate our results. There are at least a couple of hundred different types of Machine Learning models, and dozens of packages in R.[1] Also, there are many ways the researcher can fine-tune the basic models we introduce here: for different sizes and numbers of trees, for the numbers of variables or observations to randomly select, for different objective functions, and for different stopping criteria. Since the purpose of this book is to introduce the topic of Machine Learning to the issue of predicting conflict, we have minimized the number of specialized options by leaving several options at their default values.

Once you have installed the packages, load the data:

```
library(foreign)
ConflictData<-read.dta("ConflictBookData20160621.dta")
###Convert the character (string) variables into factor variables:
ConflictData$PartyExclusion <-as.factor(ConflictData$PartyExclusion)
ConflictData$Executive<-as.factor(ConflictData$Executive)
ConflictData$Regime<-as.factor(ConflictData$Regime)
ConflictData$PartyCoalitions<-as.factor(ConflictData$PartyCoalitions)
ConflictData$ParliamentRespons<-as.factor(ConflictData$ParliamentRespons)
ConflictData$System<-as.factor(ConflictData$System)
ConflictData$LegCompetitiveness <- as.factor(ConflictData$LegCompetitiveness)
ConflictData$ExecSelection <- as.factor(ConflictData$ExecSelection)
ConflictData$LegEffectiveness <- as.factor(ConflictData$LegEffectiveness)
```

Before proceeding further, note that many of our commands—assigning learning and test samples, selecting observations for the bootstrap samples, selecting the inputs for Random Forests, to name a few—use randomization. To ensure that our results are reproducible and comparable to similar work that may be done, we have used the "set.seed" command to fix the random seed in our code.

MISSING VALUES: RANDOM FOREST IMPUTATION

As we mentioned in chapter 4, missing data presents a serious problem for existing studies of conflict. Tree-based learning models have more flexibility for dealing with this than traditional regression models because they do not use standard matrix algebra to derive the decision rules. Hence, when these algorithms encounter missing data, they are able to sort them based on a "best guess" of how the observations with missing values might have been classified at a given node. This also implies a "best guess" with respect to the probable value for the missing information as well—usually the median or mode of the variable used to sort observations into that subnode.

However, parametric models do not have any such built in method for dealing with missing data: If a single variable in our specification is missing for certain observation(s), the method will drop the observation(s). Since we hope to be able to compare tree methods with more traditional parametric methods, it will be useful to impute the missing data so that we can compare them on the same sample. To do this, we use Random Forest imputation.

This method takes an average of the "best guesses" described above over hundreds of different trees. The *rfImpute* command in the *randomForest* package implements this procedure. We have used the following code to impute missing data:

```
set.seed(8976)
keeps.rfImpute<-rfImpute(DomesticPCA ~ Year + GDPpc + Trade + Investment + Area + AidAssist + Gini + Dependency + PopDensity + PopGrowth + FemalePop + RuralPop + RuralPopGrowth + UrbanPopGrowth + ChangeImportsPC + ChangeExportsPC + ChangePhonesPC + ChangeSecEnrollPC + ChangeGDPpc + ExchangeRate + ElectricPC + PhonesPC + SecEnrollPC + Inflation + TermsOfTrade + EthnicPolariz + ReligPolariz + PrimCommodityExports + DroughtIndex + DroughtIndexRange + System + LegCompetitiveness + PartyExclusion + Executive + ExecSelection + Regime + LegEffectiveness + PartyCoalitions + ParliamentRespons + GovStability + InvestmentProf + Corruption + DemAcct + BureaucraticQual + Polity2 + RegDurability + ExecYrsOffice + LIEC + EIEC + Fraud + GovHerfindahl + LegFrac + Checks + ChangeInVetoes + GovPolarization + Assassinations + Strikes + GovCrises + Purges + Riots + Demonstrations + EffectiveLeg + CabinetChgs + ExecutiveChgs + LagConflict + YearsSinceConflict + Rubicon, data = ConflictData, ntree = 500, iter = 10, maxnodes = 127, nodesize = 10, localImp = TRUE)
```

One last step to clean the data is to create dummy variables from the factor variables in order to estimate the Logit and neural network models later. Doing this now, before splitting the data will save several lines of code later. The class.ind function in R

```
i.System<-class.ind(ConflictData$System)
###Creates a new data frame of dummy variables based on the categories in the "System" variable from the learning sample.
colnames(i.System)<-paste("Sys", colnames(i.System), sep = "_")
###Names the columns of the dummy variables using the format "Sys_category," where category indicates the different categories of the System variable: "Presidential", "Parliamentary", or "AssemblyElectedPresident".
i.PartyExcl <-class.ind(ConflictData $PartyExclusion)
colnames(i.PartyExcl)<-paste("Excl",colnames(i.PartyExcl),sep = "_")
i.Executive <-class.ind(ConflictData $Executive)
colnames(i.Executive)<-paste("Exec",colnames(i.Executive),sep = "_")
i.Regime <-class.ind(ConflictData $Regime)
colnames(i.Regime)<-paste("Reg", colnames(i.Regime), sep = "_")
i.PartyCoal <-class.ind(ConflictData $PartyCoalitions)
```

```
colnames(i.PartyCoal)<-paste("Coal",colnames(i.PartyCoal),sep = "_")
i.ParlResp <-class.ind(ConflictData $ParliamentRespons)
colnames(i.ParlResp)<-paste("Resp", colnames(i.ParlResp),sep = "_")
###Repeats the steps in rows 29–30 for the Party Exclusion, Executive,
  Regime, PartyCoalitions, and Parliamentary Responsibility variables.
ConflictData.rfImpute<-cbind(ConflictData.rfImpute, i.System, i.PartyExcl,
  i.Executive, i.Regime, i.PartyCoal, i.ParlResp, ConflictData$wbcode,
  ConflictData$Conflict)
colnames(ConflictData.rfImpute)[99:100]<-c("wbcode", "Conflict")
write.dta(ConflictData.rfImpute, file = "ConflictBookDataImputed.dta")
###Combines the dummy variables with the ConflictData.rfImpute data
  frame and saves the imputed data to a *.dta (STATA data) file.
```

DATA REDUCTION: EXPLORATORY FACTOR ANALYSIS

Next, we notice that several of the proxies for institutional quality in our list of variables are correlated with one another. To avoid over-fitting our model, we want to eliminate some of the redundant variables using a data reduction technique. We have chosen to use exploratory factor analysis (EFA) for two main reasons: (1) like alternative methods such as the principle components analysis (PCA), EFA extracts a large proportion of the variance from the observed variables; and (2) unlike PCA, EFA preserves the common features of the observed variables and therefore lends itself better to interpretation.

We depart from R briefly and use STATA for the EFA because the package in R that implements EFA, *factanal*, has fewer options available for deriving and rotating the factor loadings. We prefer the principle factor method for deriving the factors because it does not make any *a priori* assumptions about the distribution of the variable. We also prefer the oblimin rotation method for which R requires the additional package, GPArotation. Also, the *factanal* function in R drops factor loadings below a certain threshold by default, which we prefer not to do. We therefore implement the following code in STATA using the factor command and the rotate and predict post-estimation command for our factor analysis:

```
use "ConflictBookDataImputed.dta"
factor GovStability InvestmentProf Corruption DemAcct Bureaucratic-
  Qual LIEC EIEC ExecYrsOffice Fraud GovHerfindahl ChangeInVetoes
  GovPolarization LegFrac Checks Polity2 RegDurability Assassinations
  Strikes GovCrises Purges Riots Demonstrations EffectiveLeg CabinetChgs
  ExecutiveChgs, factor (8)
```

```
rotate, oblimin
predict Democracy Transparency Protest Credibility WithinInstab
  RegimeInstab
saveold "ConflictBookDataImputed.dta", version(12) replace
```

Note that depending on your choice of derivation method, rotation method, and program, you may obtain the predicted factors in a different order and it may be necessary to rearrange the order of the variable names in the predict command.

LEARNING AND TEST SAMPLES

After we reduce the data using EFA, we need to load the imputed data with the new predicted factors back into R. We will use this dataset to divide our sample into learning and test subsets.

```
library(foreign)
ConflictData.rfImpute<-read.dta("ConflictBookDataImputed.dta")
ConflictData<-subset(ConflictData.rfImpute, Conflict != "NA")
```

As we divide our samples in to learning and test subsamples, we want to avoid two potential problems: (1) we do not want conflict episodes to be over or under-represented in either our learning or test samples; and (2) we do not want the same conflict episode to appear in both the learning and test samples. To avoid the first problem, we divide our sample based on whether it has ever experienced conflict in our sample period—the "Rubicon" variable.

```
# Cluster by Conflict History
ConflictData.Rubicon<-subset(ConflictData, Rubicon == "Conflict")
ConflictData.NoRubicon<-subset(ConflictData, Rubicon == "No Conflict")
```

Next, we randomly divide the observations into learning and test samples *by country*. We cluster the samples for each of the subsamples defined by conflict history in three steps: (1) create a random number for each observation; (2) average the random numbers for each country (this will create a bell-shaped distribution of random numbers); (3) create a uniform random number for each country based on the averages in (2) using the rank function.

```
set.seed(8976)
ConflictData.Rubicon$rand<-runif(nrow(ConflictData.Rubicon))
```

```
###Creates a variable with random numbers from a uniform[0,1] distribution for the countries in our sample with at least one conflict episode.
ConflictData.Rubicon$randbar<-with(ConflictData.Rubicon, ave(rand, wbcode, FUN = mean))
###Averages the random numbers for each country.
ConflictData.Rubicon$randbarp<-rank(ConflictData.Rubicon$randbar)/length(ConflictData.Rubicon$randbar)
###Redistributes the country-averaged random numbers onto a uniform[0,1] distribution using the rank function.
ConflictData.Rubicon.LS<-subset(ConflictData.Rubicon, randbarp <= 0.70)
ConflictData.Rubicon.TS<-subset(ConflictData.Rubicon, randbarp > 0.70)
###Creates a random learning and test sample for countries with histories of conflict.
set.seed(8976)
ConflictData.NoRubicon$rand<-runif(nrow(ConflictData.NoRubicon))
ConflictData.NoRubicon$randbar<-with(ConflictData.NoRubicon, ave(rand, wbcode, FUN = mean))
ConflictData.NoRubicon$randbarp<-rank(ConflictData.NoRubicon$randbar)/length(ConflictData.NoRubicon$randbar)
ConflictData.NoRubicon.LS<-subset(ConflictData.NoRubicon, randbarp <= 0.70)
ConflictData.NoRubicon.TS<-subset(ConflictData.NoRubicon, randbarp > 0.70)
###Repeats 62–68 for countries without an episode of conflict in our sample period.
ConflictData.LS<-rbind(ConflictData.Rubicon.LS, ConflictData.NoRubicon.LS)
ConflictData.TS<-rbind(ConflictData.Rubicon.TS, ConflictData.NoRubicon.TS)
###Recombines the countries with histories of conflict to those without histories of conflict for both the learning and test samples.
```

TRAINING THE MODELS AND PREDICTING CONFLICT

Now we are ready to train the models. We load the rpart, randomForest, adabag, nnet, and pROC libraries.

```
library(rpart); library(randomForest); library(adabag); library(nnet); library(pROC)
```

TRAINING THE MODELS

To build a single classification tree model, we use the rpart(y ~ X, data = frame, options) function. The required arguments for this function are (1) a function and (2) a data object. In addition, we set the options "model," "x," and "y" equal to "TRUE," the complexity parameter to 0.001, the maximum tree depth to 5, and the minimum number of observations to consider a new split to 10 using the "rpart.control" options.

```
set.seed(8976)
Conflict.rpart <- rpart(Conflict ~ Year + GDPpc + Trade + Investment + Area
  + AidAssist + Gini + Dependency + PopDensity + PopGrowth + Fema-
  lePop + RuralPop + RuralPopGrowth + UrbanPopGrowth + ChangeIm-
  portsPC + ChangeExportsPC + ChangePhonesPC + ChangeSecEnrollPC +
  ChangeGDPpc + ExchangeRate + ElectricPC + PhonesPC + SecEnrollPC
  + Inflation + TermsOfTrade + EthnicPolariz + ReligPolariz + PrimCom-
  modityExports + DroughtIndex + DroughtIndexRange + System + Party-
  Exclusion + Executive + Regime + PartyCoalitions + ParliamentRespons
  + Democracy + Transparency + Credibility + WithinInstab + Protest +
  RegimeInstab + LagConflict, data = ConflictData.LS, na.action = na.rpart,
  model = TRUE, x = TRUE, y = TRUE, control = rpart.control(cp = 0.001,
  maxdepth = 5, minsplit = 10))
```

Next, we build the bootstrap aggregating (Bagging) and gradient Boosting models. Since the adabag package uses the same control options as rpart, we use the same control options as the single trees. However, we need to add one pre-estimation command to set the random seed (for reproducibility) and one post-estimation command to label the columns of the votes object (for more attractive confusion matrix tables).

```
set.seed(8976)
Conflict.bag <- Bagging(Conflict ~ Year + GDPpc + Trade + Investment
  + Area + AidAssist + Gini + Dependency + PopDensity + PopGrowth
  + FemalePop + RuralPop + RuralPopGrowth + UrbanPopGrowth +
  ChangeImportsPC + ChangeExportsPC + ChangePhonesPC + ChangeSe-
  cEnrollPC + ChangeGDPpc + ExchangeRate + ElectricPC + PhonesPC +
  SecEnrollPC + Inflation + TermsOfTrade + EthnicPolariz + ReligPolariz +
  PrimCommodityExports + DroughtIndex + DroughtIndexRange + System
  + PartyExclusion + Executive + Regime + PartyCoalitions + Parliamen-
  tRespons + Democracy + Transparency + Credibility + WithinInstab +
```

Protest + RegimeInstab + LagConflict, data = ConflictData.LS, control = rpart.control(cp = 0.001,maxdepth = 5, minsplit = 10))
colnames(Conflict.bag$votes) <- c("Conflict", "No Conflict") set.seed(8976)
Conflict.boost <- Boosting(Conflict ~ Year + GDPpc + Trade + Investment + Area + AidAssist + Gini + Dependency + PopDensity + PopGrowth + FemalePop + RuralPop + RuralPopGrowth + UrbanPopGrowth + ChangeImportsPC + ChangeExportsPC + ChangePhonesPC + ChangeSecEnrollPC + ChangeGDPpc + ExchangeRate + ElectricPC + PhonesPC + SecEnrollPC + Inflation + TermsOfTrade + EthnicPolariz + ReligPolariz + PrimCommodityExports + DroughtIndex + DroughtIndexRange + System + PartyExclusion + Executive + Regime + PartyCoalitions + ParliamentRespons + Democracy + Transparency + Credibility + WithinInstab + Protest + RegimeInstab + LagConflict, data = ConflictData.LS, control = rpart.control(cp = 0.001, maxdepth = 5, minsplit = 10), mfinal = 25)
colnames(Conflict.boost$votes) <- c("Conflict", "No Conflict")

We then use the randomForest(y ~ x, data = frame, options) function to build the Forest. In this case, the control parameters differ slightly from the rpart function. We approximate the rpart.control options by setting maxnodes = 127 (about 5 levels for each tree) and nodesize = 10 to control the splitting rule. We also set proximity = "TRUE" so that R will calculate proximity measures among the rows, localImp = "TRUE" so that the algorithm will calculate importance in the aggregate and case-by-case; and keep Forest = "TRUE" so that the rF object will retain the individual tree structures in case we want to extract them later.

set.seed(8976)
Conflict.rF <- randomForest(Conflict ~ Year + GDPpc + Trade + Investment + Area + AidAssist + Gini + Dependency + PopDensity + PopGrowth + FemalePop + RuralPop + RuralPopGrowth + UrbanPopGrowth + ChangeImportsPC + ChangeExportsPC + ChangePhonesPC + ChangeSecEnrollPC + ChangeGDPpc + ExchangeRate + ElectricPC + PhonesPC + SecEnrollPC + Inflation + TermsOfTrade + EthnicPolariz + ReligPolariz + PrimCommodityExports + DroughtIndex + DroughtIndexRange + System + PartyExclusion + Executive + Regime + PartyCoalitions + ParliamentRespons + Democracy + Transparency + Credibility + WithinInstab + Protest + RegimeInstab + LagConflict, data = ConflictData.LS, na.action = na.roughfix, maxnodes = 127, proximity = TRUE, nodesize = 10, localImp = TRUE, keep.Forest = TRUE)

Next, we estimate the parametric models—logistic regression and neural networks. We run the logistic regression model using the glm(y ~ X, data

= frame, family = "binomial," options) function. We do not set any of the other options. These advanced options govern the initial values, weighting of observations, and optimization method. Typically, these only need to be used if there is a problem with the standard defaults.

Conflict.logit <- glm(Conflict ~ Year + GDPpc + Trade + Investment + Area + AidAssist + Gini + Dependency + PopDensity + PopGrowth + FemalePop + RuralPop + RuralPopGrowth + UrbanPopGrowth + ChangeImportsPC + ChangeExportsPC + ChangePhonesPC + ChangeSecEnrollPC + ChangeGDPpc + ExchangeRate + ElectricPC + PhonesPC + SecEnrollPC + Inflation + TermsOfTrade + EthnicPolariz + ReligPolariz + PrimCommodityExports + DroughtIndex + DroughtIndexRange + Democracy + Transparency + Credibility + WithinInstab + Protest + RegimeInstab + LagConflict + Sys_ + Sys_AssemblyElectedPresident + Sys_Parliamentary + Sys_Presidential + Excl_ + Excl_NoneExcluded + Excl_NoParties + Excl_ExtremistsExcluded + Excl_SignificantExclusion + Exec_ + Exec_Military + Exec_Monarch + Exec_Other + Exec_Premier + Exec_President + Reg_+ Reg_Civilian + Reg_Military + Reg_MilitaryCivilian + Reg_Other + Coal_ + Coal_CoalitionNoOpposition + Coal_CoalitionOpposition + Coal_NoCoalition + Coal_OneParty + Resp_ + Resp_Absent + Resp_Complete + Resp_Incomplete + Resp_Irrelevant, data = ConflictData.LS, family = "binomial")

Finally, we estimate the ANN models using nnet(y ~ X, data = frame, options). The only options we set differently from the defaults are the number of nodes in the hidden layer, which we set to size = 10, and the maximum number of weights, which we set to MaxNWts = 2200. The latter option ensures that the network will run without error. One must be a little careful however: estimating a network with too many weights relative to the size of the learning sample can sometimes invalidate the results and even cause the model to predict poorly.

set.seed(8976)
Conflict.nnet <- nnet(Conflict ~ Year + GDPpc + Trade + Investment + Area + AidAssist + Gini + Dependency + PopDensity + PopGrowth + FemalePop + RuralPop + RuralPopGrowth + UrbanPopGrowth + ChangeImportsPC + ChangeExportsPC + ChangePhonesPC + ChangeSecEnrollPC + ChangeGDPpc + ExchangeRate + ElectricPC + PhonesPC + SecEnrollPC + Inflation + TermsOfTrade + EthnicPolariz + ReligPolariz + PrimCommodityExports + DroughtIndex + DroughtIndexRange + Democracy + Transparency + Credibility + WithinInstab + Protest + RegimeInstab + LagConflict + Sys_ + Sys_AssemblyElectedPresident + Sys_Parliamentary + Sys_Presidential + Excl_ + Excl_NoneExcluded + Excl_NoParties

+ Excl_ExtremistsExcluded + Excl_SignificantExclusion + Exec_ + Exec_Military + Exec_Monarch + Exec_Other + Exec_Premier + Exec_President + Reg_ + Reg_Civilian + Reg_Military + Reg_MilitaryCivilian + Reg_Other + Coal_ + Coal_CoalitionNoOpposition + Coal_CoalitionOpposition + Coal_NoCoalition +Coal_OneParty + Resp_ + Resp_Absent + Resp_Complete + Resp_Incomplete + Resp_Irrelevant, data = ConflictData.LS, size = 10, MaxNWts = 2200, maxit = 200)

PREDICTED VALUES

We use the *predict* function to extract the predicted classes (conflict or no conflict) and probabilities of conflict for each of the learning models. For the Bagging and Boosting models, we need to use "as.factor" to make sure that the class predictions are not stored as numerical variables. We also use column #1 of the predicted probability matrix for the Bagging and Boosting models since these models store the predicted probability of each class in separate columns. We attach these predicted values immediately to the data frames. Our code for extracting and attaching these predicted values executes is:

Probabilities:

ConflictData.LS$treeProb<-predict(Conflict.rpart, type="prob")[,"Conflict"]
###Extracts the predicted probabilities based on the Single-Tree model for the learning sample.
ConflictData.TS$treeProb<-predict(Conflict.rpart, type = "prob", newdata = ConflictData.TS)[,"Conflict"]
###Extracts the predicted probabilities based on the Single-Tree model for the test sample.
ConflictData.LS$rfProb<-predict(Conflict.rF, type = "prob")[,"Conflict"]
ConflictData.TS$rfProb<-predict(Conflict.rF, type = "prob", newdata = ConflictData.TS)[,"Conflict"]
ConflictData.LS$bagProb<-predict(Conflict.bag, newdata = ConflictData.LS)$prob[,2]
ConflictData.TS$bagProb<-predict(Conflict.bag, newdata = ConflictData.TS)$prob[,2]
ConflictData.LS$boostProb<-predict(Conflict.boost, newdata = ConflictData.LS)$prob[,2]
ConflictData.TS$boostProb<-predict(Conflict.boost, newdata = ConflictData.TS)$prob[,2]
ConflictData.LS$logitProb<-predict(Conflict.logit, newdata = ConflictData.LS, type = "response")

ConflictData.TS$logitProb<-predict(Conflict.logit, newdata = ConflictData.TS, type = "response")

ConflictData.LS$nnetProb<-as.vector(Conflict.nnet$fitted.values)

ConflictData.TS$nnetProb<-as.vector(predict(Conflict.nnet, newdata = ConflictData.TS, type = "raw"))

###Repeats lines 167–169 for the Forest, Bagging, Boosting, Logit, and neural network models.

ConflictData.LS$averageProb<-(ConflictData.LS$treeProb + ConflictData.LS$rfProb + ConflictData.LS$bagProb + ConflictData.LS$boostProb + ConflictData.LS$logitProb + ConflictData.LS$nnetProb)/6

ConflictData.TS$averageProb<-(ConflictData.TS$treeProb + ConflictData.TS$rfProb + ConflictData.TS$bagProb + ConflictData.TS$boostProb + ConflictData.TS$logitProb + ConflictData.TS$nnetProb)/6

###Calculates the average predicted probabilities from the 6 models for the test and learning samples.

###Classes:

ConflictData.LS$treeClass<-predict(Conflict.rpart, type = "class")

###Extracts the predicted classes for the Single-Tree model for the learning sample by classifying all cases with probabilities of conflict greater than or equal to 0.5 as "Conflict," and cases with probabilities of conflict less than 0.5 as "No Conflict."

ConflictData.TS$treeClass<-predict(Conflict.rpart, type = "class", newdata = ConflictData.TS)

###Extracts the predicted classes based on the Single-Tree model for the test sample.

ConflictData.LS$rfClass<-predict(Conflict.rF, type = "class")

ConflictData.TS$rfClass<-predict(Conflict.rF, type = "class", newdata = ConflictData.TS)

ConflictData.LS$bagClass<-as.factor(predict(Conflict.bag, newdata = ConflictData.LS)$class)

ConflictData.TS$bagClass<-as.factor(predict(Conflict.bag, newdata = ConflictData.TS)$class)

ConflictData.LS$boostClass<-as.factor(predict(Conflict.boost, newdata = ConflictData.LS)$class)

ConflictData.TS$boostClass<-as.factor(predict(Conflict.boost, newdata = ConflictData.TS)$class)

ConflictData.LS$logitClass<-as.factor(ifelse(ConflictData.LS$logitProb < 0.5, "No Conflict", "Conflict"))

ConflictData.TS$logitClass<-as.factor(ifelse(ConflictData.TS$logitProb < 0.5, "No Conflict", "Conflict"))

```
ConflictData.LS$nnetClass<-as.factor(predict(Conflict.nnet, newdata = ConflictData.LS, type = “class”))
ConflictData.TS$nnetClass<-as.factor(predict(Conflict.nnet, newdata = ConflictData.TS, type = “class”))
ConflictData.LS$averageClass<-ifelse(ConflictData.LS$averageProb < 0.5, “No Conflict”, “Conflict”)
ConflictData.TS$averageClass<-ifelse(ConflictData.TS$averageProb < 0.5, “No Conflict”, “Conflict”)
###Obtains the predicted class for the Forest, Bagging, Boosting, Logit, neural network, and average models.
```

PREDICTIVE ACCURACY, IMPORTANCE, AND PARTIAL DEPENDENCE PLOTS

Now that we have trained our learning models and obtained the predicted probabilities and classes from the models, we need to interpret the results.

MEASURES OF PREDICTIVE ACCURACY

There are six general measures of predictive accuracy that we use to assess the performance of a model: sensitivity, specificity, positive predictive value (PPV), negative predictive value (NPV), and the overall error rate.

```
    Confusion.tree.LS <-with(ConflictData.LS, table(Conflict, treeClass))
###Creates the confusion matrix for the tree model using the learning sample.
    Confusion.tree.TS<-with(ConflictData.TS, table(Conflict, treeClass))
###Creates the confusion matrix for the tree model using the test sample.
Confusion.rf.LS <-with(ConflictData.LS, table(Conflict, rfClass))
Confusion.rf.TS<-with(ConflictData.TS, table(Conflict, rfClass))
Confusion.bag.LS <-with(ConflictData.LS, table(Conflict, bagClass))
Confusion.bag.LS <- cbind(Confusion.bag.LS[,2], Confusion.bag.LS[,1])
colnames(Confusion.bag.LS)<-rownames(Confusion.bag.LS)
Confusion.bag.TS<-with(ConflictData.TS, table(Conflict, bagClass))
Confusion.bag.TS <- cbind(Confusion.bag.TS[,2], Confusion.bag.TS[,1])
colnames(Confusion.bag.TS)<-rownames(Confusion.bag.TS)
Confusion.boost.LS <-with(ConflictData.LS, table(Conflict, boostClass))
Confusion.boost.LS <- cbind(Confusion.boost.LS[,2], Confusion.boost.LS[,1])
colnames(Confusion.boost.LS)<-rownames(Confusion.boost.LS)
Confusion.boost.TS<-with(ConflictData.TS, table(Conflict, boostClass))
Confusion.boost.TS <- cbind(Confusion.boost.TS[,2], Confusion.boost.TS[,1])
```

```
colnames(Confusion.boost.TS)<-rownames(Confusion.boost.TS)
Confusion.logit.LS <-with(ConflictData.LS, table(Conflict, logitClass))
Confusion.logit.LS <- cbind(Confusion.logit.LS[,2], Confusion.logit.LS[,1])
colnames(Confusion.logit.LS)<-rownames(Confusion.logit.LS)
Confusion.logit.TS<-with(ConflictData.TS, table(Conflict, logitClass))
Confusion.logit.TS <- cbind(Confusion.logit.TS[,2], Confusion.logit.TS[,1])
colnames(Confusion.logit.TS)<-rownames(Confusion.logit.TS)
Confusion.nnet.LS <-with(ConflictData.LS, table(Conflict, nnetClass))
Confusion.nnet.LS <- cbind(Confusion.nnet.LS[,2], Confusion.nnet.LS[,1])
colnames(Confusion.nnet.LS)<-rownames(Confusion.nnet.LS)
Confusion.nnet.TS<-with(ConflictData.TS, table(Conflict, nnetClass))
Confusion.nnet.TS <- cbind(Confusion.nnet.TS[,2], Confusion.nnet.TS[,1])
colnames(Confusion.nnet.TS)<-rownames(Confusion.nnet.TS)
Confusion.ave.LS <-with(ConflictData.LS, table(Conflict, averageClass))
Confusion.ave.LS <- cbind(Confusion.ave.LS[,2], Confusion.ave.LS[,1])
colnames(Confusion.ave.LS)<-rownames(Confusion.ave.LS)
Confusion.ave.TS<-with(ConflictData.TS, table(Conflict, averageClass))
Confusion.ave.TS <- cbind(Confusion.ave.TS[,2], Confusion.ave.TS[,1])
colnames(Confusion.ave.TS)<-rownames(Confusion.ave.TS)
## Repeats 223–224 for the Forest, Bagging, Boosting, Logit, ANN, and
average predictions.
```

We have also included code to rearrange some of the columns so that they are consistent across all learning models, and so that the correctly predicted cases line up on the diagonal going down from left to right.

After having tabulated these matrices, we must calculate the measures of predictive accuracy. These are simple row or column percentages, the code for which we provide below.

SPECIFICITY

Specificity, also known as the true negative rate, is calculated as the number of correctly predicted negative outcomes divided by the total number of observed negative outcomes. It is also equal to one minus the Type I error rate. There are several ways to calculate this value, but the most straightforward might be simply to calculate it using row one of the confusion matrix.

```
Specificity.tree.LS<-Confusion.tree.LS[1,1]/(Confusion.tree.LS[1,1] +
Confusion.tree.LS[1,2])
###Calculates the specificity for the tree model learning sample.
```

Specificity.tree.TS<-Confusion.tree.TS[1,1]/(Confusion.tree.TS[1,1] + Confusion.tree.TS[1,2])
###Calculates the specificity for the tree model test sample.
Specificity.rf.LS<-Confusion.rf.LS[1,1]/(Confusion.rf.LS[1,1] + Confusion.rf.LS[1,2])
Specificity.rf.TS<-Confusion.rf.TS[1,1]/(Confusion.rf.TS[1,1] + Confusion.rf.TS[1,2])
Specificity.bag.LS<-Confusion.bag.LS[1,1]/(Confusion.bag.LS[1,1] + Confusion.bag.LS[1,2])
Specificity.bag.TS<-Confusion.bag.TS[1,1]/(Confusion.bag.TS[1,1] + Confusion.bag.TS[1,2])
Specificity.boost.LS<-Confusion.boost.LS[1,1]/(Confusion.boost.LS[1,1] + Confusion.boost.LS[1,2])
Specificity.boost.TS<-Confusion.boost.TS[1,1]/(Confusion.boost.TS[1,1] + Confusion.boost.TS[1,2])
Specificity.logit.LS<-Confusion.logit.LS[1,1]/(Confusion.logit.LS[1,1] + Confusion.logit.LS[1,2])
Specificity.logit.TS<-Confusion.logit.TS[1,1]/(Confusion.logit.TS[1,1] + Confusion.logit.TS[1,2])
Specificity.nnet.LS<-Confusion.nnet.LS[1,1]/(Confusion.nnet.LS[1,1] + Confusion.nnet.LS[1,2])
Specificity.nnet.TS<-Confusion.nnet.TS[1,1]/(Confusion.nnet.TS[1,1] + Confusion.nnet.TS[1,2])
Specificity.ave.LS<-Confusion.ave.LS[1,1]/(Confusion.ave.LS[1,1] + Confusion.ave.LS[1,2])
Specificity.ave.TS<-Confusion.ave.TS[1,1]/(Confusion.ave.TS[1,1] + Confusion.ave.TS[1,2])
###Repeat for the other learning models.

SENSITIVITY

Sensitivity, also known as the true positive rate, is the number of correctly predicted positives divided by the total number of positives, or one minus the Type II error rate. As with the specificity, we calculate sensitivity using the confusion matrix—this time using row two.

Sensitivity.tree.LS<-Confusion.tree.LS[2,2]/(Confusion.tree.LS[2,2] + Confusion.tree.LS[2,1])
Sensitivity.tree.TS<-Confusion.tree.TS[2,2]/(Confusion.tree.TS[2,2] + Confusion.tree.TS[2,1])

```
Sensitivity.rf.LS<-Confusion.rf.LS[2,2]/(Confusion.rf.LS[2,2] + Confusion.rf.LS[2,1])
Sensitivity.rf.TS<-Confusion.rf.TS[2,2]/(Confusion.rf.TS[2,2] + Confusion.rf.TS[2,1])
Sensitivity.bag.LS<-Confusion.bag.LS[2,2]/(Confusion.bag.LS[2,2] + Confusion.bag.LS[2,1])
Sensitivity.bag.TS<-Confusion.bag.TS[2,2]/(Confusion.bag.TS[2,2] + Confusion.bag.TS[2,1])
Sensitivity.boost.LS<-Confusion.boost.LS[2,2]/(Confusion.boost.LS[2,2] + Confusion.boost.LS[2,1])
Sensitivity.boost.TS<-Confusion.boost.TS[2,2]/(Confusion.boost.TS[2,2] + Confusion.boost.TS[2,1])
Sensitivity.logit.LS<-Confusion.logit.LS[2,2]/(Confusion.logit.LS[2,2] + Confusion.logit.LS[2,1])
Sensitivity.logit.TS<-Confusion.logit.TS[2,2]/(Confusion.logit.TS[2,2] + Confusion.logit.TS[2,1])
Sensitivity.nnet.LS<-Confusion.nnet.LS[2,2]/(Confusion.nnet.LS[2,2] + Confusion.nnet.LS[2,1])
Sensitivity.nnet.TS<-Confusion.nnet.TS[2,2]/(Confusion.nnet.TS[2,2] + Confusion.nnet.TS[2,1])
Sensitivity.ave.LS<-Confusion.ave.LS[2,2]/(Confusion.ave.LS[2,2] + Confusion.ave.LS[2,1])
Sensitivity.ave.TS<-Confusion.ave.TS[2,2]/(Confusion.ave.TS[2,2] + Confusion.ave.TS[2,1])
```

POSITIVE PREDICTIVE VALUE

The positive predictive value (PPV), also known as the precision, is calculated as the number of correctly predicted positives divided by the total number of predicted positives. We calculate PPV using the *columns* of the confusion matrix—in this case column 2.

```
PPV.tree.LS<-Confusion.tree.LS[2,2]/(Confusion.tree.LS[2,2] + Confusion.tree.LS[1,2])
PPV.tree.TS<-Confusion.tree.TS[2,2]/(Confusion.tree.TS[2,2] + Confusion.tree.TS[1,2])
PPV.rf.LS<-Confusion.rf.LS[2,2]/(Confusion.rf.LS[2,2] + Confusion.rf.LS[1,2])
PPV.rf.TS<-Confusion.rf.TS[2,2]/(Confusion.rf.TS[2,2] + Confusion.rf.TS[1,2])
```

```
PPV.bag.LS<-Confusion.bag.LS[2,2]/(Confusion.bag.LS[2,2] + Confusion.bag.LS[1,2])
PPV.bag.TS<-Confusion.bag.TS[2,2]/(Confusion.bag.TS[2,2] + Confusion.bag.TS[1,2])
PPV.boost.LS<-Confusion.boost.LS[2,2]/(Confusion.boost.LS[2,2] + Confusion.boost.LS[1,2])
PPV.boost.TS<-Confusion.boost.TS[2,2]/(Confusion.boost.TS[2,2] + Confusion.boost.TS[1,2])
PPV.logit.LS<-Confusion.logit.LS[2,2]/(Confusion.logit.LS[2,2] + Confusion.logit.LS[1,2])
PPV.logit.TS<-Confusion.logit.TS[2,2]/(Confusion.logit.TS[2,2] + Confusion.logit.TS[1,2])
PPV.nnet.LS<-Confusion.nnet.LS[2,2]/(Confusion.nnet.LS[2,2] + Confusion.nnet.LS[1,2])
PPV.nnet.TS<-Confusion.nnet.TS[2,2]/(Confusion.nnet.TS[2,2] + Confusion.nnet.TS[1,2])
PPV.ave.LS<-Confusion.ave.LS[2,2]/(Confusion.ave.LS[2,2] + Confusion.ave.LS[1,2])
PPV.ave.TS<-Confusion.ave.TS[2,2]/(Confusion.ave.TS[2,2] + Confusion.ave.TS[1,2])
```

NEGATIVE PREDICTIVE VALUE

The negative predictive value (NPV) is the number of correctly predicted negatives divided by the total number of predicted negatives. We calculate it using Column one of the confusion matrix.

```
NPV.tree.LS<-Confusion.tree.LS[1,1]/(Confusion.tree.LS[1,1] + Confusion.tree.LS[2,1])
NPV.tree.TS<-Confusion.tree.TS[1,1]/(Confusion.tree.TS[1,1] + Confusion.tree.TS[2,1])
NPV.rf.LS<-Confusion.rf.LS[1,1]/(Confusion.rf.LS[1,1] + Confusion.rf.LS[2,1])
NPV.rf.TS<-Confusion.rf.TS[1,1]/(Confusion.rf.TS[1,1] + Confusion.rf.TS[2,1])
NPV.bag.LS<-Confusion.bag.LS[1,1]/(Confusion.bag.LS[1,1] + Confusion.bag.LS[2,1])
NPV.bag.TS<-Confusion.bag.TS[1,1]/(Confusion.bag.TS[1,1] + Confusion.bag.TS[2,1])
NPV.boost.LS<-Confusion.boost.LS[1,1]/(Confusion.boost.LS[1,1] + Confusion.boost.LS[2,1])
```

NPV.boost.TS<-Confusion.boost.TS[1,1]/(Confusion.boost.TS[1,1] + Confusion.boost.TS[2,1])
NPV.logit.LS<-Confusion.logit.LS[1,1]/(Confusion.logit.LS[1,1] + Confusion.logit.LS[2,1])
NPV.logit.TS<-Confusion.logit.TS[1,1]/(Confusion.logit.TS[1,1] + Confusion.logit.TS[2,1])
NPV.nnet.LS<-Confusion.nnet.LS[1,1]/(Confusion.nnet.LS[1,1] + Confusion.nnet.LS[2,1])
NPV.nnet.TS<-Confusion.nnet.TS[1,1]/(Confusion.nnet.TS[1,1] + Confusion.nnet.TS[2,1])
NPV.ave.LS<-Confusion.ave.LS[1,1]/(Confusion.ave.LS[1,1] + Confusion.ave.LS[2,1])
NPV.ave.TS<-Confusion.ave.TS[1,1]/(Confusion.ave.TS[1,1] + Confusion.ave.TS[2,1])

OVERALL ERROR RATE

The overall error rate, also known as the redistribution estimate, is the number of incorrectly predicted observations divided by the total number of observations. We calculate it by dividing the off-diagonal terms of the confusion matrix by the total number of observations.

Error.tree.LS<-(Confusion.tree.LS[1,2] + Confusion.tree.LS[2,1])/length(ConflictData.LS)
Error.tree.TS<-(Confusion.tree.TS[1,2] + Confusion.tree.TS[2,1])/length(ConflictData.TS)
Error.rf.LS<-(Confusion.rf.LS[1,2] + Confusion.rf.LS[2,1])/length(ConflictData.LS)
Error.rf.TS<-(Confusion.rf.TS[1,2] + Confusion.rf.TS[2,1])/length(ConflictData.TS)
Error.bag.LS<-(Confusion.bag.LS[1,2] + Confusion.bag.LS[2,1])/length(ConflictData.LS)
Error.bag.TS<-(Confusion.bag.TS[1,2] + Confusion.bag.TS[2,1])/length(ConflictData.TS)
Error.boost.LS<-(Confusion.boost.LS[1,2] + Confusion.boost.LS[2,1])/length(ConflictData.LS)
Error.boost.TS<-(Confusion.boost.TS[1,2] + Confusion.boost.TS[2,1])/length(ConflictData.TS)
Error.logit.LS<-(Confusion.logit.LS[1,2] + Confusion.logit.LS[2,1])/length(ConflictData.LS)

```
Error.logit.TS<-(Confusion.logit.TS[1,2] + Confusion.logit.TS[2,1])/
  length(ConflictData.TS)
Error.nnet.LS<-(Confusion.nnet.LS[1,2] + Confusion.nnet.LS[2,1])/
  length(ConflictData.LS)
Error.nnet.TS<-(Confusion.nnet.TS[1,2] + Confusion.nnet.TS[2,1])/
  length(ConflictData.TS)
Error.ave.LS<-(Confusion.ave.LS[1,2] + Confusion.ave.LS[2,1])/
  length(ConflictData.LS)
Error.ave.TS<-(Confusion.ave.TS[1,2] + Confusion.ave.TS[2,1])/
  length(ConflictData.TS)
```

Finally, we combine the predictive quality measures into a table using *cbind* and *rbind*.

```
PredictiveQuality.LS <- cbind(rbind(Specificity.tree.LS, Sensitivity.tree.
  LS, PPV.tree.LS, NPV.tree.LS, Error.ave.LS), rbind(Specificity.rf.LS,
  Sensitivity.rf.LS, PPV.rf.LS, NPV.rf.LS, Error.rf.LS), rbind(Specificity.
  bag.LS, Sensitivity.bag.LS, PPV.bag.LS, NPV.bag.LS, Error.bag.LS),
  rbind(Specificity.boost.LS, Sensitivity.boost.LS, PPV.boost.LS, NPV.
  boost.LS, Error.boost.LS), rbind(Specificity.logit.LS, Sensitivity.logit.
  LS, PPV.logit.LS, NPV.logit.LS, Error.logit.LS), rbind(Specificity.nnet.
  LS, Sensitivity.nnet.LS, PPV.nnet.LS, NPV.nnet.LS, Error.nnet.LS),
  rbind(Specificity.ave.LS, Sensitivity.ave.LS, PPV.ave.LS, NPV.ave.LS,
  Error.ave.LS))
colnames(PredictiveQuality.LS)<- c("Tree", "Forest", "Bagging", "Boost-
  ing", "Logit", "Neural Network", "Average")
rownames(PredictiveQuality.LS)<- c("Specificity", "Sensitivity", "Positive
  Predictive Value", "Negative Predictive Value", "Overall Error Rate")
PredictiveQuality.TS <- cbind(rbind(Specificity.tree.TS, Sensitivity.tree.
  TS, PPV.tree.TS, NPV.tree.TS, Error.ave.TS), rbind(Specificity.rf.TS,
  Sensitivity.rf.TS, PPV.rf.TS, NPV.rf.TS, Error.rf.TS), rbind(Specificity.
  bag.TS, Sensitivity.bag.TS, PPV.bag.TS, NPV.bag.TS, Error.bag.TS),
  rbind(Specificity.boost.TS, Sensitivity.boost.TS, PPV.boost.TS, NPV.
  boost.TS, Error.boost.TS), rbind(Specificity.logit.TS, Sensitivity.logit.
  TS, PPV.logit.TS, NPV.logit.TS, Error.logit.TS), rbind(Specificity.nnet.
  TS, Sensitivity.nnet.TS, PPV.nnet.TS, NPV.nnet.TS, Error.nnet.TS),
  rbind(Specificity.ave.TS, Sensitivity.ave.TS, PPV.ave.TS, NPV.ave.TS,
  Error.ave.TS))
colnames(PredictiveQuality.TS)<- c("Tree", "Forest", "Bagging", "Boost-
  ing", "Logit", "Neural Network", "Average")
rownames(PredictiveQuality.TS)<- c("Specificity", "Sensitivity", "Positive
  Predictive Value", "Negative Predictive Value", "Overall Error Rate")
```

RECEIVER OPERATING CHARACTERISTIC CURVES

The receiver operating characteristic (ROC) compares and plots the sensitivity against (1-specificity) as the classification threshold changes. This curve exploits the fact that as the threshold for classifying a new case as positive *increases*, the probability that the model will predict conflict (a positive outcome) correctly *increases* (i.e., the sensitivity increases), whereas the probability that the model will predict nonconflict (a negative outcome) correctly *decreases* (i.e. the specificity *decreases*). We provide the code for the ROCs below.

```
ConflictData.LS$ConflictDummy <- ifelse(ConflictData.LS$Conflict ==
  "Conflict", 1, 0)
ConflictData.TS$ConflictDummy <- ifelse(ConflictData.TS$Conflict ==
  "Conflict", 1, 0)
```

This creates a dummy variable in each subsample for conflict that takes the values {0, 1}, instead of a factor variable that takes the values {Conflict, No Conflict}.

```
roc.tree.ConflictData.LS<-roc(ConflictData.LS$ConflictDummy, Conflict-
  Data.LS$treeProb, smooth = FALSE, auc = TRUE, plot = T, add = F,
  col = "brown", lwd = 1)
roc.rf.ConflictData.LS<-roc(ConflictData.LS$ConflictDummy, ConflictData.
  LS$rfProb, smooth = FALSE, auc = TRUE, plot = T, add = T, col = "red",
  lwd = 1)
roc.bag.ConflictData.LS<-roc(ConflictData.LS$ConflictDummy, Conflict-
  Data.LS$bagProb, smooth = FALSE, auc = TRUE, plot = T, add = T,
  col = "green", lwd = 1)
roc.boost.ConflictData.LS<-roc(ConflictData.LS$ConflictDummy, Conflict-
  Data.LS$boostProb, smooth = FALSE, auc = TRUE, plot = T, add = T,
  col = "blue", lwd = 1)
roc.logit.ConflictData.LS<-roc(ConflictData.LS$ConflictDummy, Conflict-
  Data.LS$logitProb, smooth = FALSE, auc = TRUE, plot = T, add = T,
  col = "gold", lwd = 1)
roc.nnet.ConflictData.LS<-roc(ConflictData.LS$ConflictDummy, Conflict-
  Data.LS$nnetProb, smooth = FALSE, auc = TRUE, plot = T, add = T, col
  = "gray", lwd = 1)
roc.ave.ConflictData.LS<-roc(ConflictData.LS$ConflictDummy, Conflict-
  Data.LS$averageProb, smooth = FALSE, auc = TRUE, plot = T, add = T,
  col = "black", lwd = 1)
```

legend("bottomright", c("Tree", "Forest", "Bagging", "Boosting", "Logit", "ANN", "Average"), lty = c(1,1), lwd = 1, col = c("brown", "red", "green", "blue", "gold", "gray", "black"))

We also draw and combine the ROC curves for the test sample.

roc.tree.ConflictData.TS<-roc(ConflictData.TS$ConflictDummy, ConflictData.TS$treeProb, smooth = FALSE, auc = TRUE, plot = T, add = F, col = "brown", lwd = 1)
roc.rf.ConflictData.TS<-roc(ConflictData.TS$ConflictDummy, ConflictData.TS$rfProb, smooth = FALSE, auc = TRUE, plot = T, add = T, col = "red", lwd = 1)
roc.bag.ConflictData.TS<-roc(ConflictData.TS$ConflictDummy, ConflictData.TS$bagProb, smooth = FALSE, auc = TRUE, plot = T, add = T, col = "green", lwd = 1)
roc.boost.ConflictData.TS<-roc(ConflictData.TS$ConflictDummy, ConflictData.TS$boostProb, smooth = FALSE, auc = TRUE, plot = T, add = T, col = "blue", lwd = 1)
roc.logit.ConflictData.TS<-roc(ConflictData.TS$ConflictDummy, ConflictData.TS$logitProb, smooth = FALSE, auc = TRUE, plot = T, add = T, col = "gold", lwd = 1)
roc.nnet.ConflictData.TS<-roc(ConflictData.TS$ConflictDummy, ConflictData.TS$nnetProb, smooth = FALSE, auc = TRUE, plot = T, add = T, col = "gray", lwd = 1)
roc.ave.ConflictData.TS<-roc(ConflictData.TS$ConflictDummy, ConflictData.TS$averageProb, smooth = FALSE, auc = TRUE, plot = T, add = T, col = "black", lwd = 1)
legend("bottomright", c("Tree", "Forest", "Bagging", "Boosting", "Logit", "ANN", "Average"), lty = c(1,1), lwd = 1, col = c("brown", "red", "green", "blue", "gold", "gray", "black"))

Another measure of predictive accuracy that is based on the ROC curve is the C-statistic (also known as the area under the ROC curve, or AUC). A model that makes "perfect prediction" (for some threshold, and only in the sense of specificity and sensitivity equaling one[2]) will have an ROC equal to one. We extract the C-statistics from the ROC curve object using the code below:

auc.table<-cbind(rbind(roc.tree.ConflictData.LS$auc,roc.tree.ConflictData.TS$auc), rbind(roc.rf.ConflictData.LS$auc,roc.rf.ConflictData.TS$auc), rbind(roc.bag.ConflictData.LS$auc,roc.bag.ConflictData.TS$auc), rbind(roc.boost.ConflictData.LS$auc,roc.boost.ConflictData.TS$auc), rbind(roc.logit.ConflictData.LS$auc,roc.logit.ConflictData.TS$auc),

```
  rbind(roc.nnet.ConflictData.LS$auc,roc.nnet.ConflictData.TS$auc),
  rbind(roc.ave.ConflictData.LS$auc,roc.ave.ConflictData.TS$auc))
  rownames(auc.table)<-c("Learning Sample", "Test Sample")
colnames(auc.table)<-c("Tree", "Forest", "Bagging", "Boosting", "Logit",
  "ANN", "Average")
```

This creates a table that compares the AUCs for the different models across the rows, and for the learning versus the test sample down the columns.

VARIABLE IMPORTANCE

A variable in the model is more important the greater extent to which its inclusion in the specification reduces the measure of impurity. In this case, our measure of impurity is the Gini impurity index described in chapter 2. Since the different models reduce the total level of impurity by different amounts, we rank the variables' importance based on the percentage of the total reduction in the Gini impurity index that each variable contributes for each learning model. Then, we average these percentages and rank the variables based on average relative importance. The code we use to implement this ranking is:

```
Importance.rpart<-100*as.data.frame(Conflict.rpart$variable.importance)/
  sum(Conflict.rpart$variable.importance)
Importance.rF<-100*as.data.frame(Conflict.rF$importance[,4])/
  sum(Conflict.rF$importance[,4])
Importance.bag<-as.data.frame(Conflict.bag$importance)
Importance.boost<-as.data.frame(Conflict.boost$importance)
Importance.rpart$id<-rownames(Importance.rpart)
Importance.rF$id<-rownames(Importance.rF)
Importance.bag$id<-rownames(Importance.bag)
Importance.boost$id<-rownames(Importance.boost)
Importance<-merge(Importance.rpart, Importance.rF, by = "id", all = T)
Importance<-merge(Importance, Importance.bag, by = "id", all = T)
Importance<-merge(Importance, Importance.boost, by = "id", all = T)
Importance[is.na(Importance)]<-0
colnames(Importance)<-c("id", "Tree", "Forest", "Bagging", "Boosting")
rownames(Importance)<-Importance$id
Importance$Average<-(Importance$Tree + Importance$Forest + Importance$
  Bagging + Importance$Boosting)/4
Importance<-Importance[order(-Importance$Average),]
```

PARTIAL DEPENDENCE PLOTS

Finally, we use the partialPlot function from the randomForest package to draw the partial dependence plots (PDPs) for each variable in the Forest model. We have also adapted the code to draw the corresponding PDPs for the Bagging and Boosting learning models. The adapted source code for these commands are included on the website for this book as "partialPlotBagging.R" and "partialPlotBoosting.R" and these source code files must be run separately in order to make those functions available to use.

```
source('partialPlotBagging.R')
source('partialPlotBoosting.R')
#Partial Plots of Top Important Variables (Except Current Conflict)
Categoricals<-c("LagConflict", "LegCompetitiveness", "PartyExclusion",
  "Executive", "ExecSelection", "Regime", "LegEffectiveness", "PartyCo-
  alitions", "ParliamentRespons", "System")
Numericals<-rownames(Importance)[!rownames(Importance) %in%
  Categoricals]
for (i in seq_along(Numericals))
{ pdp.Bag<-partial PlotBagging(Conflict.bag, pred.data = ConflictData.LS,
  Numericals[i], xlab=Numericals[i], main = paste("Partial Dependence
  on", Numericals[i]), plot = T, col = "green")
lim.Bag<-par('usr')
pdp.rF<-par lim.rF<-par('usr tialPlot(Conflict.rF, pred.data = ConflictData.
  LS, Numericals[i], xlab=Numericals[i], main = paste ("Partial Depen-
  dence on", Numericals[i]), plot = T, col = "red")
lim.rF<-par ('usr')
pdp.Boost<-partialPlotBoosting(Conflict.boost, pred.data = ConflictData.LS,
  Numericals[i], xlab=Numericals[i], main = paste("Partial Dependence on",
  Numericals[i]), plot = T, col = "blue")
lim.Boost<-par('usr')
yLimMin<-min(lim.Boost[3], lim.Bag[3], lim.rF[3])
yLimMax<-max(lim.Boost[4], lim.Bag[4], lim.rF[4])
jpeg(filename = paste('pdp',Numericals[i],'.jpg'))
partialPlotBagging(Conflict.bag, pred.data = ConflictData.LS, Numericals[i],
  xlab=Numericals[i], main = paste("Partial Dependence on", Numericals[i]),
  add = F, col = "green", ylim = c(yLimMin, yLimMax), xlim = c(quantile
  (ConflictData.LS[,Numericals[i]],0.05), quantile(ConflictData.
  LS[,Numericals[i]],0.95)))
partialPlot(Conflict.rF, pred.data = ConflictData.LS, Numericals[i],
  xlab=Numericals[i], main = paste("Partial Dependence on", Numericals[i]),
  add = T, col = "red")
```

```
partialPlotBoosting(Conflict.boost, pred.data = ConflictData.LS,
  Numericals[i], xlab=Numericals[i], main = paste("Partial Dependence on",
  Numericals[i]), add = T, col = "blue")
dev.off()
legend("bottomright", c("Forest", "Bagging", "Boosting"), lty = c(1,1), lwd
  = 1, col = c("red","green","blue"))
```

OPTIMAL PROBABILITIES

Next, we replicate the diagnostics for the "optimal" threshold probability. We define "optimal" as the threshold on the ROC curve that corresponds to the threshold that maximizes the sum of the sensitivity and specificity of the prediction. The *roc* command used previously for the ROC curves stores this threshold, and we can extract it using the "coords(roc, x)" function in the pROC package. The argument *roc* corresponds to the roc object and "x" corresponds to the type of threshold ("all," "local maximas," or "best"). The "best" threshold is controlled by the option "best.method," which is set to maximize the sum of the sensitivity and specificity (best.method = "youden") by default. We begin by predicting the class for each learning model based on the "best" threshold.

```
ConflictData.LS$treeClassP <- ifelse(ConflictData.LS$treeProb < coords(roc.
  tree.ConflictData.LS, "best")[1], "No Conflict", "Conflict")
ConflictData.TS$treeClassP <- ifelse(ConflictData.TS$treeProb < coords(roc.
  tree.ConflictData.LS, "best")[1], "No Conflict", "Conflict")
ConflictData.LS$rfClassP <- ifelse(ConflictData.LS$rfProb < coords(roc.
  rf.ConflictData.LS, "best")[1], "No Conflict", "Conflict")
ConflictData.TS$rfClassP <- ifelse(ConflictData.TS$rfProb < coords(roc.
  rf.ConflictData.LS, "best")[1], "No Conflict", "Conflict")
ConflictData.LS$bagClassP <- ifelse(ConflictData.LS$bagProb < coords(roc.
  bag.ConflictData.LS, "best")[1], "No Conflict", "Conflict")
ConflictData.TS$bagClassP <- ifelse(ConflictData.TS$bagProb < coords(roc.
  bag.ConflictData.LS, "best")[1], "No Conflict", "Conflict")
ConflictData.LS$boostClassP <- ifelse(ConflictData.LS$boostProb < coords
  (roc.boost.ConflictData.LS, "best")[1], "No Conflict", "Conflict")
ConflictData.TS$boostClassP <- ifelse(ConflictData.TS$boostProb < coords
  (roc.boost.ConflictData.LS, "best")[1], "No Conflict", "Conflict")
ConflictData.LS$logitClassP <- ifelse(ConflictData.LS$logitProb < coords
  (roc.logit.ConflictData.LS, "best")[1], "No Conflict", "Conflict")
ConflictData.TS$logitClassP <- ifelse(ConflictData.TS$logitProb < coords
  (roc.logit.ConflictData.LS, "best")[1], "No Conflict", "Conflict")
```

ConflictData.LS$nnetClassP <- ifelse(ConflictData.LS$nnetProb < coords (roc.nnet.ConflictData.LS, "best")[1], "No Conflict", "Conflict")
ConflictData.TS$nnetClassP <- ifelse(ConflictData.TS$nnetProb < coords (roc.nnet.ConflictData.LS, "best")[1], "No Conflict", "Conflict")
ConflictData.LS$averageClassP<-ifelse(ConflictData.LS$averageProb<coords (roc.ave.ConflictData.LS, "best")[1], "No Conflict", "Conflict")
ConflictData.TS$averageClassP<-ifelse(ConflictData.TS$averageProb<coords (roc.ave.ConflictData.LS, "best")[1], "No Conflict", "Conflict")

Next, we build the confusion matrices based on the optimal thresholds.

Confusion.tree.LSp <- table(ConflictData.LS$Conflict, ConflictData.LS$tree ClassP)
Confusion.tree.TSp <- table(ConflictData.TS$Conflict, ConflictData.TS$tree ClassP)
Confusion.rf.LSp <- table(ConflictData.LS$Conflict, ConflictData.LS$rf ClassP)
Confusion.rf.TSp <- table(ConflictData.TS$Conflict, ConflictData.TS$rf ClassP)
Confusion.bag.LSp <- table(ConflictData.LS$Conflict, ConflictData.LS$bag ClassP)
Confusion.bag.TSp <- table(ConflictData.TS$Conflict, ConflictData.TS$bag ClassP)
Confusion.boost.LSp<-table(ConflictData.LS$Conflict,ConflictData.LS$boost ClassP)
Confusion.boost.TSp<-table(ConflictData.TS$Conflict,ConflictData.TS$boost ClassP)
Confusion.logit.LSp<-table(ConflictData.LS$Conflict,ConflictData.LS$logit ClassP)
Confusion.logit.TSp<-table(ConflictData.TS$Conflict,ConflictData.TS$logit ClassP)
Confusion.nnet.LSp<-table(ConflictData.LS$Conflict,ConflictData.LS$nnet ClassP)
Confusion.nnet.TSp<-table(ConflictData.TS$Conflict,ConflictData.TS$nnet ClassP)
Confusion.average.LSp <- table(ConflictData.LS$Conflict, ConflictData. LS$averageClassP)
Confusion.average.TSp <- table(ConflictData.TS$Conflict, ConflictData. TS$averageClassP)

Finally, we calculate the measures of predictive quality for the predicted classes based on the "best" thresholds.

SPECIFICITY

```
Specificity.tree.LSp<-Confusion.tree.LSp[1,1]/(Confusion.tree.LSp[1,1] + Confusion.tree.LSp[1,2])
Specificity.tree.TSp<-Confusion.tree.TSp[1,1]/(Confusion.tree.TSp[1,1] + Confusion.tree.TSp[1,2])
Specificity.rf.LSp<-Confusion.rf.LSp[1,1]/(Confusion.rf.LSp[1,1] + Confusion.rf.LSp[1,2])
Specificity.rf.TSp<-Confusion.rf.TSp[1,1]/(Confusion.rf.TSp[1,1] + Confusion.rf.TSp[1,2])
Specificity.bag.LSp<-Confusion.bag.LSp[1,1]/(Confusion.bag.LSp[1,1] + Confusion.bag.LSp[1,2])
Specificity.bag.TSp<-Confusion.bag.TSp[1,1]/(Confusion.bag.TSp[1,1] + Confusion.bag.TSp[1,2])
Specificity.boost.LSp<-Confusion.boost.LSp[1,1]/(Confusion.boost.LSp[1,1] + Confusion.boost.LSp[1,2])
Specificity.boost.TSp<-Confusion.boost.TSp[1,1]/(Confusion.boost.TSp[1,1] + Confusion.boost.TSp[1,2])
Specificity.logit.LSp<-Confusion.logit.LSp[1,1]/(Confusion.logit.LSp[1,1] + Confusion.logit.LSp[1,2])
Specificity.logit.TSp<-Confusion.logit.TSp[1,1]/(Confusion.logit.TSp[1,1] + Confusion.logit.TSp[1,2])
Specificity.nnet.LSp<-Confusion.nnet.LSp[1,1]/(Confusion.nnet.LSp[1,1] + Confusion.nnet.LSp[1,2])
Specificity.nnet.TSp<-Confusion.nnet.TSp[1,1]/(Confusion.nnet.TSp[1,1] + Confusion.nnet.TSp[1,2])
Specificity.ave.LSp<-Confusion.ave.LSp[1,1]/(Confusion.ave.LSp[1,1] + Confusion.ave.LSp[1,2])
Specificity.ave.TSp<-Confusion.ave.TSp[1,1]/(Confusion.ave.TSp[1,1] + Confusion.ave.TSp[1,2])
```

SENSITIVITY

```
Sensitivity.tree.LSp<-Confusion.tree.LSp[2,2]/(Confusion.tree.LSp[2,2] + Confusion.tree.LSp[2,1])
Sensitivity.tree.TSp<-Confusion.tree.TSp[2,2]/(Confusion.tree.TSp[2,2] + Confusion.tree.TSp[2,1])
Sensitivity.rf.LSp<-Confusion.rf.LSp[2,2]/(Confusion.rf.LSp[2,2] + Confusion.rf.LSp[2,1])
Sensitivity.rf.TSp<-Confusion.rf.TSp[2,2]/(Confusion.rf.TSp[2,2] + Confusion.rf.TSp[2,1])
```

Sensitivity.bag.LSp<-Confusion.bag.LSp[2,2]/(Confusion.bag.LSp[2,2] + Confusion.bag.LSp[2,1])

Sensitivity.bag.TSp<-Confusion.bag.TSp[2,2]/(Confusion.bag.TSp[2,2] + Confusion.bag.TSp[2,1])

Sensitivity.boost.LSp<-Confusion.boost.LSp[2,2]/(Confusion.boost.LSp[2,2] + Confusion.boost.LSp[2,1])

Sensitivity.boost.TSp<-Confusion.boost.TSp[2,2]/(Confusion.boost.TSp[2,2] + Confusion.boost.TSp[2,1])

Sensitivity.logit.LSp<-Confusion.logit.LSp[2,2]/(Confusion.logit.LSp[2,2] + Confusion.logit.LSp[2,1])

Sensitivity.logit.TSp<-Confusion.logit.TSp[2,2]/(Confusion.logit.TSp[2,2] + Confusion.logit.TSp[2,1])

Sensitivity.nnet.LSp<-Confusion.nnet.LSp[2,2]/(Confusion.nnet.LSp[2,2] + Confusion.nnet.LSp[2,1])

Sensitivity.nnet.TSp<-Confusion.nnet.TSp[2,2]/(Confusion.nnet.TSp[2,2] + Confusion.nnet.TSp[2,1])

Sensitivity.ave.LSp<-Confusion.ave.LSp[2,2]/(Confusion.ave.LSp[2,2] + Confusion.ave.LSp[2,1])

Sensitivity.ave.TSp<-Confusion.ave.TSp[2,2]/(Confusion.ave.TSp[2,2] + Confusion.ave.TSp[2,1])

POSITIVE PREDICTIVE VALUE

PPV.tree.LSp<-Confusion.tree.LSp[2,2]/(Confusion.tree.LSp[2,2] + Confusion.tree.LSp[1,2])

PPV.tree.TSp<-Confusion.tree.TSp[2,2]/(Confusion.tree.TSp[2,2] + Confusion.tree.TSp[1,2])

PPV.rf.LSp<-Confusion.rf.LSp[2,2]/(Confusion.rf.LSp[2,2] + Confusion.rf.LSp[1,2])

PPV.rf.TSp<-Confusion.rf.TSp[2,2]/(Confusion.rf.TSp[2,2] + Confusion.rf.TSp[1,2])

PPV.bag.LSp<-Confusion.bag.LSp[2,2]/(Confusion.bag.LSp[2,2] + Confusion.bag.LSp[1,2])

PPV.bag.TSp<-Confusion.bag.TSp[2,2]/(Confusion.bag.TSp[2,2] + Confusion.bag.TSp[1,2])

PPV.boost.LSp<-Confusion.boost.LSp[2,2]/(Confusion.boost.LSp[2,2] + Confusion.boost.LSp[1,2])

PPV.boost.TSp<-Confusion.boost.TSp[2,2]/(Confusion.boost.TSp[2,2] + Confusion.boost.TSp[1,2])

PPV.logit.LSp<-Confusion.logit.LSp[2,2]/(Confusion.logit.LSp[2,2] + Confusion.logit.LSp[1,2])

```
PPV.logit.TSp<-Confusion.logit.TSp[2,2]/(Confusion.logit.TSp[2,2] + Confusion.logit.TSp[1,2])
PPV.nnet.LSp<-Confusion.nnet.LSp[2,2]/(Confusion.nnet.LSp[2,2] + Confusion.nnet.LSp[1,2])
PPV.nnet.TSp<-Confusion.nnet.TSp[2,2]/(Confusion.nnet.TSp[2,2] + Confusion.nnet.TSp[1,2])
PPV.ave.LSp<-Confusion.ave.LSp[2,2]/(Confusion.ave.LSp[2,2] + Confusion.ave.LSp[1,2])
PPV.ave.TSp<-Confusion.ave.TSp[2,2]/(Confusion.ave.TSp[2,2] + Confusion.ave.TSp[1,2])
```

NEGATIVE PREDICTIVE VALUE

```
NPV.tree.LSp<-Confusion.tree.LSp[1,1]/(Confusion.tree.LSp[1,1] + Confusion.tree.LSp[2,1])
NPV.tree.TSp<-Confusion.tree.TSp[1,1]/(Confusion.tree.TSp[1,1] + Confusion.tree.TSp[2,1])
NPV.rf.LSp<-Confusion.rf.LSp[1,1]/(Confusion.rf.LSp[1,1] + Confusion.rf.LSp[2,1])
NPV.rf.TSp<-Confusion.rf.TSp[1,1]/(Confusion.rf.TSp[1,1] + Confusion.rf.TSp[2,1])
NPV.bag.LSp<-Confusion.bag.LSp[1,1]/(Confusion.bag.LSp[1,1] + Confusion.bag.LSp[2,1])
NPV.bag.TSp<-Confusion.bag.TSp[1,1]/(Confusion.bag.TSp[1,1] + Confusion.bag.TSp[2,1])
NPV.boost.LSp<-Confusion.boost.LSp[1,1]/(Confusion.boost.LSp[1,1] + Confusion.boost.LSp[2,1])
NPV.boost.TSp<-Confusion.boost.TSp[1,1]/(Confusion.boost.TSp[1,1] + Confusion.boost.TSp[2,1])
NPV.logit.LSp<-Confusion.logit.LSp[1,1]/(Confusion.logit.LSp[1,1] + Confusion.logit.LSp[2,1])
NPV.logit.TSp<-Confusion.logit.TSp[1,1]/(Confusion.logit.TSp[1,1] + Confusion.logit.TSp[2,1])
NPV.nnet.LSp<-Confusion.nnet.LSp[1,1]/(Confusion.nnet.LSp[1,1] + Confusion.nnet.LSp[2,1])
NPV.nnet.TSp<-Confusion.nnet.TSp[1,1]/(Confusion.nnet.TSp[1,1] + Confusion.nnet.TSp[2,1])
NPV.ave.LSp<-Confusion.ave.LSp[1,1]/(Confusion.ave.LSp[1,1] + Confusion.ave.LSp[2,1])
NPV.ave.TSp<-Confusion.ave.TSp[1,1]/(Confusion.ave.TSp[1,1] + Confusion.ave.TSp[2,1])
```

OVERALL ERROR RATE

```
Error.tree.LSp<-(Confusion.tree.LSp[1,2] + Confusion.tree.LSp[2,1])/ nrow
  (ConflictData.LSp)
Error.tree.TSp<-(Confusion.tree.TSp[1,2] + Confusion.tree.TSp[2,1])/ nrow
  (ConflictData.TSp)
Error.rf.LSp<-(Confusion.rf.LSp[1,2] + Confusion.rf.LSp[2,1])/ nrow
  (ConflictData.LSp)
Error.rf.TSp<-(Confusion.rf.TSp[1,2] + Confusion.rf.TSp[2,1])/ nrow
  (ConflictData.TSp)
Error.bag.LSp<-(Confusion.bag.LSp[1,2] + Confusion.bag.LSp[2,1])/ nrow
  (ConflictData.LSp)
Error.bag.TSp<-(Confusion.bag.TSp[1,2] + Confusion.bag.TSp[2,1])/ nrow
  (ConflictData.TSp)
Error.boost.LSp<-(Confusion.boost.LSp[1,2] + Confusion.boost.LSp[2,1])/ nrow
  (ConflictData.LSp)
Error.boost.TSp<-(Confusion.boost.TSp[1,2] + Confusion.boost.TSp[2,1])/
  nrow(ConflictData.TSp)
Error.logit.LSp<-(Confusion.logit.LSp[1,2]+Confusion.logit.LSp[2,1])/nrow
  (ConflictData.LSp)
Error.logit.TSp<-(Confusion.logit.TSp[1,2]+Confusion.logit.TSp[2,1])/nrow
  (ConflictData.TSp)
Error.nnet.LSp<-(Confusion.nnet.LSp[1,2]+Confusion.nnet.LSp[2,1])/nrow
  (ConflictData.LSp)
Error.nnet.TSp<-(Confusion.nnet.TSp[1,2]+Confusion.nnet.TSp[2,1])/nrow
  (ConflictData.TSp)
Error.ave.LSp<-(Confusion.ave.LSp[1,2] + Confusion.ave.LSp[2,1])/ nrow
  (ConflictData.LSp)
Error.ave.TSp<-(Confusion.ave.TSp[1,2] + Confusion.ave.TSp[2,1])/ nrow
  (ConflictData.TSp)
PredictiveQuality.LSp <- cbind(rbind(Specificity.tree.LSp, Sensitivity.tree.
  LSp, PPV.tree.LSp, NPV.tree.LSp, Error.ave.LSp), rbind(Specificity.
  rf.LSp, Sensitivity.rf.LSp, PPV.rf.LSp, NPV.rf.LSp, Error.rf.LSp),
  rbind(Specificity.bag.LSp, Sensitivity.bag.LSp, PPV.bag.LSp, NPV.bag.
  LSp, Error.bag.LSp), rbind(Specificity.boost.LSp, Sensitivity.boost.LSp,
  PPV.boost.LSp, NPV.boost.LSp, Error.boost.LSp), rbind(Specificity.logit.
  LSp, Sensitivity.logit.LSp, PPV.logit.LSp, NPV.logit.LSp, Error.logit.
  LSp), rbind(Specificity.nnet.LSp, Sensitivity.nnet.LSp, PPV.nnet.LSp,
  NPV.nnet.LSp, Error.nnet.LSp), rbind(Specificity.ave.LSp, Sensitivity.
  ave.LSp, PPV.ave.LSp, NPV.ave.LSp, Error.ave.LSp))
colnames(PredictiveQuality.LSp)<- c("Tree", "Forest", "Bagging", "Boost-
  ing", "Logit", "Neural Network", "Average")
```

```
rownames(PredictiveQuality.LSp)<- c("Specificity", "Sensitivity", "Positive
  Predictive Value", "Negative Predictive Value", "Overall Error Rate")
PredictiveQuality.TSp <- cbind(rbind(Specificity.tree.TSp, Sensitivity.tree.
  TSp, PPV.tree.TSp, NPV.tree.TSp, Error.ave.TSp), rbind(Specificity.
  rf.TSp, Sensitivity.rf.TSp, PPV.rf.TSp, NPV.rf.TSp, Error.rf.TSp),
  rbind(Specificity.bag.TSp, Sensitivity.bag.TSp, PPV.bag.TSp, NPV.bag.
  TSp, Error.bag.TSp), rbind(Specificity.boost.TSp, Sensitivity.boost.TSp,
  PPV.boost.TSp, NPV.boost.TSp, Error.boost.TSp), rbind(Specificity.logit.
  TSp, Sensitivity.logit.TSp, PPV.logit.TSp, NPV.logit.TSp, Error.logit.
  TSp), rbind(Specificity.nnet.TSp, Sensitivity.nnet.TSp, PPV.nnet.TSp,
  NPV.nnet.TSp, Error.nnet.TSp), rbind(Specificity.ave.TSp, Sensitivity.
  ave.TSp, PPV.ave.TSp, NPV.ave.TSp, Error.ave.TSp))
colnames(PredictiveQuality.TSp)<- c("Tree", "Forest", "Bagging", "Boost-
  ing", "Logit", "Neural Network", "Average")
rownames(PredictiveQuality.TSp)<- c("Specificity", "Sensitivity", "Positive
  Predictive Value", "Negative Predictive Value", "Overall Error Rate"
```

PREDICTING BEYOND THE TIME SAMPLE

The last year in which we observe our target variable—whether a country will experience conflict in the next five years—ends in 2009, for the period 2010–2014. The last year in which we observe our input variables—the values of economic, demographic, geographic, and institutional characteristics of a country—ends in 2014. Hence, the input data corresponding to the last year of our dataset, 2014, does not correspond to any observed information about the target variable. So, while our validation set for the period 1950–2009 includes *countries* that the forecasting set also includes, it does not overlap with any incidences of conflict that had already been counted in construction of the dependent variable for the sample that ended in 2009.

PREDICTED VALUES

First, we predict the probability of conflict for whether each country for the period 2015–2019.

```
ConflictData.rfImpute$treeProb <- predict(Conflict.rpart, newdata = Con-
  flictData.rfImpute, type = "prob")[,"Conflict"]
ConflictData.rfImpute$rfProb <- predict(Conflict.rF, newdata = ConflictData.
  rfImpute, type = "prob")[,"Conflict"]
```

```
ConflictData.rfImpute$bagProb <- predict(Conflict.bag, newdata = ConflictData.rfImpute)$prob[,1]
ConflictData.rfImpute$boostProb <- predict(Conflict.boost, newdata = ConflictData.rfImpute)$prob[,1]
ConflictData.rfImpute$logitProb <- 1-predict(Conflict.logit, newdata = ConflictData.rfImpute, type = "response")
ConflictData.rfImpute$nnetProb <- 1 - as.vector(predict(Conflict.nnet, newdata = ConflictData.rfImpute, type = "raw"))
ConflictData.rfImpute$averageProb <- (ConflictData.rfImpute$treeProb + ConflictData.rfImpute$rfProb + ConflictData.rfImpute$bagProb + ConflictData.rfImpute$boostProb + ConflictData.rfImpute$logitProb + ConflictData.rfImpute$nnetProb)/6
```

And just to be sure we are using the forward data from 2014, we create a new dataframe for that subset.

```
Data2014.rfImpute <- subset(ConflictData.rfImpute, year == 2014)
```

Next, we predict whether a country will be expected to have a conflict or not for the period 2015–2019. We use the "optimal" cutoffs described in the previous section.

```
ConflictData.rfImpute$treeClassP <- ifelse(ConflictData.rfImpute$treeProb < coords(roc.tree.ConflictData.rfImpute, "best")[1], "No Conflict", "Conflict")
ConflictData.rfImpute$rfClassP <- ifelse(ConflictData.rfImpute$rfProb < coords(roc.rf.ConflictData.rfImpute, "best")[1], "No Conflict", "Conflict")
ConflictData.rfImpute$bagClassP <- ifelse(ConflictData.rfImpute$bagProb < coords(roc.bag.ConflictData.rfImpute, "best")[1], "No Conflict", "Conflict")
ConflictData.rfImpute$boostClassP <- ifelse(ConflictData.rfImpute$boostProb < coords(roc.boost.ConflictData.rfImpute, "best")[1], "No Conflict", "Conflict")
ConflictData.rfImpute$logitClassP <- ifelse(ConflictData.rfImpute$logitProb < coords(roc.logit.ConflictData.rfImpute, "best")[1], "No Conflict", "Conflict")
ConflictData.rfImpute$nnetClassP <- ifelse(ConflictData.rfImpute$nnetProb < coords(roc.nnet.ConflictData.rfImpute, "best")[1], "No Conflict", "Conflict")
ConflictData.rfImpute$averageClassP <- ifelse(ConflictData.rfImpute $averageProb < coords(roc.ave.ConflictData.rfImpute, "best")[1], "No Conflict", "Conflict")
```

We can do all of the things with the predicted probabilities and classes using these forward predications as we have done in the previous sections (such as creating confusion matrices, plotting the ROC curves, calculating the measures of predictive quality, etc.). In the interest of space, we forego this exercise for this chapter.

HEAT MAPS

A graphical tool that helps to visualize the predictions of the out-of-sample time period is a heat map. For this, we need to load the library rworldmap. This tool will create a map of the world with countries experiencing lower probabilities of conflict shaded in yellow, and countries experiencing higher probabilities of conflict shaded in red. First, we have to join our dataset to a map file.

```
library(rworldmap)
ConflictMap <- joinCountryData2Map(Data2014.rfImpute, nameJoinColumn = "wbcode")
```

Now that we have joined the data, we can plot any variable from the dataset to a world heat map. We will use the predicted probabilities.

```
mapCountryData(ConflictMap, nameColumnToPlot = "treeProb", catMethod = "fixedWidth")
mapCountryData(ConflictMap, nameColumnToPlot = "rfProb", catMethod = "fixedWidth")
mapCountryData(ConflictMap, nameColumnToPlot = "bagProb", catMethod = "fixedWidth")
mapCountryData(ConflictMap, nameColumnToPlot = "boostProb", catMethod = "fixedWidth")
mapCountryData(ConflictMap, nameColumnToPlot = "logitProb", catMethod = "fixedWidth")
mapCountryData(ConflictMap, nameColumnToPlot = "nnetProb", catMethod = "fixedWidth")
mapCountryData(ConflictMap, nameColumnToPlot = "averageProb", catMethod = "fixedWidth"
```

SUMMARY

We have posted R source code files, as well as the raw data for the analysis described in this chapter (and the book overall) on the book's webpage. We hope that practitioners will be able to use this code to predict ongoing conflicts, and even update the dataset and model parameters to experiment with different types of models and even improve the predictions.

NOTES

1. A not-necessarily-complete list of these models and the packages that support them can be found at https://topepo.github.io/caret/modelList.html.

2. We should note that a model could achieve the ideal level of sensitivity and specificity without actually predicting positive outcomes well at all. Note that the specificity (or "true negative rate") is equal to P(Predicted Negative Outcome | Negative Observed Outcome), whereas the sensitivity (or "true positive rate") equals P(Predicted Positive Outcome | Positive Observed Outcome). In the extreme, as our model approaches predicting *zero* cases to be "positives" (failed states), the specificity and sensitivity both converge to one. However, one could hardly argue this to be "perfect prediction since the positive predicted value will be zero! Hence, all of the measures of predictive quality deserve some consideration.

Chapter 6

Methods and Results

In this chapter, we first discuss the methodology we use to identify the best predictive models before turning to our main result, the best predictors of conflict. We run a number of different Machine Learning technologies to identify the sets of variables that best predict conflict. We then compare their results using misclassification rates to help identify the best predictive methodology. Our algorithm then ranks the most important predictor variables in these models. Please note that although we choose a particular technology for our purposes, there are other ways of choosing predictive technologies to suit different purpose.

METHODOLOGY: THE "BEST" PREDICTIVE TECHNOLOGIES

In this section, we provide a sense of how Machine Learning technologies can improve on traditional parametric estimates. Then, we describe our methodology. We find that, for our purposes, tree-based technologies are the best for finding those variables that are 'best' at predicting conflict.

Why Machine Learning? The kind of cross validation that Machine Learning entails (described below) is theoretically agnostic and somewhat automatic—we let the size of the misclassification rates decide which models work best rather than cherry pick the model that tells our story the best. In short, our approach reduces the risk of researcher biases and as such gives us some scientific confidence in our model. Researchers often use *p*-values to say that a hypothesis is correct. Recent guidance from the American Statistical Association (when responding to the fact that a spate of studies that could not be replicated) suggests that this interpretation is a misuse of the

p-value. It is more accurate to say that a p-value of 0.01 suggests that if the null hypothesis is true then there is a 1% chance of finding another result at least as extreme as the observed result. In other words, a significant p-value can come about through sheer chance. Journals tend not to publish insignificant results. Given the low cost of running regressions, researchers may be tempted to run thousands of regressions purely with the intent of hitting upon this significance by chance. And this may explain the difficulty of replicating published results. We suggest that Machine Learning technologies can strengthen the social sciences by adding the element of prediction. A variable with a significant p-value but which does not predict the outcome well may well be significant by pure chance. Arguably, a highly significant causal variable (as opposed to one that has, by chance, a low p-value) should be able to predict out-of-sample. Thus, prediction adds a layer of discipline to investigative results and reduces the incentive to publish that one significant result that happened by chance to the detriment of the hundreds that did not make that cut. Even without assuming ulterior motives, a researcher may be tempted to run to publication with the first significant result. Thus, Machine Learning-induced predictive discipline may be useful given the disarray in the conflict literature we allude to in chapter 1.

Now onto our methodology. First, we divide our dataset into a learning and a test sample. Then, we train our models on the learning sample,[1] using the following Machine Learning technologies; Single-Tree, Bagging, Gradient Boosting, Forest, Artificial Neural Network (ANN), and Logit. A model is considered trained when it minimizes misclassifications of the target variable within the learning sample. Once the models are trained, we expose them to the test sample to see how well each model reduces misclassification errors. This is the true measure of a trained model's predictive power: how well it reduces misclassification errors on any number of dimensions in a test sample it has never seen before.

We use the area under the curve (AUC) of the Receiver Operator Characteristic (ROC), a common evaluation metric for binary classification problem, to compare the predictive capacities of these technologies. AUCs can be calculated for both the learning sample and the test sample. We argue that the best technologies should be the best predictive models; that is, have the highest out-of-sample AUCs. Predicting well in-sample is less of a feat because the model already "knows" the data and explicitly uses this data to find the best classification: in-sample good prediction is therefore somewhat tautological. A model that predicts outcomes well out-of-sample is, quite literally, predicting, since it tells us what should happen in a sample it has never seen. Then, if the model is largely correct, it should have the highest AUC. We report different manifestations of these error rates in Table 6.1. Table 6.2 reports p-values for pairwise comparisons of the predictive capability of different technologies. In short, we validate the trained models in the test sample. The model with the lowest misclassification rate in this test sample is therefore the most "valid" or predictive model.

The story goes that receiver-operating characteristic originated when the British started using radar to identify enemy aircraft in World War II. As they increased radar sensitivity, they began to pick out more enemy aircraft—but also more flocks of birds. Thus, increasing radar sensitivity increased the error rate, that is, the identifications became less specific. The ROC curve takes this problem into account. A model's true positive identification rate (sensitivity) is measured on the vertical axis while the model's false positive rate (lack of specificity) is measured on the horizontal axis. In more general statistical terms, specificity is (1-Type 1 error), while sensitivity is (1-Type 2 error). The ROC curve reflects how well the model trades off sensitivity and specificity, true positives and false positives. Notice that an ROC graph measures proportions along the axes. Since it is not possible to get more than 100% correct classifications (or for that matter misclassifications) the axes are limited to 0, 1 and the graph is a unit square. If the ROC is coincident with a 45-degree line in this graph, the model is no better than a coin toss as a predictive tool. The area under such an ROC would be 50% of the unit square. To be better than a coin toss, then, any predictor model must have more than 50% of the unit square under the ROC. A model with an AUC of 100% would be a perfect predictor.

How do our models perform in terms of the AUCs? Table 6.1 reports the AUCs for the ANN, Bagging, Boosting, Forest, Logit, and Single-Tree models as a C-Statistic. We look at the results of choosing a classical threshold. The classical threshold for classifying a new observation into a class assumes that all of the categories of the target (output) variable are equally likely. The class with the highest predicted probability above that threshold is the predicted class. In the case of a binary target (Conflict/No Conflict), an observation is classified as a "positive" outcome (Conflict) if the probability of the positive outcome (Conflict) is greater than 0.5.

First, we notice that the Logit technology seem to have the highest out-of-sample predictive power with a C-statistic of 0.886. Its closest competitors are the Forest and the Boosting methodologies with C-statistics of 0.883 and 0.882, respectively. Next, we see that the ANN model performs relatively poorly in the test sample with the lowest C-Statistic of 0.537, which is frankly, a bit of a relief! It is quite hard to interpret ANNs because the very nature of the technique involves the existence of complicated interrelationships between variables. Thus, ANNs are likely to be good predictors only if the complicated interrelationships between variables matter more for predicting an outcome. The low C-Statistic suggests that the potential interrelationships between variables are probably less important than the direct

Table 6.1 Area Under the Curve (AUC)

Machine Learning Technologies	ANN	Bagging	Boosting	Forest	Logit	Single-Tree	Average*
C-Statistic	0.537	0.850	0.882	0.883	0.886	0.844	0.889
"Classical" Threshold (p^* = 0.5)							
Specificity (1-Type 1 error)	0.998	0.984	0.948	0.985	0.971	0.957	0.985
Sensitivity (1-Type 2 error)	0.002	0.598	0.619	0.548	0.603	0.565	0.573
Positive Predicted Value	0.200	0.891	0.731	0.894	0.825	0.749	0.895
Negative Predictive Value	0.815	0.915	0.917	0.906	0.915	0.907	0.911
Overall Error Rate	0.186	0.088	0.112	0.095	0.097	0.115	0.091
"Best" Threshold (p^* varies)							
p^*	0.177	0.045	0.404	0.178	0.204	0.215	0.188
Specificity (1-Type 1 error)	0.116	0.788	0.833	0.762	0.855	0.784	0.774
Sensitivity (1-Type 2 error)	0.966	0.736	0.741	0.801	0.762	0.761	0.814
Positive Predicted Value	0.198	0.440	0.502	0.432	0.544	0.444	0.449
Negative Predictive Value	0.937	0.929	0.934	0.944	0.941	0.935	0.948
Overall Error Rate	0.727	0.221	0.184	0.231	0.162	0.220	0.219

* 'Average' is the AUC of the average of the predictions, not the average of the AUCs of the predictions.

predictive effects of the variables themselves. This is, of course, an indication rather than a scientific test. However, the poor predictive performance of ANNs could be further explored, especially since some subsets of our variables may in fact have important theoretically plausible interrelationships. We do not pursue this path in this book.

Let's look at another comparison of the Single-Tree, Bagging, Boosting, Forest, and Logit models, since their C-statistics are so close. Table 6.2

Table 6.2 *p*-values of Pairwise Comparisons of Individual Predictors, Out-of-sample

	Single-Tree	*Forest*	*Bagging*	*Boosting*	*Logit*	*ANN*
Single-Tree	.					
Forest	0.0000	.				
Bagging	0.2380	0.0000	.			
Boosting	0.0000	0.0800	0.0033	.		
Logit	0.0000	0.2743	0.0005	0.4345	.	
ANN	0.0000	0.0000	0.0000	0.0000	0.0000	.

provides the p-values for a pairwise statistical test of the whether the AUCs or C-statistics significantly differ from each other in making out-of-sample predictions. There is a 43.45% chance that the Logit and the Boosting models are the same, and a 27.43% chance that the Forest and the Logit models are the same. In short, these pairs do have significantly different predictive accuracy. However, we cannot statistically choose between Logit and the Bagging models, or any other pair. We therefore build a "combined" model by calculating the average predictions of all the technologies, and then building an AUC on this average.[2] This combined "average of the predictors" model (Table 6.1, last column), possibly because it aggregates information from all the technologies, has by far the highest out-of-sample AUC (88.9%). Thus, if our goal is to predict only the likelihood of conflict, the combined technology should be our choice. We can envisage a policy maker at the US Department of Defense using this combined model to predict the likelihood of conflict in specific countries, and then using these likelihoods to determine grand strategy.

However, what if the goal is to explore the effect of each variable on the likelihood of conflict? The combined model does not allow for that. The Logit model can help specify the variables and, to a certain extent, explore their marginal effects on the likelihood of conflict. However, neither model allows us to specify and rank variables according to their predictive ability.

Ranking variables according to their predictive capabilities is an important feature of tree-based Machine Learning technologies. In that capacity, Tree-based technologies allow us to choose the most predictive theoretical models among competing modeling approaches. We discuss this in detail in chapters 7 and 10. In chapter 7, we show how the ranking allows investigators first to choose a particular theoretical modeling approach, and then to empirically narrow down the list of causal factors using more traditional econometric techniques. In addition, ranking variables according to how well they predict conflict allows us to identify the kinds of data that should be collected, and moves us toward the path of a unique theory of conflict. We discuss such a possible path in chapter 10. Further, to the extent that ranking is validated by out-of-sample predictive power, we can have scientific confidence in our choice of the most predictive theoretical model.

The ability to rank also lends confidence to the policy maker when she evaluates a particular policy lever relative to another. If credibility is a better predictor of conflict than, say, aid assistance, the policy maker should probably focus more on thinking about investing in institutions of a particular type than soliciting more aid. For a different kind of policy maker, differences in institutional capacity along the credibility dimension may serve as an "early warning system" for conflict.

In addition to identifying and ranking variables that may matter most for peace, policy makers are also concerned about *how* they matter for peace.

In other words, what are the marginal effects of the 'best' variables? Again, the combined model cannot do this. The Logit model can, but it cannot rank these variables as policy levers. Tree models, however, are amenable to creating partial dependence plots that relate how *changes* in the magnitude of the independent variable change the likelihood of conflict. Logit models only provide a point parameter that effectively "averages" over this complex relationship. To that extent, Tree models provide more nuance to the exploration of marginal effects. These nuances are important to the academic, but also is of practical import to the policy maker. Where policy is concerned, the devil is in the details. Chapter 9 discusses this feature in more detail.

The ability of the Tree technologies to rank variables according to their predictive ability, and the fact that they lend themselves to partial dependence plots for these variables makes them quite useful. These technologies allow us to embark on a theoretical journey to explore causality as well as to identify variables that should be targets of data collections. Moreover, the partial dependence plots for these "important" variables can help predict the impact of specific policy changes. This ability to rank is therefore important for peace, policy, and theory.

We suggest that tree-based technologies should probably be the models of choice if we wish to move beyond pure prediction and use Machine Learning as part of a process toward developing a theory of conflict. We therefore reiterate that the Single-Tree, Boosting, Bagging, and Forest technologies actually have a very similar predictive performance to the combined model as well as the Logit model. Thus, we feel quite confident in using the tree-based technologies to explore both pathways to a unique theoretical predictive model of conflict, as well as the policy implications from the marginal effects of the important variables identified by these methods.

We now turn to a slightly finer grained analysis of the error rates reported in Table 6.1. The "best" threshold is the threshold corresponding to the point on the ROC curve that maximizes the sum of the Specificity and the Sensitivity. Graphically, this chooses the point on the ROC that maximizes the perpendicular distance from the 45-degree line. In the case of the Logit model, for example, the combined Specificity and Sensitivity achieves a maximum when we predict all observations with a probability of conflict greater than 0.204 as "Conflict." Choosing this "best" threshold (compared to the classical threshold) increases the combined Logit Specificity/Sensitivity for the test sample from 1.574 (0.971+0.603) to 1.617 (0.855+0.762). This is a small increase. While this trend is largely the case, the Bagging technique shows a small decline in this sum for the "best" predictor. Notably too, the overall error rate worsens for any given empirical modeling technology and absolutely jumps for the ANN (0.186 to 0.727). Thus, these "best" thresholds do not always offer better predictive results than the classical approaches. We therefore stick to the C-statistic for choosing between predictive model technologies for all the reasons described above. Nevertheless, we continue to suggest that the choice of model technologies should also be sensitive to the purpose of an inquiry. We make this point a little clearer with a deeper dive into Table 6.1.

In Table 6.1, we report specificity as (1-Type 1 error) and sensitivity as (1-Type 2 error). Type 1 error happens if our model predicts conflict when the observed outcome was peace. A Type 2 error occurs if our model predicts peace when the observed outcome was conflict. A risk-averse policy maker may be more concerned about missing a likely conflict. She may therefore wish to avoid Type 1 errors and maximize specificity. This policy maker would rather overpredict conflict than miss a real conflict. One supposes that organizations like the UN or NATO would rather be prepared for a conflict that doesn't happen, than miss one that does. The world should regret having missed the genocide in Rwanda. A focus on specificity may have avoided that regret and potentially saved the lives of thousands.

On the other hand, sensitivity over predicts peace. Thus maximizing sensitivity might actually oversell how well the model predicts peace. Now notice that the "best" threshold for prediction quality tends to increase sensitivity relative to the classical threshold. For example, notice that for the Boosting method, the classical threshold gives us a sensitivity score of 0.619, while the "best" threshold gives us a score of 0.741. Clearly, the incidence of Type 2 error is smaller for the "best" threshold. On the other hand, the opposite is true for specificity: For Boosting, the classical threshold offers a 0.948 specificity, while the "best" threshold offers 0.833.

In this book, we care unabashedly for reducing Type 1 errors for all the reasons we explained. We are of the "better safe than sorry" camp. Thus, to the extent that we want to use these models to develop policies leading to peace, choosing a policy based on technology with high sensitivity may not be nearly as effective in keeping the peace. Investigators with a different purpose may choose to focus on sensitivity. We prefer to pick those with higher specificity. This further justifies our reliance on the classical threshold for choosing the modeling technology.

Our discussion in this section points us toward one direction—choosing the tree-based technologies for giving us the most predictive empirical model. In the next section, we show the results of this choice. Table 6.3 ranks the "most" important variables based on the tree methods. This forms the basis for our discussion throughout the remaining part of this chapter and the rest of the book.

THE "BEST" PREDICTIVE SPECIFICATIONS

As noted, classification tree models have a big advantage over other models because they can rank variables by their predictive power. We use the Gini Impurity Index (not to be confused with the Gini income inequality coefficient) to get a sense of the predictive power of a specific variable within the "best" predictive model. Recall that Machine Learning models ask, "By how much would the predictive accuracy deteriorate if a variable was excluded from the model?" The algorithm then ranks the variables according to how much the predictive accuracy of the model would be reduced if a variable were removed. Variables that reduce model accuracy more if they are removed are more "important." We present our results in Table 6.3, where we list variables according to their importance as measured by the average.

According to the C-statistic in Table 6.1, the Forest technology is probably the "best" predictive technology. The Boosting technology has a C-statistic of 0.882 relative to the Forest's 0.883, while the Bagging and the Single-Tree have C-statistics of 0.85 and 0.84, respectively. Thus, the Forest tree probably should be the technology we use to identify the variables that predict conflict the best and rank them. Nevertheless, the predictive power of the Forest and the Boosting technology are statistically the same since we fail to reject the null hypotheses that the pairwise predictors are the same (the p-value reported in Table 6.2 is 0.08). But it also appears that the Bagging technology is statistically *different* from both the Forest and the Boosting technologies. Moreover, even though the ranking of the variables by the different tree methods are very similar to each other, there are some notable differences (see the last four columns in Table 6.3 which show the actual rank of a variable identified by a particular modeling technology). We therefore try to reconcile all these differences by averaging over the percentage decrease in the Gini Impurity Index for each variable and then ranking the variables. This weighted Gini therefore captures variable importance information from all the tree models. We would not suggest doing this if the AUCs or the misclassification rates for the models were wildly different. But they are not in this case. And it does give a sense of consistency to the variable importance. We clarify this with examples in the next paragraph.

A glance over Table 6.3 shows that the models ranked all the variables reasonably consistently, with a few exceptions. Trade, for example, is ranked higher as a predictor of conflict by the Boosting and Forest tree technologies relative to the other two models. Trade, if taken out of the model, reduces the predictive power of the Single-Tree technology by 0.769% and the predictive power of the Forest technology by about 2.84%. On the other hand, the Forest technology has a slightly (0.043) higher C-statistic than the Single-Tree

Table 6.3 Variables Ranked According to their Predictive Powers

	% of Decrease in Gini Impurity Index				
	Average	Bagging	Boosting	Forest	Single-Tree
LagConflict	53.435	81.159	34.427	33.601	64.553
GDPpc	5.359	1.492	12.244	3.884	3.814
RuralPop	4.021	2.608	4.391	5.105	3.982
Transparency	3.725	2.394	5.721	3.015	3.770
Credibility	2.469	0.606	3.104	4.257	1.909
SecEnrollPC	2.327	1.541	3.669	1.463	2.636
ElectricPC	2.003	0.326	1.738	4.017	1.932
Dependency	1.439	0.367	1.404	2.524	1.463
ReligPolariz	1.375	0.226	2.295	2.942	0.036
Trade	1.374	0.694	1.191	2.842	0.769
UrbanPopGrowth	1.291	0.558	1.035	1.696	1.875
Gini	1.263	0.405	0.457	2.794	1.395
PartyExclusion	1.140	0.565	1.836	1.317	0.842
Inflation	1.127	0.345	2.074	1.547	0.542
Area	1.084	0.384	0.568	1.724	1.658
RegimeInstab	0.972	0.607	2.201	1.081	0.000
PopGrowth	0.940	0.245	0.655	1.356	1.505
PopDensity	0.906	0.363	1.571	1.618	0.072
Regime	0.905	0.606	1.786	0.893	0.334
PhonesPC	0.895	0.209	1.245	1.502	0.623
Year	0.877	0.107	1.390	1.025	0.985
RuralPopGrowth	0.840	0.366	1.589	1.406	0.000
FemalePop	0.804	0.305	1.426	1.341	0.146
TermsOfTrade	0.801	0.104	1.460	0.921	0.719
EthnicPolariz	0.773	0.372	0.873	1.327	0.521
PrimCommodityExports	0.769	0.285	0.774	0.982	1.033
ExchangeRate	0.760	0.188	1.105	1.467	0.282
ParliamentRespons	0.672	0.173	1.160	0.987	0.367
AidAssist	0.665	0.396	0.702	1.265	0.295
System	0.498	0.034	0.568	0.401	0.987
ChangeGDPpc	0.475	0.201	1.100	0.600	0.000
WithinInstab	0.471	0.281	0.541	1.039	0.022
Democracy	0.429	0.197	0.558	0.963	0.000
Investment	0.400	0.211	0.116	1.275	0.000
Executive	0.400	0.219	0.152	0.863	0.367
PartyCoalitions	0.390	0.069	0.453	0.597	0.439
DroughtIndex	0.381	0.162	0.814	0.547	0.000
ChangePhonesPC	0.335	0.132	0.553	0.653	0.000
Protest	0.333	0.187	0.055	0.986	0.105
ChangeImportsPC	0.250	0.101	0.369	0.530	0.000
ChangeSecEnrollPC	0.239	0.090	0.135	0.707	0.022
DroughtIndexRange	0.217	0.035	0.360	0.473	0.000
ChangeExportsPC	0.171	0.083	0.132	0.470	0.000

technology.[3] Thus, even though the difference between the two predictive technologies is statistically significant (Table 6.2), it is small. The other examples of inconsistencies are in the ranking of SecEnrollPC, ElectricPC, Dependency, and ReligPolariz.

In order to reconcile this, we average over the % decrease in Gini over all the technologies for each variable—given that the models predictive powers were similar—to provide a consistent ranking of variables that did not throw away "importance" information. We calculate the average mean decrease Gini for the all the variables and report them in first column in Table 6.3. The top five variables, however, are consistency ranked across all the technologies.[4] They are LagConflict (conflict in the past), GDPpc (per capita GDP), RuralPop (the proportion of the population that is rural), transparency, and credibility.

How can a consistent ranking of variables help us understand conflict better? Blattman & Miguel (2010) in their masterful review of the civil conflict literature suggest that theories of conflict remain largely untested—particularly against each other. In other words, there is an evidence gap for which type of theoretical model best predicts conflict. Our methodology of ranking variables, to the extent that these variables can represent particular theoretical modeling strands, can potentially delineate an initial horse race between these theoretical models. Of course, we use variables here that *have* been used to test particular theoretical strands, for example in the greed versus grievance debates started by Colllier and Hoeffler (2004) and Fearon and Laitin (2003). There is always some debate about the theoretical salience of a particular variable—does income inequality represent greed or grievance? We discuss our general findings about the sort of theoretical models that are most predictive given these caveats in the next chapter, after pointing out some specific examples of what we mean by a horse race between theories here. Moreover, we note that Table 6.3 says nothing about the direction of the predictive effect of a variable. For example does transparency increase or decrease the likelihood of conflict? Nevertheless, in this chapter we would like to reassure the reader that these directional effects are intuitive and theoretically justified. We thereofore refer to the direction of the predictive impact on the likelihood of conflict here without more formal justification. That justification is, however, forthcoming in chapter 9.

The lagged conflict variable is the most important predictor of future conflict for ALL the tree-based models. This suggests that factors that encourage path dependence and/or inter-temporal calculations about war and peace must play an important role. We suggest that this particular predictor of conflict is never studied *directly* in a literature replete with competing theories. Having said that, current theories of conflict may well be implicitly connected to this finding. We will discuss this in more detail in the next chapter.

For now, let's keep in mind that *the potential ability to rank theories of conflict* based on the ranks of variables is a key feature of tree-based Machine Learning technologies. Certain variables are more likely to matter in certain theories. Thus, if a variable has greater predictive powers, the theory behind why that variable matters may be more important than the theory behind others. For example, notice that both the percentage change in per capita exports (ChangeExportspc) and percentage change in per capita imports (ChangeImportsPC) have lower predictive power than LagConflict. A theoretical model that suggests that sudden shocks in trade balances help explain conflict may be a less useful predictive theory of conflict than say commitment problems leading to bargaining failure. The latter modeling approach may more readily explain path dependence in peace and war.

As an overall trend, we find that variables that capture economic opportunity tend to be better predictors of conflict than political structure variables. Thus, for example, credibility and transparency are better predictors of conflict than how an executive is selected, or legislative competitiveness (Table 6.1 lists the variables that go into each factor). We also find that of the top ten predictors of conflict only one, transparency, represents some form of political expression.[5] Moreover, actual structural expressions may matter more than the structure itself. For example, transparency captures elements of democratic accountability, corruption, bureaucratic quality, and to a lesser extent, investment profile. These are expressions of political structures that provide economic opportunity and political voice. Our democracy factor on the other hand, while capturing elements of democratic accountability tends to focus on political structures like legislative and executive electoral competition, checks on power, executive's years in office, and so on. Therefore, even if one were to argue that conflict is a political rather than an economic pursuit, political expression seems to matter more than political structure.

Even within a particular theoretical modeling strand, certain variables matter more than others. This holds true for economic variables as well. For example, the credibility of economic institutions predicts conflict more than actual investment, aid assistance to a country, or even ChangeGDPpc, that is economic growth. This suggests to us that the credible possibility of economic opportunity may be a better way of avoiding conflict than actual wealth. In fact, contrary to the idea that poverty causes conflict, often justified by complicated econometrics that we will discuss in later chapters, many poor nations are quite peaceful. If poverty is a cause of conflict, all poor nations should be aflame. Poverty itself therefore cannot be a cause of conflict. Any real theory of conflict should be able to identify not only why people engage in conflict but also why they stay in peace. This really brings into question modeling techniques that do not account for this kind of equilibrium switch. Nevertheless, we make a larger point here. Current models of conflict are not always predictive. These approaches therefore cannot be theories of conflict. We argue that a theory of conflict should be generalizable and be able to predict conflict. We therefore suggest that any theory of conflict should focus on economic opportunity and government responsiveness rather than economic outcomes like investment, and political structures like the existence of a competitive legislature.

Our findings therefore appear to have important implications for both our understanding of civil conflict and policy. For example, we suggest that fundamental expressions of economics and politics matter more for predicting conflict than the structure of a political system or the dollar amount invested in or given to a country. Demographics matter as well (the rural population, secondary school enrollment per capita, and dependency ratios make it into the top ten predictors of conflict). To the extent that economic institutions and their expressions seem to predict conflict better than political institutions (even though some *expressions* of political institutions like democratic accountability and corruption seem to matter as well) we suggest that the causes of conflict are fundamentally economic. This argument is strengthened with the predictive salience of demographic variables that we know have important economic implications.

Moreover, as a matter of policy, it may not be enough to have the right institutional trappings or more wealth. For example, GDP per capita is a really important predictor of conflict. Nevertheless, the economic inputs that go into creating a higher GDP, other than economic opportunity, are not. Thus, investment, terms of trade, exchange rate, monetary policy as measured by inflation rates, aid assistance together do not predict conflict well. Indeed, income inequality itself, as measured by the Gini index, is not a salient predictor of conflict. Taken holistically, this suggests that investing in economic opportunity with the *possibility* of more wealth may be a better policy for reducing conflict than direct transfers aimed at reducing poverty or income inequality. Moreover, even though investment is necessary for economic growth and wealth creation, the fact that actual investment does not predict conflict well also suggests that economic opportunity and the consequent hope for the future really matters a lot for reducing conflict.

What might all this mean for actual policy? Poorer countries with more economic opportunity for citizens may be less likely to suffer from conflict than richer countries with no such opportunity. After all, if poverty were a cause of conflict then a simple redistribution of wealth would reduce conflict. That would not explain why a richer Middle East is in flames while many poorer African or Asian countries are relatively peaceful.

Our study also suggests that policies that reduce conflict should concentrate on fundamental types of change in the expressions of political and economic structures. For example, in order to reduce conflict effectively, a legislature needs to be democratically accountable. Mere elections are not enough. This dynamic may be a reason for the July 2016 Turkish coup attempt and the unrest leading up to it. Moreover, credible economic institutions that foster trade are more important for reducing conflict than the actual dollar amount of investment into a country. The apparent success of post genocidal Rwanda may reflect this, though we might add that the increasing lack of democratic accountability there also poses future conflict risks.

In this chapter, we base our conclusions on the ranking of variables. This method allows us to say which variables matter most for conflict, but not how they matter. Nevertheless, how these variables matter is important for both our understanding of conflict and for policy makers. Does democracy increase or decrease conflict? These questions are important. The tree methodology (luckily the source of our "best" models!), provides a unique opportunity to answer these questions using the partial dependence plot technology. We will also describe how this technology helps us understand the impact of the important variables on conflict in chapter 9. We have now set the stage for a deeper understanding of what kinds of theories matter for understanding conflict, the important variables that identify these theories, and how these variables influence conflict.

TAKEAWAYS

Our technological approach reduces researcher bias by adding a predictive component to investigations in the social sciences. A variable may have a low *p*-value by sheer chance. Such a variable though is unlikely to predict very well out-of-sample. Machine Learning technologies can help identify such variables. We should have increased confidence in a result that is not only statically significant, but also has strong out-of-sample prediction powers. Such a result should direct us to investigate causality within a subset of results that are both significant and predictive.

Machine Learning techniques come built in with out-of-sample generalizability. In fact, the entire Machine Learning process is uniquely focused on predictive generalizability. While out-of-sample predictions are certainly doable in more traditional econometric methods, they are not necessary, and as a result, are simply not done. Nevertheless, a theory by definition is generalizable. Thus, both theoretical and empirical modeling approaches can benefit from the Machine Learning approach. We suggest that the most predictive variables identified in this chapter should form the core of an iterative process leading to a theory (as opposed to a model) of conflict. We show just such a path over the next four chapters.

We make a further general point. Machine Learning is not an automated black box panacea to econometric problems. We discuss this in more detail in the later chapters. Nevertheless, even here, we note that the choice of technology depends on a researcher's goals. Thus, while the combined model was the most predictive and therefore useful in a predictive practical sense, the tree-based technologies were more nuanced and help us move toward a theory of conflict. Last, we find that expressions of economic opportunity and responsive inclusive governments should be part of any theory of conflict and should inform policies to help reduce conflict.

NOTES

1. We describe this process in more detail in chapter 4.
2. Thus we have calculated the AUC of the average of the predictors, and not the average AUC of the predictors.
3. See Table 6.1. The out-of-sample AUC for the Single-Tree model is 0.84 while that for the Bagging model is 0.88. The Single-Tree model performs considerably worse.
4. The Machine Learning algorithms choose the variables to test predictive power randomly in the learning sample. Thus, there is a risk that depending on the starting randomization "seed" the algorithms may give different variable rankings. We therefore tested our algorithms with three separate seeds. We found consistent rankings for any given model even when the randomization seeds were different.
5. We could probably count transparency as an economic opportunity variable since corruption is well known as a form of economic predation.

Chapter 7

Choosing from Among Seminal Models of Conflict Theory

In the previous chapter, our Machine Learning methodology identified the empirical models that best predict conflict. Can these models also help identify the "best" theoretical model? The answer has deep implications for humanity and society. A unique model, or even a parsimonious set of similar models, can help move us toward a theory of conflict. Such a theory of conflict would be useful in generating conflict policy, in the same way that theoretical physics generates engineering capabilities. This is not an argument for social engineering. It is an argument for a unified understanding of social processes that underlie war and peace. We suggest that our methodology allows us to give a higher priority to certain models over others. It also identifies theoretical gaps that require further investigation. At the same time, we gain insights into the extent to which certain factors matter more than others do.

The fact of the matter is that civil wars are costly and increasingly more likely than interstate wars (see e.g. Coyne and Mathers, 2011 pp. 177–194 for a review of the literature on the prevalence, costs, and consequences of civil war). It is therefore important to understand why they happen and how to restore peace. At the most basic economic level, the question is one of production or predation. After all people can get what they need either by making what they need and trading with others, or by taking what they need. The former requires specialization and trade and has the potential to make humanity better off. The latter is more of a zero sum game in the short run, and may make everyone worse off in the medium to long term. Stated as baldly as this, war appears to be irrational. Nevertheless, it is not. Yet we do not have a unified theory explaining this crucial, apparent contradiction. A number of economic *models* and corresponding evidence suggest that war is quite rational. However, we do not have a *theory* of civil conflict that yields this conclusion. The reader will notice that we are making a distinction between *models* of conflict, and a *theory* of conflict.

Economists explicitly use models as part of a toolkit to investigate how and why humans make decisions. This is standard procedure. This is certainly true for the conflict literature, probably more so than other areas of economic investigation given the complex nature of conflict. So, what we have is an array of models of conflict. Which of these predict conflict the best? Investigators have hunches but do not know the answer in any validated or cohesive way.

We have assembled a dataset that includes, political, economic, institutional, demographic, and geographical variables that represent a wide array of the sorts of variables usually identified as correlates of conflict. In this chapter, we will first rank the most important variables that predict conflict, and then explore what these identified variables imply for our understanding of conflict.

DISTINGUISHING BETWEEN SEMINAL MODELS OF CONFLICT

Seminal conflict models suggest that conflict is an artifact of a lawless world where political processes are resolved with bullets rather than ballots. That covers a rather wide range of reasons for conflict. We will look at distinguishing features in these seminal theoretical approaches, and see if our empirical models can separate these theoretical models into classes that differ by their ability to predict conflict. We suggest that the class of theoretical models that predict conflict the best might be the most important approach to understanding conflict. A good general model should be able to predict conflict well.

One seminal strand of the conflict literature looks at the economic, sociological, and psychological motivations behind conflict. Predatory leaders try to grab resources because they are greedy or have the opportunity to do so. These leaders capture natural resources like diamonds or oil, the proceeds from illegal trades, or straight out tax the populace (Collier and Hoeffler, 2007). Thus, rents from natural resources drive civil war. On the other hand, grievance may drive civil war. Typically, this grievance may stem from those political structures that close off avenues through which certain groups may better themselves or may make their voices heard. This kind of closure is easier if excluded groups are identifiable in particular ways like by ethnic or religious differences (Fearon and Laitin, 2003 p. 76 of course suggest that these forces cannot be identified as specific correlates for conflict even if they do play a role). These differences, however, may play an important role in fomenting conflict when exogenous shocks make economic conditions particularly bad (Gurr, 1968 and Tellis et al., 1997, pp. 86–96). Sudden scarcity may exacerbate conflict between social groups while enhancing the importance of kinship ties (Hirshleifer, 1998). Thus, grievance-motivated conflicts should be more apparent in multiethnic countries faced with exogenous economic shocks.

Moreover, recent experimental work in behavioral economics shows that people care about fairness at a neuro–physiological level. Individuals seem to prefer punishing social norm violators even when punishment costs are nontrivial (Charness and Rabin, 2002). Indeed, Choi and Bowles (2007) argue that this sort of conflict helps group selection. Our country level data cannot directly test the validity of this class of grievance models. Nevertheless, presumably such measurable things like the unequal distribution of resources and income should stir the instinct for fairness and predict conflict robustly if a desire for justice, that is, grievance, is the most important motivator of conflict.

Rational choice theory centers on another seminal source for conflict models, one in which individuals decide on peace of war, but do not interact. Contest models (originating with Haavelmo, 1954 and continuing with Hirshleifer, 1988, 1989 and Skaperdas, 1992 among others) suggest that leaders choose predation if the benefit of predation (which includes the opponent's economic production in addition to their own production—exceeds the costs (the diversion of productive resources toward guns). These models famously initiated the modern conversation on developing models of conflict that are rooted in rational choice. Grossman (1991) complicates this by adding the individual participation problem to the conflict calculus—leaders need to convince people to be soldiers. These models, however, like in the greed/grievance debate, largely ignore how agents interact with each other while choosing between predation and production, and the consequences of these interactions. Moreover, in these models, conflict is unlikely whatever the grievance, as long as the net benefit of conflict does not exceed the net benefit of peace.

This comparison of net benefits and net costs appear to be a simple thought in itself and perfectly in tune with standard economic rational choice models. Nevertheless, even at this level, things are complicated. For example, these models suggest that empirically, poverty and civil war should be correlated. Indeed, GDP is considered a fundamental correlate of conflict (Blattman and Miguel, 2010). Notice that the general structure of the models we cite here suggest that more national assets should create more war since at the very least the winner will get the right to tax. Further, people in poorer countries may be more easily persuaded to fight but they also have less to fight for. Thus, in equilibrium, a higher GDP should be correlated with more war (Garfinkel and Skaperdas, 2007). However, a lower GDP reduces the opportunity cost of war for individuals so that a lower GDP should be correlated with more war. Indeed, the two effects may cancel each other out (Fearon, 2007), particularly if coordination costs are high. Thus, the theoretical problems pertaining to understanding conflict even at this fundamental level remains problematic.

This particular theoretical Gordian knot can be resolved only if we know whether GDP is an important predictor of conflict relative to other variables. Even if one ignores the rampant endogeneity that bedevils the conflict literature, standard econometric techniques have no methodology that can rank variable importance. Of course, endogeneity cannot be wished away either. Lower GDP may increase conflict (and remember even that is theoretically unclear) but increased conflict may lower GDP as well. Then there is always the possibility of a third variable that can influence both GDP and conflict. These problems would lead to parametric estimates that are inconsistent and biased—in short, meaningless. Thus, the relative magnitude of parametric estimates themselves may say nothing about the importance of GDP relative to other factors in promoting conflict.

Further, econometric attempts to control for this sort of endogeneity using instrumental variables have also been problematic. Instrumental variables can resolve the endogeneity problem only if, for example, there is an instrument for GDP that is correlated with GDP but not with conflict. Miguel et al. (2004) use annual rainfall as such an instrument. However, as Blattman and Miguel (2010, pp. 25) point out, the use of rainfall as an instrument is itself problematic. Crop failure because of low rainfall may reduce the opportunity cost of conflict for individuals. However, it may increase the opportunity cost of conflict if people have to forage for food—armies famously do not march on empty stomachs. Then again, crop failure may reduce government revenues and state capacity (more on state capacity later). Oh what a tangled web.

Machine Learning provides a perspective that bypasses this web and ranks variables by out-of-sample validations of their predictive power. There are two issues here. First, if the opportunity cost rational choice model is a good theoretical model for understanding conflict, then at the very least, per capita GDP should predict conflict well. In fact, per capita GDP, and the conditions that increase per capita GDP, should be important predictors of conflict if there is causal link between the opportunity cost of conflict and conflict. Second, if we can show that that likelihood of conflict increases or decreases with higher per capita GDP, and the conditions that increase per capita GDP, then we can resolve some of the confusion above. We will investigate this latter idea in a later chapter.

The two seminal approaches discussed above incorporate purely psychological and sociological explanations, as well as rational choice cost–benefit analyses of conflict. But in these models people act alone—they are pure utility maximizing Homo Economicus. A warlord makes a rational decision on the benefit of war relative to the opportunity costs. If the benefit outweighs the cost, he (and warlords are usually "he") prosecutes war. The warlord may have to worry about side payments to his troops, or may even use grievance as the glue to keep his troops fighting, but he remains a unitary actor. The general miasma of grievance, on the other hand, may motivate people to start a rebellion. However, here too, the implicit assumption is that grievance helps individuals internalize the external benefits of rebellion. Thus, the idea that rebellion can redress injustice becomes part of the internal calculus of an individual's motivation to go to war. Grievance increases the benefits of rebellion relative to the costs. Once again, implicitly, the aggrieved person is Homo Economicus.

A second feature distinguishes these models. People in this model are already aggrieved or greedy to enjoy the spoils of war. Their only restraints are the costs of war. But what of peace? Arguably, the benefits of peace enter into their calculus as an opportunity cost, if at all. But it is a lonely peace. Because actors here are unitary, they cannot understand that peace may, for example, change the opportunity cost of war if other people peacefully trade with them. In these models, therefore, war is the natural state for the unitary agent. Peace is a mere by product of the calculus for war. Apart from being a depressing view of humanity, this ignores the reality that conflict is rare even in poor countries.

A third related strand in the conflict literature suggests that conflict may be a matter of state capacity. Weak states that cannot respond to grievances (as opposed to strong states that squelch grievances) can create the conditions for conflict. This may happen for a number of reasons. Rebels with grievances, for instance, may ignore a weak state and try to control resources to help their particular ethnic group. In this case, the weak state has nothing to offer rebels. Thus, weak states may provide the opportunity for conflict that may be motivated by either greed or grievance. Moreover, any deals with weak states may be problematic because they may not be able to insure against time inconsistency. For example, once a peace deal is struck, the relative strength of the warring factions may change in the future. Factions will take this future into account as they make current decisions about war and peace. Any faction that feels that it may become relatively weaker in the future will be unlikely to sue for peace now. In equilibrium, rebels would be unlikely to make deals, particularly if the whole problem could be avoided by taking down the weak state in the current period rather than wait for an uncertain future. Unstable regimes may therefore be more likely to be opportunities for conflict. Notice here that the focus is on instability rather than the nature of the state. Thus, both stable autocracies and stable democracies may not be conducive to conflict. Strong autocracies may squelch legitimate grievance while stable democracies may have mechanisms to voice grievances that channel and redress grievances positively. States in between—and particularly states in transition from one to the other—may practice both repression and be open enough to allow aggrieved groups to mobilize (Hegre et al., 2001, p. 33). This line of reasoning suggests that unstable regimes should be a good predictor of conflict.

A fourth modeling approach takes a rational choice approach in a *strategic* setting. In these models, bargaining failure between two individuals drives conflict. There is a notable distinction in this class of rational choice models. Here, individuals have a choice between production and predation, but their choices interact. Bargaining implies there is something worth the bargain. The size of this bargaining pie, therefore, matters, and depends on the interactions of agents in this model. For example, agents may choose to trade, and in the process, enjoy gains from trade, gains that may be lost with conflict. These models therefore capture a significant reality—if peace can provide clear benefits and war is costly, why do people choose conflict? After all, conflict can happen in rich or poor countries, even if they are more likely in poorer ones. And shouldn't conflict be even less likely in poor countries because people in these countries have most to gain from peace? Fearon (1995) suggests that bargaining failure has three reasons. First, leaders may be irrational or just make mistakes about the cost–benefit calculus. Second, the leaders may be rational, but the costs of conflict may be disproportionately borne by others. This would increase the leader's private net benefit from going to war even when peace is a viable option. Last, leaders may be rational and their private costs and benefits may reflect reality, but they may face a problematic information structure. Agents may not bargain if they have private information about the costs and benefits of war. They may know they have the economic capacity for war while their opponent does not, making the bargaining table less attractive. Or, they may choose to lie about their capacity for war. Nevertheless, this approach is not very convincing because if asymmetric information leads to costly war then agents also have an incentive to invest in mechanisms to reduce the information asymmetry, such as spying.

A more promising mechanism for bargaining failure could be commitment failures. Commitment failures occur when one of the two agents engaged in the bargaining process find an advantage from reneging on bargained solution. Powell (2006), for example, suggests that commitment problems can lead to bargaining failure even when all parties have complete information. For example, say a state makes a peace deal with rebels. Consequently, the state may get a peace dividend and gain in the future. At that point, the state may renege on the bargain. The expectation of reneging may reduce the rebel's desire to negotiate the initial peace deal. In any case, these models explicitly model strategic interactions between agents who, unlike Homo Economicus, are no longer islands. In the process, they also explain realistic conflict when peace is an attractive alternative.

A fifth source of conflict may be what Fearon (1995) defines as part of his argument for conflict arising from bargaining failure. In his telling, religion is part of a subset of general bargaining failure that necessitates conflict. In our opinion though, religion may rank as a separate seminal source for theoretical conflict models because it does not quite fit the mold of the general tenor of the approaches being described here. Fearon (1995) himself notes that religion feeds bargaining failure because in some senses it is indivisible. That is, one can fight for or against religion, but not over it. After all, it would be foolish to say that I have won a war by keeping 51% of my idea of God. Jackson and Morelli (2011) nevertheless point out that religious wars can be rational as well as long as leaders in these conflicts choose and optimize by using religion to, for example, inspire followers to overcome differences and join a conflict. Fearon's religious leader might not optimize as long s/he thinks religion is indivisible, but Jackson and Morelli's leader uses religion as a tool to prosecute a rational cost–benefit war. The latter case fits the rational choice modeling approach but the former requires a category by itself. This 'indivisible religion' approach to conflict suggests that religious polarization should increase the likelihood of war. The more polarized people are over religious factors, the less likely they will compromise since the very indivisibility of religion reduces the likelihood of compromise.

A final approach to conflict is psychological. Hardie et al. (2011) summarizes the literature on the psychological causes of war by focusing on three major kinds of biases that they suggest make war "irrational." We place the word "irrational" in quotes because there is a great deal of controversy about whether many of these experimentally verified biases fit the rational choice paradigm. Nevertheless, these approaches do suggest that psychological biases may cause agents to miscalculate the true costs of war. Thus, for example, fundamental attribution errors and social identity theories may help explain why certain groups of people may be viewed as enemies. Prospect theory may then help explain why agents are be willing to gamble more even when facing the certain losses from war with those enemies. At the end, these biases move them toward conflict.

Economic investigations of conflict, however, tend to be of the rational choice variety. This may be an artifact of the utility optimization approach to decision making preferred by economists. Cramer (2002) argues that as a result, economists' empirical investigations tend to be limited to reinforcing economic interpretations. We have assembled a dataset that includes both economic and noneconomic variables. We want to respond to Cramer by analyzing the results of the horse race between important variables. At the same time, we try to gain some insight into whether certain classes of models are better predictors of conflict. Eliminating certain classes of models may also help us develop a theory of conflict by shining a light on the channels of conflict that truly matter. So what does matter? Let us take look at these seminal models through the lens of Machine Learning.

A PATH TOWARD CHOOSING THE MOST PREDICTIVE THEORETICAL MODEL

We would like to bring the reader's attention to the top ten predictors of conflict in Table 6.3 We rank the variables according to the *average reduction* in the Gini Impurity Index from the Tree class of models. Notice, though, that there is some variation in the ranking of the variables across the three methods. Thus, religious polarization is ranked the 9th most important predictor of conflict on average. However, it is ranked 31st by the Single-Tree method, and 7th by the Forest and Boosting variations of the tree methodology, respectively. The reader will also notice that this sort of variation is much smaller among the top five variables. We will focus on the top ten variables in this list as we discuss our model choices below. Nevertheless, we remain most confident about the top five among this list. Why the top ten? This is largely a judgment call. We would invite the reader to go further down the list. However, we think they will continue to find that the broad outlines of our story below will remain undisturbed.

Greed as an explanation of conflict—at least in the sense that rebel groups are motivated to capture rents—seems to be a loser in our horse race. Recall that if greed is a motivator of conflict then easily captured rents should facilitate conflict. Primary commodities are well-known proxies for such easily captured rents. Primary commodity exports, however, are not even in the top 20 most important variables on both the average ranking and in all the models except in the Single-Tree model (where it ranks a low #13). Can such a poor predictor of conflict ever be an important cause for conflict? We think not. However, this variable represents the salience of greed as well. Collier et al. (2009) rename their greed variables as feasibility variables. This places them more in line with the opportunity cost reasoning for war approach where people choose war because of a decrease in the opportunity cost of war as a matter of rational choice. They find that rough terrain, proportions of young men in the population along with a population's dependence on commodity exports correlate with civil conflict. Our data matches theirs, except for the primary commodity exports. Nevertheless, we find that area as a proxy for terrain, and the percentage of women in the population as proxy for the role of demographics, are not salient predictors of conflict. These findings suggest that greed—at least to the extent it implies resource grabbing—and some types of opportunity costs, ought not to be part of a validated model of conflict and therefore probably should not be featured in a theory of conflict. Of course, there are other kinds of rents to pursue—taxation revenues for one. We are not claiming that we have the definitive answer to the model selection problem here. We do however suggest that our methodology provides the means toward solving the model selection problem and in that sense help us gain insight in to a true theory of conflict.

What about grievance? Recall that in our discussion above, conflict motivated by grievance should at least be predicted by ethnic fractionalization, income inequality, and exogenous shocks. We do have income inequality (the Gini coefficient of income inequality) and ethnic fractionalization explicitly in our models. Unfortunately, none of these variables ranks particularly highly. If variables have a significant causal impact on conflict, they also should be important predictors of conflict. To the extent that our grievance variables (and these are grievance variables that are commonly used elsewhere in the literature) do not rise up to the challenge, could it be that a grievance based model of conflict is not a good contender for a theory of conflict?

Of course, one might argue that these variables do not capture the psychological factors that drive grievance. It may even be that these variables are capturing something other than grievance. For example, income inequality may be driving greed—"if X has more than me why shouldn't I have more?" Such a telling of the story nevertheless misses the holistic point. To quote Miguel and Blattman (2010, pp. 10–11):

> [T]he distribution of income and wealth—whether across individuals or sectors—is central in explaining the economic incentives for rebellion. Civil war seems more likely when state wealth is easily appropriated or divorced from the citizenry, as with some natural resource wealth and foreign aid flows.

Our validated methodology suggests that neither greed (nor the updated "feasibility" redefinition of greed type variables) nor grievance predict conflict well. Incidentally, foreign aid flows, contrary to the emphasis placed on it by Miguel and Blattman (2010), either as a proxy for greed or grievance, is not an important predictor of conflict either. Friedman (2006) suggests that economic growth may fuel "greater opportunity, tolerance of diversity, social mobility, commitment to fairness, and dedication to democracy." The converse then can have the opposite effect. Friedman suggests that when we cannot compare our current economic situation to our past favorably, for example during an economic downturn, we are more likely to compare our economic situation with others. At this point, relative affluence becomes a source of grievance and potential conflict. The predictive salience of GDP per capita may capture some of this. Nevertheless, both the change in GDP per capita and the Gini coefficient have low predictive powers in our empirical model. Thus, while Friedman's argument for moral decay during bad economic times may be valid, it does not seem to predict all-out conflict.

Thus, a predictive theoretical model that looks to either greed or grievance may be deeply problematic. Note further that these models focus on the motivation behind conflict. On the greed side, unitary actors make a rational choice decision to choose war if the opportunity costs are low enough, and on the grievance side, they choose war merely because they are aggrieved. In both cases though, conflict is an underlying feature and peace merely a hiatus from conflict. Our results therefore are quite important for both theory and policy. For one, it appears that focusing on the motivation for conflict without any concomitant sense of the motivation for peace does not make a good predictive theoretical model of conflict. As a matter of policy too, redistribution programs by themselves may not stave off conflict by redressing grievance. Moreover, we also seem to have put paid to the "greed" argument since the availability of resources and some of the other variables that according to Collier et al. (2009) influence the feasibility of conflict also appear to be poor predictors of conflict.

We do however note that religious polarization ranks higher than all the potential grievance variables in our models. This may be a reflection of grievance though it seems unlikely since in the holistic context the other greed/grievance variables don't seem to predict conflict very well. Religious polarization often fractures along ethnic lines. For example, in conflict-torn Iraq, the Yazidi are ethnically and religiously different from the Shia (more Persian) and the Sunni (more Arab). Here, both ethnic fractionalization *and* religious fractionalization should be important predictors of conflict. In fact, Reynal-Querol (2002) makes precisely this point. To the extent that religious fractionalization seems to predict conflict much better than ethnic fractionalization, natural resources, and income inequality, something other than the greed/grievance paradigm must be at play here. Moreover, religious conflict may be different from the state capacity models or the rational choice models if religion is indivisible and therefore cannot be fought over. The salience of religious fractionalization in this context therefore suggests that a theory of conflict should somehow encompass the role of indivisible religion.

Let us look at another strand among the seminal models of conflict. Earlier in this chapter, we noted that unstable regimes promote conflict because they cannot completely avoid repression nor can they repress enough to prevent the formation of rebel groups. This approach suggests that neither stable democracy nor strong autocracies are particularly conducive to conflict. In other words, both democracy and autocracy should strongly predict peace, that is, the lack of conflict. In short, if the state capacity model is a good theory of conflict, unstable regimes, democracy, and autocracy together should be strong predictors of conflict.

Au contraire, we find that none of the political structure variables rank very highly as predictors of conflict. Party Exclusion is the highest ranking of the political structure variables. This variable measures whether and how political parties are excluded from the political process. This may hint at the importance of state capacity as a predictor of conflict. Nevertheless, it does not break the top ten. The two most direct measures of political instability and state capacity are regime instability and within instability. Regime Instability captures an institutional dimension that may indicate sources of instability stemming from fissures within the regime, specifically the frequency of cabinet changes and executive changes. Within instability, on the other hand, captures a broader political instability arising from the concentration of government and legislative fractionalization. Democracy—which captures the institutional dimensionality from democratic accountability: whether a regime is autocratic or not, the extent of electoral competition for the executive and the legislature—is ranked even lower. In short, the state capacity argument seems to be losing as a predictive theory as well.

Next, we investigate whether psychological factors may help predict conflict follows a similar pattern. Hardie et al. (2011) suggest that psychological causes for war find expression in observable variables. They first suggest that while psychological biases are part of the human condition, their most perverse expressions are most likely in autocracies rather than democracies. Biases are more likely to result in conflict in an autocracy than in a democracy because there are no checks and balances in autocracies (Kowert, 2002). Even within democracies, biases may overwhelm checks and balances if regimes tend to be concentrated and efficient and information flows are controlled (Desch, 2008). However, our democracy variable, which captures the essential features of a democracy like democratic accountability, checks on power, government polarization, electoral competition, and so on, is not a predictor of conflict. If psychological biases are indeed more likely to result in conflict in autocracies, then the democracy variable should at least be a salient predictor of conflict. It is not.

Another way that psychological biases may emerge is when, within democracies, the decision-making structure is centralized so that it is likely to transfer biases into policy, leading to conflict. Yet our within instability variable is *also* not a salient predictor of conflict. Recall that this variable captures the variation emanating from government concentration and legislative fractionalization. Thus, if certain psychological biases matter, they certainly do not seem to operate through the political structures suggested in the literature.

On the other hand, transparency is a salient predictor. Transparency is sourced from variables like corruption, democratic accountability, and bureaucratic quality. This variable captures the sort of open decision-making processes wherein different views are valued—a classic characteristic of democratic structures. More diverse decision-making groups are more likely to avoid biases because they are more likely to have countervailing voices. Thus, if different people with different biases are represented, existing biases may cancel each other out. Hardie et al. (2011) make a similar point about the decision-making process from a psychological perspective. Therefore, more competitive decision-making systems are less likely to be biased in any particular, overconfident, direction, and less likely to lead to war. Again, this suggests that governments/autocracies that are more concentrated are prone to war, while more competitive political systems are not.

So, even though democracy and within stability are not important predictors of conflict, the broad point of this literature—that truly democratic processes may help place a check on psychological biases playing out into conflict—is captured in our transparency variable. Thus, our results certainly do not rule out the causal and experimentally verified impact of psychological biases on decision-making. However, our results add nuance to this idea by bringing into question the role of the structures of democracy vis-à-vis democratic processes. In short, elections and multiparty democracy may not be enough to avert conflict if democratic processes emphasizing free and open discussion of policy making are clogged.

The saliency of transparency has a further implication. A third expression of psychological bias, urgency, may also have an effect on the likelihood of conflict. Psychological biases may be most relevant when there is no time to think things through. From a rational choice perspective, it may merely mean that our brain's capacity constraints kick in to emphasize the present over the future. Urgency may also ensure that even in even in democratic and competitive systems, debates, and checks and balances, of different biases may not find their way into a coherent policy. For example, conflict prone biases may become more salient if decision makers are under stress (Rosen 2004) and emotions cloud their judgment (McDermott 2004). We have no variable that tests this point directly and note that it may be hard to do in a cross-country study. Nevertheless, the predictive salience of transparency in our empirical model is broadly consistent with the role of urgency. Urgency is less likely to lead to conflict if multiple brains are yoked together in adversarial ways in the decision-making process, thus alleviating the resource constraint element of brain capacity, while emphasizing the effect of different types of biases.

Is there then any hope for rational choice approaches to conflict? Notice the variables in the top ten list. Of course, LagConflict is the elephant in the room. It is important enough to earn a completely separate chapter. Therefore, we will wait to talk about it since it hints at a new approach to modeling a theory of conflict. Nevertheless, almost all the variables in this list suggest a rational cost–benefit analysis of conflict may be our best shot at a formal predictive theory of conflict.

First, we note that per capita GDP (as noted by the rational choice contest models) is the second most important predictor of conflict. Other important variables in this parsimonious list like credibility, transparency, education (secondary school enrollment), electricity, trade, dependency, all influence *economic* opportunity. Now, the direction of such influence matters, and we will take this up in a later chapter (Hint: they predict conflict in the "right" intuitive direction). *Nevertheless, the salience of these variables, taken together, suggests the predictive primacy of rational choice models that focus on the opportunity cost of conflict over other theoretical modeling paradigms.*

This is not to say that grievance, state capacity, or psychological biases do not matter. We suggest that the sort of grievance that matters is centered on economic opportunity. Further, political structures that give us a sense of state capacity and stability may be important insofar as they facilitate economic opportunity. As a matter of policy, economic opportunity may thus be more important than political structures that give voice to grievances in reducing civil conflict. If state capacity matters, it is probably to the extent that the state allows a framework for economic opportunity to flourish and negate grievances. Indeed, the sorts of structures that support economic opportunity may also intercede in placing a check on the psychological biases that may lead to war. Religious polarization, as we have alluded to earlier, may be a slightly different animal. In any case, the effect of religiosity in predicting conflict is small relative to the combined predictive power of what we are calling the economic opportunity variables. A unique theory of conflict may then well be formulated around open governments and economic opportunity.

TAKEAWAYS

Why does identifying a *predictive* theoretical model matter apart from assuaging some academic need for intellectual coherence? It matters for policy. Policy makers implement a policy with the hope of some future impact. Theoretical models that perform well as predictors are therefore more useful to policy makers because these models highlight the possible salience of the effect of a policy. So, if people choose conflict by weighing its costs and benefits, rather than because of whether they feel repressed, policies designed to allow people a structure to air their grievance may fail if the goal is to reduce civil conflict. Elections and new parliament buildings may therefore be poor investments in conflict reduction while improvements in transparency and credibility may be better policies to reduce conflict.

Further, we often hear from political science "realists" that certain regions like the Middle East may avoid conflict if only dictators there have a firm grip on power. But this sort of policy is predicated on a sense that regime stability, whatever the sort of regime, is a bulwark against conflict. Our results suggest that variables like regime instability, or, for that matter, political structure variables (like executive selection), are not important predictors of conflict. Therefore, policies that target those variables may not be effective for reducing civil conflict. Propping up regional dictators like Saddam Hussein, or for that matter, the Shah of Iran are the mainstay of "realist" policy. But if the goal of such policy is to reduce the likelihood of conflict in the Middle East, then our technology suggests it is likely to fail.

Recall Cramer's (2002) criticism of economists focus on economic variables: It is a valid criticism in general. However, we may have lucked out while considering conflict. As a matter of *predictive* salience, among a wide array of variables that capture elements of the psychological, political structure, greed/grievance approaches to modeling conflict, those variables that capture economic activity and opportunity seem to matter the most. But what tips a country from peace into conflict or vice versa? We delve into that question in the next chapter.

Chapter 8

Choosing Among Microeconomic Models of Conflict

In the last chapter, we noted several of the seminal approaches to understanding conflict and our algorithms chose the most salient predictor of conflict among them. Nevertheless, human history is not solely the history of conflict. So what tips a country from peace into conflict or vice versa? In the last chapter, we suggested that variables that represent rational choice approaches to conflict seem to predict civil conflict the best. In this chapter, we will discuss some of the rational choice approaches to modeling conflict and discuss whether our algorithms have any specific recommendations for developing a unique predictive theory of conflict from among them.

CHOOSING RATIONALLY BETWEEN THEORETICAL RATIONAL CHOICE MODELS

The seminal contest models and the strategic models of bargaining failure we described in the last chapter were fundamentally rational choice models. Our algorithms suggest that the cost–benefit modeling style of these rational choice models was more predictively salient than the other approaches, with the possible exception of a relatively lower ranked religious indivisibility understanding of conflict and certain psychological biases. The contest models, while seminal, are unsatisfying. In those models, conflict leaders appear to act in a vacuum, as if Homo Economicus lived alone on a desert island. There is no strategic interaction between opposing players of the conflict game. As a result, conflict rages undeterred by anyone else in those models. Whether conflict happens or not is purely the rational choice decision of a savant like utility maximizer who is ignorant of other people's desires and actions. That is somewhat unrealistic. Moreover, it fails to explain why conflict happens some of the time but not others. Rationally, since war is costlier than peace, a cheaper bargaining solution should always be possible. If so, then peace should be the dominant outcome. Also, recall that while GDP per capita remains a salient predictor of conflict, other variables that should be important for the lonely rebel's calculus of war are emphatically not salient predictors of conflict. Collier et al.'s (2009) opportunity cost reasoning for war approach where people choose war because of a lowering of the opportunity cost of war as a matter of rational choice reports statistically significant correlations between civil conflict and "feasibility" or "greed" variables like resource availability, proportion of young men, and rough terrain, among others. As noted in the last chapter, our proxies for these feasibility variables remain disappointingly non-predictive. All this suggests that the unitary actor making decisions to go to war based on a direct cost–benefit analysis may not be the best approach to predicting civil conflict. Of course, the standard neoclassical models assume perfect information. Modern approaches to this problem follow two patterns that relax the perfect information assumption. This relaxation of the perfect information assumption results in multiple equilibria where conflict happens in some equilibria. In these models, nations tip into conflict from peace or vice versa.

Fearon (1995) suggests that bargaining failure is the root cause of conflict. He points out that bargaining failure may be a result of (a) irrational leaders who are susceptible to emotions, (b) rational leaders with costs that can be externalized but with private benefits, and (c) rational leaders with internalized cost who nevertheless choose war. Much of the current theoretical work concentrates on this third sort of bargaining failure. Notice that actors are quite rational here. Fearon (1995) however, further suggests that this third sort of rational conflict may happen for three reasons. First, asymmetric information where the parties involved in the conflict have private information about say military strength may encourage them to lie about these strengths (or weakness) and these actions may lead to war. Second, the parties involved in potential conflict may not be able credibly to commit to peace for reasons we will outline below. Last, the conflict may be about indivisible issues like religion. Religious differences guarantee bargaining failure since by definition there can be no bargaining over indivisible things. In any case, models of conflict as a rational choice take a two-pronged approach; one path looks at information asymmetry and the other at incomplete contracting or bargaining failure.

Akerloff (1970) has suggested that information asymmetry is a source of market failure. In a general equilibrium sense, this relationship between information asymmetry and market failure merely suggests that information is valuable and the information asymmetry is a market opportunity. Business models for Standard and Poors, or even Carfax, are based on information asymmetries. Moreover, any market must have information asymmetries to create arbitrage opportunities. Thus, just pointing toward information asymmetry as a source of conflict is problematic. If information asymmetry is a potential source of conflict, and if conflict is costly, then all parties have an incentive to invest in information gathering and signal strength (Fearon, 1995). Spy agencies are an investment in reducing conflict. Large defense expenditures or acts of terrorism can also surmount information asymmetries if they credibly signal strength. Arguably, Pakistan's ill-disguised involvement in the Mumbai attack was just such a signal to Indian forces. Even in the intrastate context, Maoists in a wide swath of India exert influence by occasional attacks on government forces. These attacks on police convoys and paramilitary forces have effectively deterred the Indian state from any meaningful retaliation and indeed removed the Government of India's writ from large parts of eastern India. In short, information asymmetry need not devolve into all out insurgency. It is certainly possible to envisage a stable equilibrium that avoids conflict with an optimum investment in information gathering or signaling.

Moreover, even if a conflict starts as a result of asymmetric information about say the relative strength of the two parties, the actual prosecution of the conflict should reveal the true strength during the duration of the conflict. At that point, the costs of conflict should become obvious to the weaker party who should then sue for peace. Therefore, if asymmetric information is a source for conflict, then there needs to be some structural problem that hampers the evolution of an optimum investment in gathering information or signaling (Blattman and Miguel, 2010, pp. 12).

Hirshleifer (1995) suggests that divergent perceptions about the *net* benefits from a war may reduce the opportunity space where bargaining is possible, thus making it harder to negotiate. In his model, two agents have the option of coming to an agreement about the distribution of a scarce resource, represented by a production possibilities curve, through say trade, or through acquiring the resources through war. War requires expenditure of resources. Thus, Hirshleifer explicitly models the costs of war in a way that ensures that any outcome of war must lie *inside* some production possibilities frontier. Clearly, this modeling approach makes war less desirable than a bargaining solution where the two agents can be *on* the production possibilities frontier. However, if, because of asymmetric information, an agent's (or both agents) estimates of his or her opponent's opportunity cost of war diverges from the opponent's actual estimates, the share of resources that can be haggled over falls. Hirshleifer then suggests that it becomes harder to come to a bargained solution if there are fewer resources to haggle over. Simply put, asymmetric information about resource distribution after a war may result in bargaining failure. Thus, if this sort of asymmetric information is a cause of war, one might expect variables that reduce the resource space that can be haggled over, and institutions that restrict information flows, to predict the likelihood of conflict.

Another set of models incorporates asymmetric information as a direct cause of conflict. Esteban and Ray (2001) model multiple players. They show that the Pareto improving social decision making—about say a transfer of resources from one group to another—is impossible when each player has imperfect information about the others cost of conflict. In their model, unlike Hirshleifer's, information asymmetry among multiple agents is the direct cause of conflict rather than a force merely exacerbating the likelihood of bargaining failure between two agents. Ray (2009) extends this model to show that even complete contracting cannot stave off conflict. His model shows that that if multiple groups have to come together to make social decisions, such interactions are more likely to result in conflict even if these groups have perfect information and contracts. Thus, bargaining failure comes about as a sort of collective action problem.

Societies of course are often fractured around ethnic, religious, age, or class fault lines. Since such diversity implies the existence of information asymmetry, this modeling approach suggests that conflict is more likely in such societies. Thus, for example, ethnically diverse societies, that is, societies divided along multiple ethnic fault lines, arguing about social security, might devolve into conflict, and particularly more so if an older generation is of a different ethnicity than the younger generation. In short, ethnically fractured societies are less likely to have cohesive social capital and therefore more prone to conflict.

The same argument could be made for societies with high levels of income inequality or ones with a large proportion of very young or very elderly people (dependents). Such societies may be less likely to agree on social security transfers say than relatively homogenous societies. Indeed, there have been numerous papers on the role of social capital leading to successful transfer policies in the more traditional economics literature. Moreover, if social divisions hamper social decisions, shouldn't democratic institutions designed to mediate theses division ameliorate conflict?

Chassang and Padro-i-Miquel (2009) incorporate information asymmetry as a direct source of conflict within the context of global games. Their model suggests that temporary economic shocks—like a sudden terms-of-trade shock or a drought—interact with asymmetric information to cause conflict. Say one of the two agents in a potential conflict has more information about a terms-of-trade shock or the widespread effect of a drought. At least one of the agents therefore has some uncertainty about future economic conditions. This reduces the present value of a bargained peace. On the other hand, an immediate conflict victory has immediate gains. Thus, agents may choose to go for the immediate spoils of war rather than wait for the uncertain fruits of peace. Agents in this class of models have a distinct advantage from moving preemptively. One nice thing about this modeling approach, as Blattman and Miguel (2010) point out, is that it generates some clearly testable predictions: Negative income shocks and volatile national incomes should increase the likelihood of armed conflicts while higher expected GDP growth should reduce conflict.

Dal Bo and Powell (2009) suggest that commitment problems may increase the likelihood of conflict in the presence of exogenous income shocks. Their model focuses on the commitment problem rather than on these exogenous shocks. Commitment problems tend to arise when parties to a conflict are aiming for peace deals. Paying off an aggressor may buy peace. Nevertheless, history is replete with examples documenting the failure of such attempts. Rudyard Kipling in Dane-Geld says:

It is always a temptation to an armed and agile nation
To call upon a neighbour and to say:—
"We invaded you last night—we are quite prepared to fight,
Unless you pay us cash to go away."

And that is called asking for Dane-geld,
And the people who ask it explain
That you've only to pay 'em the Dane-geld
And then you'll get rid of the Dane!

It is always a temptation for a rich and lazy nation,
To puff and look important and to say: —
"Though we know we should defeat you, we have not the time to meet you.
We will therefore pay you cash to go away."

And that is called paying the Dane-geld;
But we've proved it again and again,
That if once you have paid him the Dane-geld
You never get rid of the Dane.

It is wrong to put temptation in the path of any nation,
For fear they should succumb and go astray;
So when you are requested to pay up or be molested,
You will find it better policy to say: —

"We never pay *any*-one Dane-geld,
No matter how trifling the cost;

For the end of that game is oppression and shame,
And the nation that pays it is lost!"

Why does this ransom bargain not work? Say the government has more information about the state of the economy than rebels do. When the government tries to pay off the rebels, the rebels may not believe that the government is making a good offer. This may lead them to ask for more. However, if only the government has a sense of the true extent of the damage from a negative shock to the economy, "more" may not be forthcoming! This could make conflict more likely. Once again, observationally, an economic shock makes conflict more likely in this model because the government's commitment to peace is not credible to the rebels who do not have access to the state's private information.

There may be yet another source of assault on the credibility of a negotiated settlement: Say the government agrees to share power with the rebels. Arguably, this power sharing agreement could buy rebels time to increase power, and therefore, ultimately overthrow the state. Rational actors in government would preempt this possibility by being unwilling to share power; thus making conflict more likely. Either agent could be somewhat tone deaf to overtures for peace under these circumstances.

Psychological factors may also exacerbate commitment problems. In the last chapter, we noted how social identity theory and fundamental attribution errors could make enemies. Prospect theory can then explain why agents may be overconfident about the benefits of war. These psychological biases can taint the discussion process going into brokering the peace and cause them to fail. This, as we noted earlier, can be particularly pertinent when the threat of war is imminent or ongoing so that peace is an urgent business.

The commitment problems described above can arise when there is perfect information (Walter, 1997). Even when everyone has the same information about the economy, or about relative strengths, or about any other factor that goes into the calculus of conflict, the future is always uncertain. The outcome of a current conflict, therefore, may be more certain than the outcome of a future conflict since the relative power of the agents may change during the peaceful interlude. In fact, Powell's (2006) theoretical model suggests that that these commitment problems are the sole result of large shifts in future power. In his telling, a weak state may be willing to pay ransom to strong rebels. However, when this peace generates an economic dividend through straight out legitimate economic activity, or through revenues from primary commodity exports or tranches of foreign aid assistance, the state benefits rather than the rebels. The state thus may gain power relative to rebels. In a perfect information world, the rebels know this possibility and therefore would rather strike while they can get a larger, and surer, net benefit.

A similar logic applies when the state (or rebels) can gain a strategic advantage by wiping out their opponents (McBride and Skaperdas, 2007). Simply put, a victory now can lead to permanent future gains. Indeed, the reduction in uncertainty from the conflict actually increases the present value of the future peace dividend, ceteris paribus. This is the calculus for a bloody war and possibly even rational genocide. Assad may have just such a calculus in mind in Syria.

The literature on commitment problems as a source of conflict thus suggests that the element of time, and mechanisms that bridge time in a way that reduces uncertainty about the future, should matter. North (2005, pp. 13–22), for example, argues that conflict arises when agents who believe they live in an ergodic world find themselves in non-ergodic situations. This happens because experience of the past cannot prepare one for a non-ergodic event. This lack of preparedness for the possibility of non-ergodic events can lead to social failure. He goes on to suggest that social institutions that can manage risk and increase certainty are the bedrock of civilization itself. This question brings us nicely to one of the important questions: What sorts of institutions manage future uncertainty and pave the way for a civilized peace?

Contracts are one such social institution. They can manage intertemporal uncertainty. Efficient contracts deter reneging through two mechanisms that incorporate the shadow of the future. Penalties can credibly deter reneging by increasing the present value of future punishment. Alternatively, reputation effects can deter default if agents have a stake in future interactions. In either case, Game Theory's Folk Theorem suggests that a more certain future deters conflict. In other words, contracts can deter conflict when agents negotiating the contract are patient enough to avoid future punishment by repeatedly fulfilling their obligations. This sort of certainty about the future requires stable state institutions to enforce contracts. Ergo, states with weak institutions are less likely to overcome commitment problems because an uncertain future makes contracts less likely to be enforced. These states are therefore more likely to devolve into violence. Fearon and Laitin (2003), La Ferrara and Bates (2001) and Skaperdas (2008) all suggest that states with weak governance structures and fewer checks on executive power are, as a result, more likely to be driven to conflict. Moreover, uncertainty about the future makes decisions more urgent and centered on the here and now. Given that human psychological biases make war likely, consideration of varied viewpoints, and the consequent countervailing psychological biases, are less likely to interrupt the decision to wage war. Thus, if conflict arising out of bargaining failure and/or information asymmetry can be mediated by institutional context, we must be open to the idea that social capital embedded in this institutional structure may be important in delineating a unified theory of conflict. Can Machine Learning shed some light on this claim?

A PATH TOWARD CHOOSING THE "BEST" RATIONAL CHOICE MODELS

The models described in this chapter provide some testable hypotheses. Indeed, these hypotheses *have* been tested, separately. However, to the best of our knowledge, no one has run a horse race to see whether some models are "better" than others. Recall that a main argument in this book is that good models of conflict can claim to be a theory only if they predict well. Do our Machine Learning algorithms shed any light here?

As in the last chapter, let us continue to concentrate on the top ten (see Table 6.3), and particularly, the top five most important variables—Lag-Conflict, GDPpc, RuralPop, transparency, credibility. The most important variable in our model is lagged conflict. This variable says that past conflict is the best predictor of future conflict. This seems obvious. Nevertheless, this conclusion, when taken together with the other important variables of our model, allows us to make an important distinction between those approaches that model commitment problems as the source of bargaining failure and those that model asymmetric information alone as a source of bargaining failure. We can say that the former may predict conflict better than the latter.

Recall that Esteban and Ray (2001) suggest that asymmetric information alone hampers the process of social decision-making. Consequently, in their modeling approach, ethnic fractionalization is a major source of conflict. In our predictive model, however, ethnic polarization is a remarkably poor predictor of conflict—not even breaking into the ranks of the top ten predictors. One explanation for this unimportance could be that even if social divisions hamper social decision-making and tip countries into conflict, democratic political institutions that are designed to give voice to these grievances would mitigate that effect. In other words, in our model, ethnic polarization is unimportant because we include 'democracy.'

Of course, democratic political institutions can help or hinder conflict: on the one hand, they can help clear the air and heal social differences by giving voice to the silent, while on the other hand such voice may vitiate preexisting divisions. Our democracy variable focuses on the political structure of democracy. It is sourced from (EFA table) democratic accountability, bureaucratic quality, the Democracy-Autocracy index, political competition (e.g., legislative fractionalization, etc.), checks on power, government polarization etc. Recall that asymmetric information should be a source of conflict only if there are structural reasons to prevent information search. It appears though, that political structures, or the lack thereof, do not predict conflict. The fact that democracy is a poor predictor of conflict suggests that structural asymmetric information may not be a convincing path toward a predictive theory of conflict. Even political instability within a regime (Within Instability) does not predict conflict well suggesting that the argument that weak states may exacerbate the information asymmetry problem in ethnically polarized states may itself be weak. The relative predictive unimportance of all the other political structure variables we use in our Machine Learning models merely strengthen this view.

Incidentally, measurement errors may be rife in these political and social measures. The political measures are of course somewhat subjective artifacts. Ethnicity may be too fluid a concept to be measured in any meaningful way to capture polarization. Nevertheless, such measures are used often and consequent results are published in respected peer reviewed journals that note such caveats. The good news is that we may dispense with these measures for accurate prediction.

We can draw two lessons here. Those models that suggest that asymmetric information in socially fractured societies explain conflict are not very good predictors of conflict. Therefore, they cannot lay claim to a theory of conflict. On the other hand, if the variables mentioned above are poor measures of the political and social elements they purport to capture, maybe such variables do not represent the models well. In that case, we would be hard pressed to eliminate these theoretical asymmetric information models as good predictors of conflict. We take the former view since it seems unlikely that ALL these variables are so fraught with errors as to render them useless as predictors. Moreover, recall that our factors extract common sources of variation from several institutional variables. That mitigates the measurement errors.

Our transparency factor is sourced from bureaucratic quality, corruption, democratic accountability, electoral fraud, government polarization, investment profile, and regime durability. Overall, therefore, transparency measures the degree to which the state is able to curb corruption and efficiently execute bureaucratic functions in a manner that is credibly open to the citizenry. Societies that are more transparent should have less asymmetric information. Transparency therefore militates against the divergent perceptions that reduce the resource space and lead to bargaining failure in the Hirshleifer model. The predictive salience of transparency therefore seems to strengthen the role of asymmetric information as a predictive model of conflict.

A similar argument can be made for the credibility factor. Government stability and investment profile define this factor. Credibility, then, relates to the confidence the public is able to place in the predictability of government policies and the relative freedom from expropriation of profits and property by the government. Markets work well with credible economic institutions.

Asymmetric information is less likely when a country's economic and political markets work better because of credible transparent economic and political institutions. The predictive salience of transparency and credibility therefore suggest that asymmetric information may be a source of bargaining failure and conflict. However, in our view, commitment issues are probably a better modeling approach. This inference is strengthened when we look at the second strand of theoretical modeling initiated by Chassang and Padro-i-Miquel (2009).

Chassang and Padro-i-Miquel (2009) suggest that if asymmetric information is a source of conflict then negative income shocks, less volatile national incomes, and income growth should be good predictors of conflict. We note, however, that in our empirical prediction model, terms of trade shocks that proxy negative income shocks (as a matter of standard treatment in the literature) is not a good predictor of conflict. Economic growth (ChangeGDPpc), the exchange rate, the drought index, or its range, are not good predictors either. Changes in exports and imports per capita also make up the predictive tail end. Taken together, this suggests that asymmetric information as a source of conflict is a poor predictor of conflict. In fact, the variables here do not have the same criticism as the "softer" social division and political variables. These variables are hard measures. Even so, they do not predict well. In addition, as we explain below, transparency and credibility also fit with commitment failures as a source of the bargaining failure that leads to conflict. Overall, then, we conclude that theoretical models that look to asymmetric information as a source of conflict do not perform well as conflict predictors. We are reluctant to give these models the mantle of predictive theory.

However, we do have a contender. Let's review the Hirshleifer bargaining model we described earlier in this chapter. In that model, bargaining failure is a consequence of a reduction in available bargaining opportunities within the resource space. Presumably, richer countries have larger bargaining opportunities. GDP per capita's predictive salience (GDPpc, ranked 2) is perhaps unsurprising in this context. Moreover, we note that transparency (ranked 4), credibility (ranked 5), and trade (ranked 10), along with education (SecEnrollPC, ranked 6) and electricity (ElectricPC, ranked 7), are important among the top ten salient predictors. All these variables are associated with positive economic growth in theoretically well-known ways (Sala-I-Martin, 1997). Keep in mind that economic growth per capita (ChangeGDPpc, ranked 31) or actual investment (investment, ranked 34) are themselves not good predictors of civil conflict. However, the conditions that allow investment and the consequent economic growth *are* important predictors. This finding suggests that it may not be actual economic growth that matters: it is the environment of economic well-being that matters more for modeling conflict. These results, juxtaposed against the poor predictive performance of variables that should matter for asymmetric information as a source for conflict, suggest that while bargaining failure may be a proximate predictor of conflict, it is probably not a consequence of asymmetric information.

Let's take another look at credibility, ranked five in our top ten predictors (Table 3) in this context. Credibility measures the quality of economic institutions. These economic institutions (captured in the investment profile component of the credibility factor) safeguard contracts and private property. Recall that weak contract enforcement is a key source of commitment problems in those models that look to commitment problems as a source of bargaining failure and subsequent civil conflict. Contracts bridge temporal uncertainty and, in that sense, provide a civilizational basis of the sort recommended by Douglass North. This civilizational imperative of enforceable contracts reduces conflict precisely by mediating commitment problems.

The role of institutions in enforcing contracts, as measured by credibility, therefore is critical for peace. At one level, enforced contracts create a sense of trust. When trust permeates a society, it becomes easier to make deals that people know will be honored in the future. At another level, it reduces the urgency in making deals, thereby reducing psychological biases. This very possibility may make deal making unnecessary in the realm of conflict.

Recall further the predictive salience of transparency. Perceptions are less likely to diverge in a transparent world. Thus, divergent perceptions are unlikely to generate conflict in the way suggested by the Hirshleifer model. Moreover, a transparent society also provides a basis for trust. People in these societies are more likely to believe that a government is not lying to them or is not corrupt. The endemic corruption of the Iraqi government makes it less likely for people to trust enough in the "system" to take the risk of starting a scalable business. At another level, anger over the government's active and covert support for Shia over Sunni has spilled over into outright conflict and Sunni support for the Daesh. The Daesh, unlike the Iraqi state, enforces contracts quite transparently in their own sickeningly brutal way. In any case, given the opaque decision process of an Iraqi government whose leaders are largely tribal leaders, no rebel will be willing to parley with them for all the time inconsistencies suggested in the models described. A similar situation probably exists in Afghanistan and in much of conflict driven continental Africa.

At the same time, this sense of trust, undergirded by transparency and credible economic institutions, also allows individuals to specialize in production. Notice that trade is the last of our top ten important predictors in Table 3. Trade of course correlates with specialization. Neither trade nor specialization is plausible without a culture of trust. Trade correlates with a larger GDP, in effect increasing the bargaining space between agents and thus reducing the likelihood of conflict. A large GDP per capita is the second most salient predictor of conflict. Incidentally, electricity, as a proxy for energy use, is also correlated with healthy economies and to that extent instrumental in influencing the bargaining resource space.

Education or human capital is an important theoretical input into expanding the bargaining pie. The predictive salience of secondary school enrollment captures this importance. All these variables therefore create the conditions for a sunnier future where people can fulfill their destinies without predation. In effect, credibility and transparency provide both the basis for a culture of trust and economic opportunity.

Trust and economic opportunity reduce commitment problems. Fearon, Skaperdas, and others model commitment mechanisms as stable state institutions. Stable state institutions can credibly enforce deals and thereby reduce uncertainty about the future. Thus, in the event of conflict, peace deals become a credible possibility. Moreover, states with credible and transparent institutions also tend to provide citizens with an environment of opportunity thus obviating the need for conflict. It therefore seems to us that the economic variables that proxy wealth and opportunity, in combination with these two institutional factors, direct us to the best predictive theoretical models of conflict in a way that models rooted in asymmetric information do not. We recognize that some of these predictive variables can be foot soldiers carrying the banner of both asymmetric information and commitment problems. Nevertheless, a holistic analysis suggests that the preponderance of predictive power seems to side with commitment problems as the more predictive source of conflict. In other words, predictive theoretical models should probably concentrate on strategic rational choice approaches that model commitment problems. Further, our results suggest that any unifying theoretical model of conflict should also emphasize the role of social capital (as measured by the institutional structure of credibility and transparency) in mediating the collective action problem inherent in the sort of commitment failures that lead to bargaining failure and then conflict.

The salience of lagged conflict also supports our view. That past conflict is a predictor of future conflict suggests path dependency in conflict. That past conflict is the *most* important predictor of conflict suggests that this path dependency is important. Unfortunately, throwaway acknowledgment aside, very little work has illuminated this path dependency. Nevertheless, path dependency's predictive salience suggests that it should be an important factor while developing theoretical models of conflict. In fact, commitment problems may be broadly consistent with path dependency. We will come back to this in a subsequent chapter. Here though it should suffice to raise a few points of consistency.

Conflict itself creates uncertainty both among individuals, who have no idea if they will live tomorrow or not, and within institutions, by weakening them. For example, conflict may reduce tax revenues by hampering economic activity, and may, in turn, defund, and destabilize state institutions. Increased uncertainty about the future makes peace deals less likely by making any future punishment for breaking a peace deal less powerful. Thus, current cooperation between parties become less likely when deviations from a cooperative path are less likely to be punished credibly. This collective action failure reduces the commitment to peace deals through an inversion of the Folk theorem. This also points to the importance of social capital theory in understanding conflict that arises out of a failure to commit to cooperative solutions.

In terms of econometrics, this cooperative failure also presents an endogeneity problem. Future conflict becomes more likely when current conflict increases uncertainty about the future. Knowledge of this future possibility cast a shadow on any current commitment to peace. Fortunately, our empirical modeling approach need not worry about such endogeneity since it is not dependent on any assumptions about the distribution of error terms—merely focused as it is on validated predictability. Nevertheless, econometric modeling aside, any quest for a true predictive theory of conflict, in our opinion, must incorporate a rationale for path dependency of conflict by explaining the relationships between institutional transparency, credibility, and economic opportunity. In turn, such a theoretical model may provide us with clues about other variables we may need to focus on to show evidence of causality.

So far, our important predictors are consistent with variables that suggest commitment failures lead to bargaining failures and conflict. Nevertheless, we notice that religious polarization (RelogPolariz, ranked 9) is also a somewhat salient predictor of civil conflict. Is there a rational choice explanation for this? Probably not. Of course, given the low predictive salience of religious polarization relative to the other variables that represent rational choice models, we could ignore it. However, we do believe that religious polarization fits the bargaining failure hypothesis, if not the theoretical rational choice models. Recall Fearon's (1995) position that religion is indivisible and therefore is not to be bargained. Thus, bargaining failure is to be expected with religious polarization. In other words, conflict over indivisible ideas may provide a competing theoretical modeling approach. Notably though, the low predictive salience of religious polarization combined with the even lower predictive salience of ethnic polarization (EthnicPolariz, ranked 25) suggests that Reynal-Querol's (2002) argument is probably not very relevant for predicting civil conflict.

TAKEAWAYS

Let us recap our main points in this chapter. Of all the classes of theoretical models that pepper the conflict literature, we think that bargaining failure arising out of commitment problems may provide the best approach yet for a validated predictive theory of conflict. This theory should also emphasize the path dependency of conflict insofar as the deeply entwined relationship between institutions that build trust (i.e., social capital) in an environment of openness and economic opportunity also influence the likelihood of conflict. Last, conflict over religion cannot be avoided: bargaining failure over religion is inevitable given that it is indivisible. This suggests that maybe the only way to avoid religious war is to learn to coexist. In fact, stable institutions may allow for such coexistence. We may get further hints toward a predictive theory of conflict by looking at *how* these important variables that predict conflict actually influence conflict. This we do in the next chapter.

Chapter 9

Bargaining Failure, Commitment Problems, and the Likelihood of Conflict

In the last chapter, we suggested that theoretical models of bargaining failure arising out of commitment problems seem to be the best predictors of conflict. The variables deemed important by these models are the ones that have the most predictive salience for our Machine Learning algorithms. The next test for these theoretical models should be whether they hypothesize the correct *direction* of the influence of these variables. Does transparency or lagged conflict increase or decrease the likelihood of conflict? If the theoretical models are correct, they should correctly predict what should happen to the likelihood of conflict as these predictive variables change. Partial dependence plots generated by Machine Learning algorithms capture this directional effect.

Estimates by standard parametric econometric approaches not only tell us whether a parameter is significant, but also provide a sense of the direction of the effect of the parameter. Thus, these techniques might tell us that transparency matters for conflict, but also that an increase in transparency reduces conflict. On the other hand, these techniques are peculiarly sensitive to the actual distribution of data. The problem of endogeneity, for example, biases these parametric estimates in unpredictable ways, and the conflict literature is rife with endogeneity problems. Even when instruments are available, parameter estimates seem to be sensitive to empirical model specification (Miguel et al., 2004). In other words, parametric estimates in the conflict literature are very likely to be both individually inaccurate as well as fail robustness checks.

Machine Learning algorithms do not require any assumptions about the underlying probabilistic distributions of the variables or any error term. They just "find" preexisting patterns in the data and identify the patterns that best predict some target variable. Thus, the question of endogeneity is irrelevant for this empirical approach. To put it differently, Machine Learning does not estimate parameters, so the issue of biased and inconsistent parameters is moot.

What about marginal effects? Machine Learning models report partial dependence plots or PDPs. These can help visualize how, all else equal, a change in a particular covariate affects the probability of conflict in the learning sample.[1] Thus, these PDPs give us a sense of the threshold effects of a discrete change in a variable on the likelihood of civil conflict. In this sense, they mimic the marginal effects of parametric econometric estimates without the concomitant problems of inaccurate parametric estimates. They answer the following question in our context: What does our Machine Learning algorithm say will happen to the likelihood of conflict within the reported range of the predictive variable? We use the most important predictors identified in Table 6.3 to answer this question.

We first take up the important predictors that conform to the commitment-problem-based bargaining failure models to check whether the PDPs confirm the theoretical predictions of those models. Next, we look at the effects of some other interesting and predictively important variables in the context of the wider literature on conflict—with a particular indictment of some of the "corrective" empirical techniques and results. We see that the effects of these important variables on the likelihood of conflict may be more complicated than that suggested by parametrically estimated marginal effects.

Figures 9.1 through 9.10 present the PDPs. In each, the horizontal axis measures the ranges of the variable of interest and the vertical axis measures an odds ratio expressed on a logarithmic scale for the likelihood of conflict.[2] All the figures presented represent PDPs from the Forest, Bagging, and Boosting methods. We present PDPs for each variable over all three methods to get a sense of the robustness of our results. There are of course variations between the methodologies since the outputs are sensitive to the sampling techniques. We focus on the general trends in the PDPs from the three methodologies.

THE LIKELIHOOD OF CONFLICT: WHAT DO OUR PREDICTORS SAY?

Before we dive into the specifics of the effect of variables on the likelihood of conflict, we would like to note that "year" is not a very good predictor of conflict (Figure 9.1). This suggests that time trends do not predict the likelihood of civil conflict. If some of the popular twitterized narratives for civil conflict were true, then for example, the march of globalization over time should have had a higher predictive impact on the likelihood of conflict. Figure 2 shows a relatively constant effect of year on the likelihood of conflict. In other words, the likelihood of civil conflict relative to peace does not appear to have changed much over time.

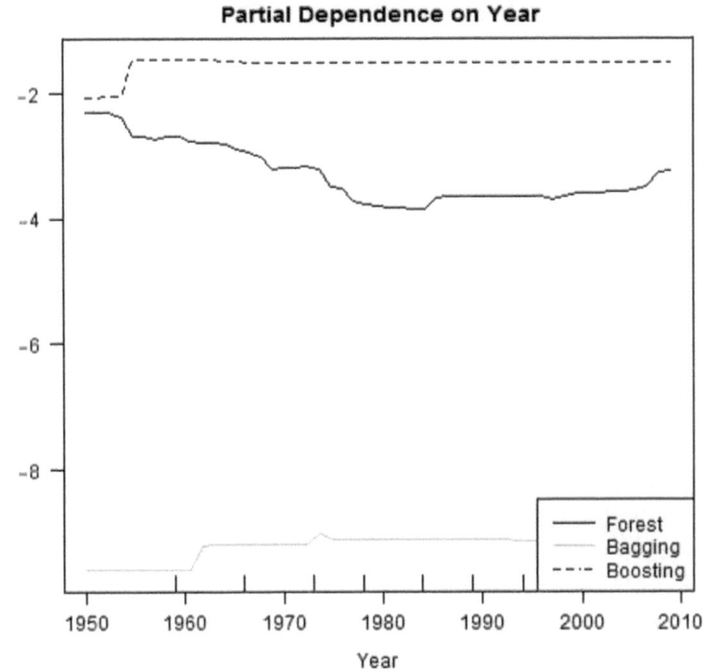

Figure 9.1 Do Time Trends Predict Conflict?

This is perhaps heartening in a world where the news suggests that civil conflict is on the rise. Of course, a world where likelihood of civil conflict diminishes over time would be better. What would be the sorts of policies that would move humanity toward peace? Lagged conflict is the most obvious, and the most predictive of all our variables. This hints that any meaningful predictive theoretical model should capture the time independent pathways of path dependency. However, its usefulness as a policy variable is limited to "if you want to stop conflict you need to stop conflict," which is very limited indeed. We will therefore not attempt to draw blood from this stone in this chapter. In the following chapter we will, however suggest ways in which path dependency can be incorporated in theoretical modeling. Other policy parameters can be influenced to make a better, more peaceful, world.

Figure 9.2 suggests that richer countries are also more peaceful. GDP per capita is the third most important predictor of conflict across all three methodological approaches. Two crucial elements stand out here. First, a country need not be rich for the likelihood of conflict to drop: the biggest impact on the likelihood of conflict seems to be in the $5,000 to $15,000 per capita GDP range. Second, there is a precipitous drop in the likelihood of conflict over this range of per capita GDP, with very little change in the impact of

GDP on the likelihood of conflict thereafter. These results have important policy consequences: the impact of per capita GDP in richer countries like Saudi Arabia will be more limited than poorer countries like Rwanda. This finer point is completely absent in parametric point estimates from the conflict literature since such estimates average the total impact of a variable on the likelihood of civil conflict. This glosses over how the impact may change for certain ranges of the variable of interest.[3]

The result reported in Figure 9.2 has theoretical implications as well. It suggests that there are equilibrium shifts from war to peace, rather than a continuous reduction in the likelihood of conflict. Such equilibrium shifts cannot be captured by point parameter estimates. That we have evidence for such equilibrium shift increases the credibility of theoretical strategic rational choice models as predictive theoretical models; that is, the kind of theoretical models Machine Learning technologies seem to prefer over unitary actor rational choice models or indeed other structural or psychological theoretical modeling techniques. In fact, the reader will note that this kind of equilibrium shift seems quite common for the other "most" important predictors in our discussion below.

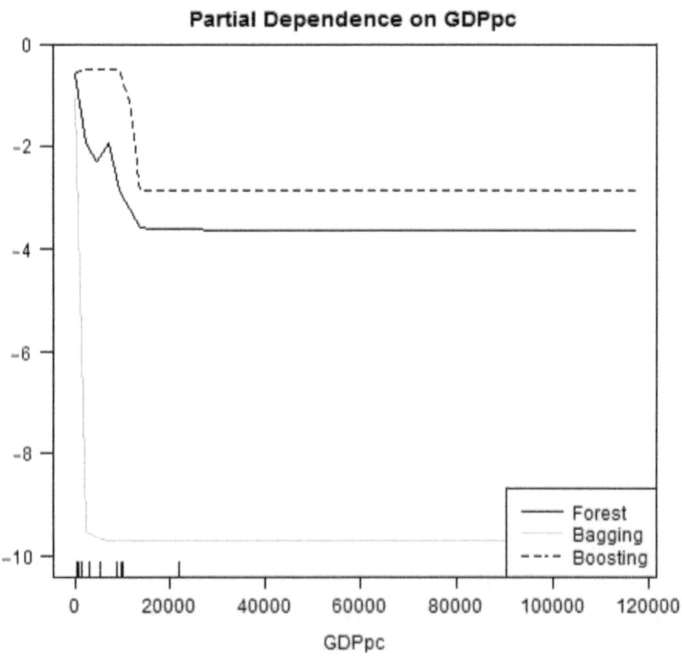

Figure 9.2 Effect of Per Capita GDP on the Likelihood of Conflict.

From a policy perspective, Transparency is the most important variable predicting conflict. Transparency is the degree to which the regime is able to curb corruption and efficiently execute bureaucratic functions. Higher numbers indicating greater transparency—less corrupt governments that respond to the people, more honest bureaucrats who do not succumb to political pressure. Figure 9.3 presents the PDPs for transparency. The horizontal axis measures standard deviations for transparency. Thus, a +0.5 suggests a 0.5 standard deviation improvement over the average level of global transparency while a –0.5 suggests a 0.5 standard deviation worsening.

Transparency gets its variation from variables like investment profile, democratic accountability, corruption, bureaucratic quality, election fraud, and regime durability. Thus, transparency is a good proxy for a consistent culture of openness in a society. Generally, Figure 9.3 suggests that societies that are more open are less likely to have civil conflict. The outcome of war may be most obvious to people in an open society where it is hard to keep information private and thus engender miscalculations about the likely outcomes of war. In the last chapter, we suggested that given the preponderance of evidence, this explanation was less likely than one where openness may generate a culture of trust. Trust, as we know from reading Smith's *Wealth of Nations*

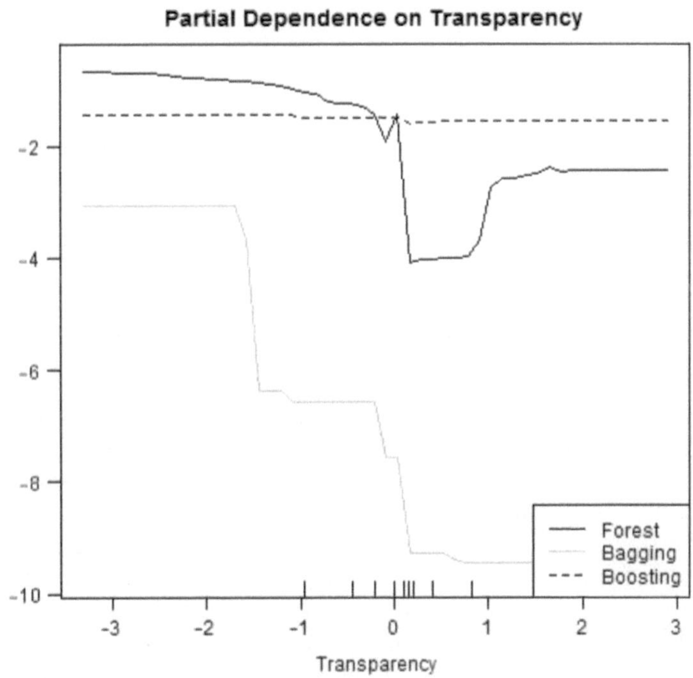

Figure 9.3 Effect of Transparency on the Likelihood of Conflict.

as well as *Moral Sentiment*, is a key element of economic specialization and the wealth generated by that specialization. In retrospect, it may seem obvious that conflict is less likely in societies where people trust each other. Keep in mind the policy issue here. Conflict is less in societies that are more open—we are merely intelligently speculating that trust channels this mechanism. What then is required to reduce conflict as a matter of policy—is it more democratic accountability, less corruption, honest bureaucratic performance? We offer our finding that the democracy variable is not particularly predictive as evidence that political structures of democracy are not enough. An elected parliament where political parties vie for seats is insufficient to prevent civil conflict. Honest democratic accountability and efficiently open societies matter. That is at least one font of peace. Our data—culled as it is from the 20th and 21st centuries—might hint at a longer antecedent for this idea. Horace's "blood of innocent Remus" may have exacted retribution during Rome's civil wars in a similar way; relatively open elections brought Tiberius Sempronius Gracchus to power but a corrupt senate anxious to hold on to their lands and wealth murdered him. Beard (2015, pp. 216–218) suggests that events such as these precipitated Rome's civil war by exposing the internal corruption of elected leaders. At that point, stability and trust could only be restored by a Leviathan, Augustus.

As a matter of policy, we also notice that the effect of transparency on conflict is sharpest (for at least two of the three tree approaches reported) where society is about half a standard deviation better than the average level of global transparency. Any improvements in transparency beyond that point appears to have little further effect on the likelihood of conflict. Opaque societies worse than the average level of global transparency are of course most likely to devolve into conflict. Nevertheless, beyond this half standard deviation range, countries that are much less transparent are unlikely to have an increased risk of conflict. For that matter, improvements in transparency beyond a half standard deviation does not appear to decrease the likelihood of conflict either. This suggests that initial returns to transparency increasing policies are quite high in terms of reduced conflict and that further improvements in openness has less of an impact. That is quite hopeful in a way. A society need not have to transform itself from a bribery-driven bureaucratic culture of political toadying to a Jeffersonian democracy in order to reduce conflict. Baby steps can accomplish a lot in this regard. Of course, as we know from the salience of lagged conflict as a predictor, the initial peace, because of baby steps in a culture of transparency, may cascade into lasting peace. Peace is also handmaiden to prosperity. transparency, possibly by undergirding a culture of increasing trust, can increase prosperity. That in turn, as we have noted above, also predicts peace. But so do the other important predictors of conflict.

The credibility variable also has a similar effect (Figure 9.4). Credibility is mainly sourced from the government stability and investment profile variables. Notice that both the Forest and Bagging methods yield a predictive trend, but the Boosting methodology does not. The first two methods capture a reduced likelihood of conflict with increased credibility, though this trend is clearer in the Bagging method. Credibility thus reduces the odds of conflict suggesting that stable government policies emphasizing property rights and contract enforcements increase the chances of peace. This is consistent with other parts of the conflict literature, as well as with the Machine Learning algorithm's findings about the predictive salience of credibility—the Forest method ranks credibility as more predictive than either the Bagging or the Boosting (though the Boosting method ranks it lower as a predictive variable than the Bagging method).

Our findings though suggest further details. The Forest method suggests that there is a "sweet spot" in credibility that captures most of the effect of credibility on peace: a country that has too little credibility, that is, its credibility measures are 2 standard deviations below the global mean, or has too much credibility, that is, 1 standard deviation above the global mean, is likely to experience more conflict. This suggests that there is an optimum amount of

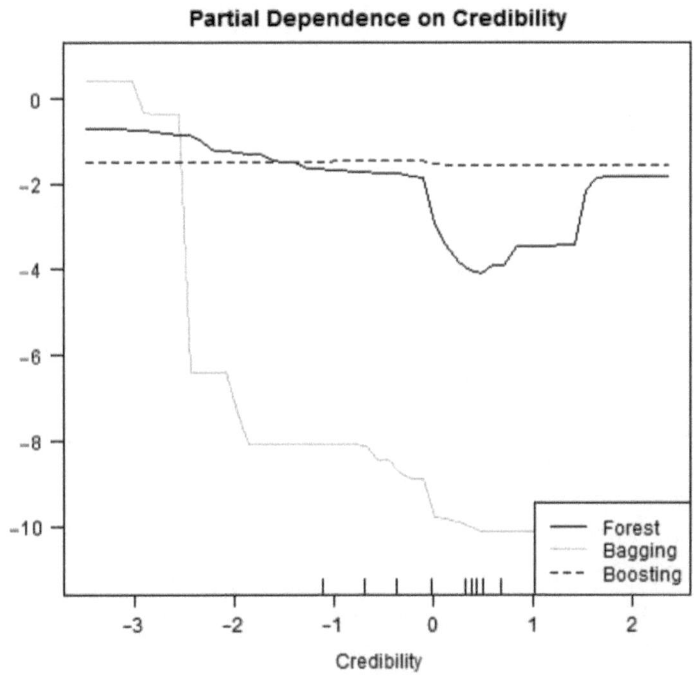

Figure 9.4 The Effect of Credibility on Likelihood of Conflict.

improvement in property rights protection and contract enforcement. It is not surprising that a country with weak property rights and so on may be prone to conflict. However, the idea of "too much" credibility is not intuitive—can there be such a thing as too many rules enforcing property rights? Clearly, credibility requires deeper future investigation, both as part of a unified predictive theory of conflict as well a subject of interest by itself. In fact, this is exactly what we mean by Machine Learning as part of an iterative process; even as we reveal the nuanced effect of credibility on the likelihood of conflict, we find deeper layers that need further investigation.

So, Figures 9.3 and 9.4 show the predictive salience of institutional quality as expressed in the transparency and credibility variables, provided they exist. Public choice theory additionally suggests that institutions themselves are "invented" only if it is cheaper to provide public goods through the state rather than via private decisions (Mueller, 2003, pp. 10–13). Thus, private security may be cheaper and therefore more likely to be the norm in Somalia than a state police force. Genicot and Skaperdas (2002) famously suggest that poorer countries may not invest in relatively more expensive institutions but cheaper war tools instead. Thus, there are two issues here with inherently similar tradeoffs. Institutions that promote transparency and credibility will exist only if the transactions costs related to their formation are relatively low. Second, improvements in the quality of transparency and credibility must also overcome these transactions cost problems. A cost-benefit comparison between different institutional elements therefore lies at the very heart of choosing policies designed to reduce conflict. It therefore becomes important to be able to identify the kinds of institutions that may help reduce conflict the most. We suggest that institution building ought to focus on transparency and credibility factors rather than say on a swanker parliament or intricate voting systems enshrined in constitutions.

The importance of credibility and transparency also ties in with the predictive salience of some of the other nakedly economic variables. Both credibility and transparency reflect a culture of trust and openness that also stimulate economic activity. Thus, the predictive salience of GDP per capita ought not to surprise us. We also know that energy is a key component of economic activity. Thus, in Figures 9.5 and 9.6, the predictive salience of per capita electricity production and rural population, as well as their role in reducing the likelihood of conflict, is consistent with our understanding that economic opportunity makes people wealthier and helps reduce conflict. Notice though, that just like GDP per capita, the largest effects of both electricity and rural populations on the likelihood of conflict are at relatively lower levels. This suggests that countries in the process of transforming themselves from poor, rural traditional economies to more open, modern economies with more transparent and credible institutions are most likely to see less conflict as a

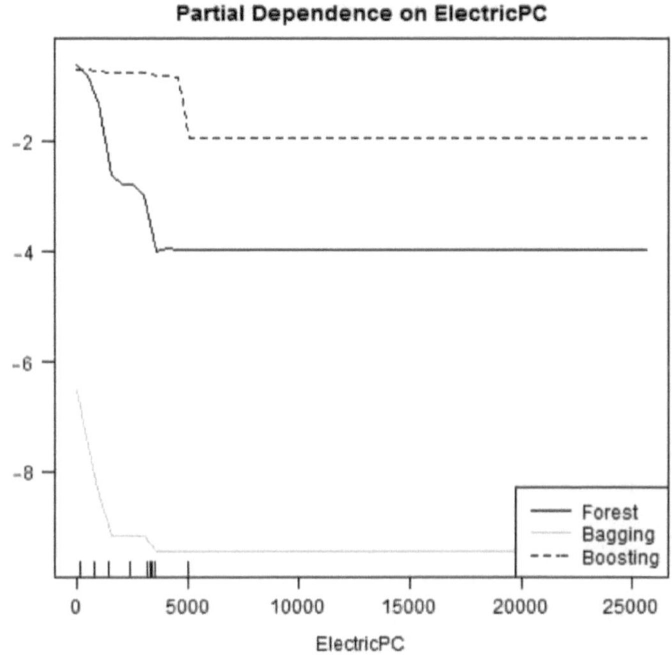

Figure 9.5 Effect of Gross Per Capita Electricity Generation on the Likelihood of Conflict.

result. In short, conflict may die away long before these countries are mature rich economies. Indeed, countries do not need to be paragons of freedom and economic opportunity for this effect to work. This should be a matter of hope for anyone interested in reducing civil conflict. Nations do not need to make huge institutional and economic leaps to conquer conflict.

We have discussed three of the top five predictors of conflict in some detail. Lagged conflict remains at the top of this list, but we will focus on it more as a way forward to a predictive theory of conflict in the next chapter, since, as noted above, we cannot say much more than "conflict should be stopped" as a matter of policy. However, let us emphasize the other four.

We made the case above that transparent open societies with credible economic institutions are likely to be peaceful and rich. Further, it is the process of economic upliftment that matters for peace since, beyond a certain point, increases in transparency, credibility, and incomes (GDP per capita) do not further increase the likelihood of peace. Our argument that it is economic opportunity that matters is strengthened when we see that instant wealth does not influence conflict. So, wealth from primary commodity exports does not predict conflict in any meaningful way, nor do investment or economic growth (change in per capita GDP). Further, terms of trade shocks or

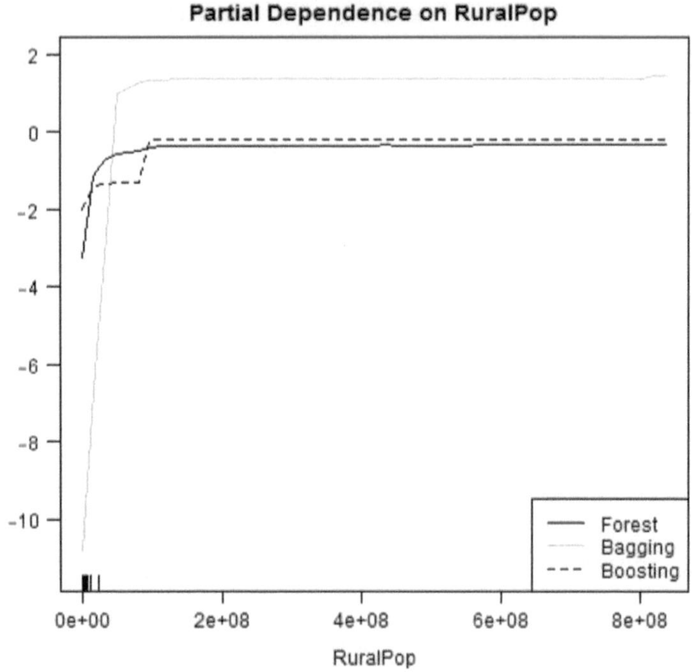

Figure 9.6 Effect of Increases in Rural Population on the Likelihood of Conflict.

exchange rate variations, which may have immediate impacts on aggregate wealth levels, are not predictive of conflict either. Similarly, the argument that aid assistance influences conflict by increasing average wealth levels and access to consumption goods like health care, or that aid assistance helps the powerful (e.g., by letting elites stay in power by increasing access to guns), exacerbates income inequality and so fuel conflicts, are suspect as well. In either case, aid assistance should be an important predictor of conflict. We find that it is not.

What about income inequality? While the Gini inequality coefficient does predict the likelihood of conflict, it is not in the top ten list of salient predictors of conflict, let alone the top five. The economic growth variable (ChangeinGDPpc) and terms of trade shocks also perform poorly as predictors. Therefore, the argument that economic growth exacerbates income inequality or that transient wealth shocks worsen income inequality fueling grievances and conflict, does not hold water.

The size of the rural population is in the top five. Figure 9.6 shows that the likelihood of conflict jumps up with an increase in the size of the rural population, and stays constant beyond a certain size. In other words, states with higher levels of rural population are likely to experience more conflict, up to a point. Clearly, this means that the size of the urban population matters. Does this agree with our argument that economic opportunity in transparent societies tends to reduce conflict? Glaeser (2011) points to cities as engines of economic opportunity. He calls cities "our specie's greatest invention." He suggests that living in close quarters makes people innovative as they bounce ideas off each other. At the same time, proximity reduces the transactions costs of specialization since services and goods need only to be traded short distances. This argument does indeed fit with our argument that economic opportunity is an engine of both peace and prosperity. As we have noted, elsewhere credibility and transparency enhance trust between people and allows them to specialize. If Juan specializes in making franks and Billy specializes in hot dog buns, then Ishmael can sell hot dogs at the street corner confident that Juan and Billy will provide supplies every week. If they renege on any contract, a court of law will enforce the contract. And police will protect Ishmael from thieves. That all this can happen over a smaller space in a city reduces the transactions costs of providing credible security, and in doing so injects certainty into the human condition. We know that certainty increases coordination between specialized people who then have the opportunity to reap the gains from trade.

Trade, one of the top ten predictors of conflict, certainly reduces the likelihood of conflict (Figure 9.7). This trend is more pronounced in the Bagging and Forest methods. Our trade variable captures international trade, but is consistent with the point we make about cities helping trade by encouraging specialization. In fact, Dr. Glaeser points out, "there's a lot to like about urban poverty." He suggests that the urban poor are better off than rural populations because of the economic opportunity urban centers provide.

In short, our top five predictors (other than lagged conflict) tell us a consistent story about economic opportunity in transparent societies as a bulwark to conflict. In the next chapter, we show a way in which the predictive salience of lagged conflict can plausibly make a similar point in developing a theory of conflict.

Figure 9.8 suggests that dependency increases the likelihood of conflict. Dependency measures the proportion of children (under 15) and the elderly (65 and over) to the working-age population (aged 15–64). At first glance this appears to be consistent with the Collier et al. (2009) story which suggests that a higher proportion of young men makes conflict more likely by making it cheaper to get a rebel army together. But as we have noted elsewhere, the other suggested correlates of conflict by a unitary rational choice theoretical model of conflict does not quite fit our predictive approach. Dependency ratios may also be a potential source of grievance. The working population may resent having to support what they consider unproductive citizens. This may particularly be an issue if these dependents tend to be of different

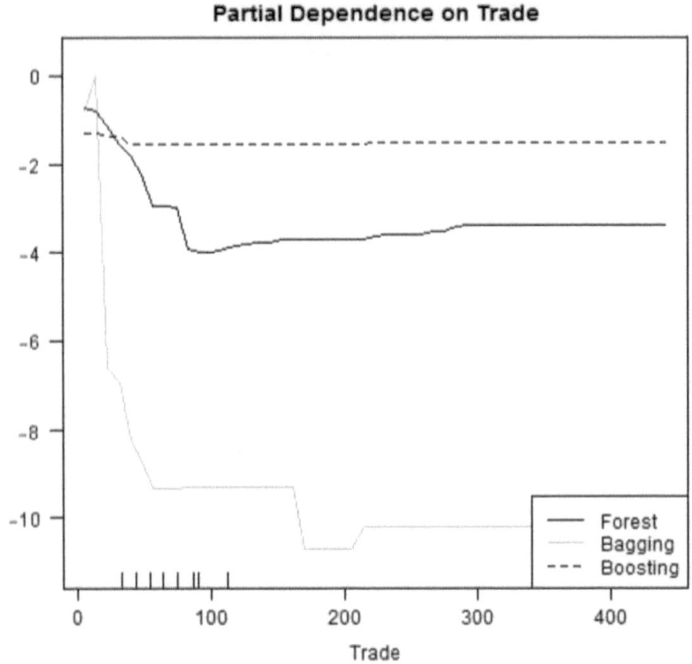

Figure 9.7 Effect of Trade on the Likelihood of Conflict.

ethnicities or religions. We think this link probably bears further investigation. At the same time, we note that other correlates of grievance like ethnic polarization and income inequality do not predict conflict very well. This suggests that the curious effect of dependency ratios on the likelihood of conflict may have other competing explanations.

Higher dependency ratios usually reflect rapid population growth. This "hidden momentum of population growth" can stretch an economy's capability to provide jobs, for example, by curtailing savings and consequently investment. Recent empirical work also suggests that rapid population growth may harm economic development by reducing economic growth, exacerbating inequality, restricting parents' ability to educate children, posing health risks to mothers and children, depleting resources, and promoting international migration. On the other hand, population growth is a necessary condition for sustainable economic growth by ensuring both a market and a labor force (see Todaro and Smith, 2012, pp. 269–303 for a complete survey of this literature). So when is population growth bad and when is it good? The key issue here is the context of population growth. Our results suggest that all else equal, for example for a given level of institutional quality (as measured by say the transparency variable), a higher dependency ratio increases the risk

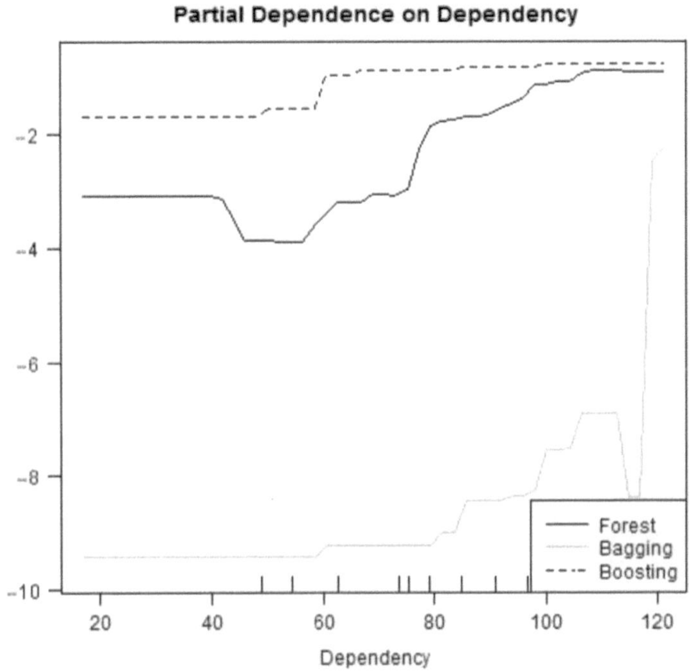

Figure 9.8 Effect of Dependency on the Likelihood of Conflict.

of conflict. It may be that rapid population growth, if it outstrips a country's institutional capability to provide economic opportunity, may lead to conflict as a larger population vies for limited resources. The institutional role becomes critical in avoiding conflict and may be the flip side of Acemoglu and Robinson's (2012) argument about the centrality of inclusive institutions in providing economic opportunity.

Education also has an interesting effect on the risk of conflict (Figure 9.9). We have data on secondary school enrollment per 10,000 people. Notice that for both the Forest and the Bagging methods an increase in the ratio of students enrolled relative to the population reduces the likelihood of conflict. However, all else equal, an increase in secondary education enrollment beyond the 15% mark seems to *increase* the likelihood of conflict. This is a counterintuitive result, if somewhat consistent with our findings on dependency ratios. A more educated population can benefit from access to education *for a given level* of institutional quality. It may be though that institutional quality is "lumpy." Thus, as the percentage of students increases, the opportunities available from a particular level of institutional quality are exhausted. This may range from overworked bureaucrats, to the inability of the executive to find and punish corrupt officials, to elected representatives

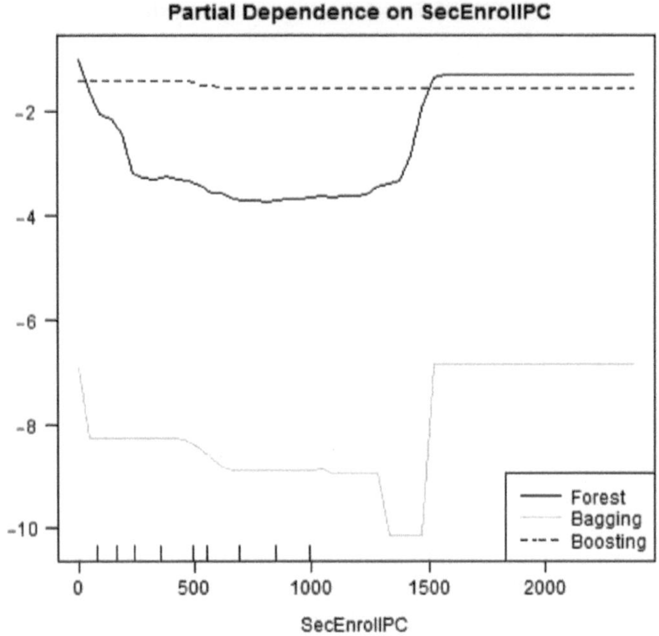

Figure 9.9 Effect of Secondary School Enrollment (per 10,000) on the Likelihood of Conflict.

unable to meet with the increasing number of constituents, given limited resources. All this limits economic opportunity. Over time, this may reduce GDP itself and place the country in a low-level equilibrium economic trap. In short, our results for both secondary school enrollment and dependency ratios suggest that conflict may ensue if for some reason economic opportunity fails to keep pace with the demographics of a country. The reader will note a certain amount of guided guesswork in our discussion over the last two paragraphs. This is largely because students of conflict have tended to focus on ethno/religious aspects of demographics. We suggest that conflict may be more fruitfully studied by bringing in the more traditional development economics literature on demographics and population dynamics.

Last, religious polarization is among our top ten predictors of conflict. This index tracks how threatened one group feels by the presence of another group, the threat being measured by the size of the other group. So, for example, polarization is at its maximum value when there are two groups of equal size. In Figure 9.10, religious polarization increases the likelihood of conflict after 0.5 according to the Forest method and after 0.7 by the Bagging method. The Forest method shows a spike up at around 0.4 to 0.5, and then the upward trend continues until 0.6, exists but is less prominent beyond 0.6.

The Bagging method shows a sharp increase in conflict in the 0.6–0.8 range, and then almost no increase beyond 0.8. Therefore, beyond that point, any further increase in religious polarization does not appear to have much of an impact on the likelihood of conflict. Further, according to the Forest method, there is a sharp increase in the likelihood of conflict when religious polarization is between 0.3 and 0.4, but no such increase below 0.3. This appears to be generally true for the Bagging method in that there is no increase in the likelihood of conflict below 0.6.

This is the same pattern that we see in many of our other results, that there are significant jumps in the likelihood of conflict for small ranges of the predictor. This suggests equilibrium shifts consistent with our "best" choice theoretical models of strategic interaction. Nevertheless, here the general trend suggests that increased polarization increases the likelihood of conflict. As we noted in the previous two chapters, Fearon's (1995) suggestion that religion is indivisible and as such may lead to bargaining failure and conflict appears to be borne out by our results. This result also poses a conundrum for a policy maker. States with two religious groups of relatively equal size may be more likely to succumb to the flames of passionate destruction than much

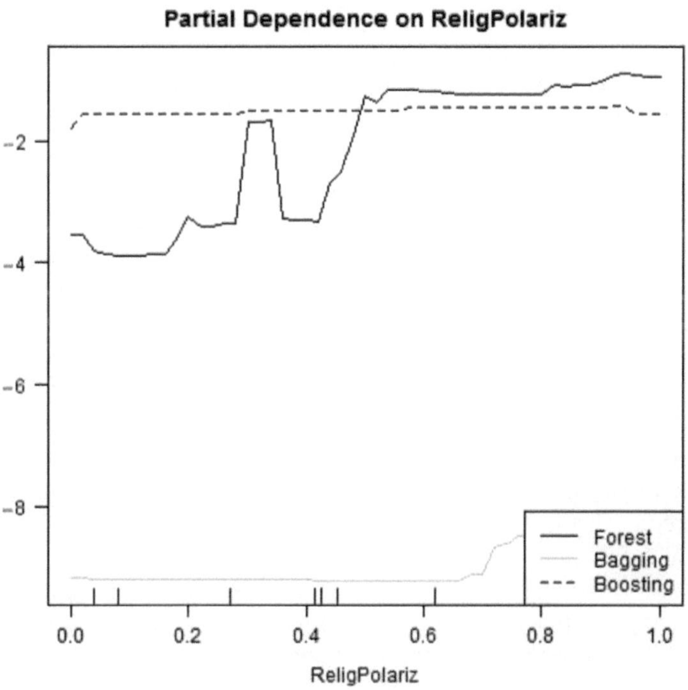

Figure 9.10 Effect of Religious Polarization on the Likelihood of Conflict.

more religiously diverse spaces. A parting of national ways may be the only solution to civil conflict in these religiously polarized places.

THE DOGS THAT DID NOT BARK: VARIABLES THAT SHOULD PREDICT BUT DID NOT

Hegre and Sambanis (2006) use extreme bounds analysis to run thousands of regressions in an effort to identify robust correlates of civil war. They find that low per capita income, slow income growth, rough terrain, large population size, recent political instability, small government militaries, and war-prone neighbors are consistently correlated with civil conflict. We do not have terrain, war-prone neighbors, or the size of small government militaries in our dataset. However, the reader by this time will have noticed that other than per capita income, none of their remaining variables that are also included in our dataset offer much predictive hope. Blattman and Miguel (2010) point out that many of these variables are endogenous which certainly biases the parametric estimates. Nevertheless, the poor predictive power of these variables suggest that we need to look for causation elsewhere. This argument could be extended to other potentially causal variables suggested by theoretical models. For instance, is ethnic polarization truly a mere correlate and not causal? After all, there are theoretical models and econometric evidence that suggest it should be important. How do we reconcile all this?

Machine Learning techniques say nothing of causation. We therefore try steering clear of suggesting any causal links between our variables and the likelihood of conflict, instead choosing to focus on our policy-oriented ability to predict conflict. But can prediction and causality be completely delinked?

Just because A predicts B does not mean that A causes B. There is a famous if somewhat apocryphal story that ice cream consumption is one of the best predictors of drowning deaths. However, no policy maker in their right mind would suggest restricting ice cream consumption as a way of reducing drowning deaths. This is where theory comes in to play an important role. Could it be that both ice cream consumption and swimming is more likely over summer at the beach? Well now we may move toward the glimmer of a causal predictive theory of death by drowning. However, if for example dog barks do not predict deaths by drowning then it is unlikely to be associated with any causal factors and may be safely ignored as part of a predictive theory.

We take a somewhat similar approach here. We have built a case over the last few chapters that suggest a determinable theoretical link between our most predictive variables and the likelihood of conflict. We have done this very explicitly by linking our predictive variables with elements of different theoretical modeling approaches. We have then chosen the most predictive theoretical modeling approach from among them. Thus, the individual variables discussed in this chapter have theoretical heft. We propose the search for causal links should therefore begin among these variables and their "known associates." As far as the variables that do not predict conflict, how can any variable that causes conflict fail to predict it? Prediction is causation's hand maiden. If gravity *causes* us to fall to earth, it should also *predict* Icarus's fate as his wings melt. We suggest that variables that do not predict ought not to be causal either.

The search for causality in the econometric analyses of conflict is fraught. For example, as noted above, the literature suggests that low income and income shocks are correlated to conflict. However, the causality between conflict and low-income levels and income shocks can potentially run both ways. An instrumental variables approach, where the instrument is correlated with an explanatory variable but clearly independent of the target variable, alleviates this problem. Miguel et al. (2004) use rainfall as an instrument for income. Since rainfall cannot be caused by conflict but is often correlated with GDP in poorer agricultural countries, it appears to be a good instrument. It is statistically significant, suggesting that random climate related income shocks may increase the risk of conflict. Ciccone (2011) finds similar results after controlling for democratic institutions and ethno-linguistic fractionalization. Together these results suggest that income shocks may indeed cause conflict. We, on the other hand, find that neither rainfall (as measured by the DroughtIndex and the DroughtIndexRange) nor income shocks (as measured by for example ChangeGDPpc, TermsofTrade, investment, ChangeExportspc, and ChangeImportspc) are actually predictive of conflict. This certainly questions the role of income shocks as a direct causal pathway to conflict. Nevertheless, this kind of inconsistency is quite common in the conflict literature. Bazzi and Blattman (2014) for example suggest that the relationship between trade shocks and political instability is sensitive to the variables chosen to represent an econometric model. Blattman and Miguel (2010) therefore ask why income shocks do not consistently destabilize regimes. Given the predictive salience of institutions that support dimensions like credibility and transparency and the lack of predictive salience of income and climate shock variables, we suggest that these institutions may act as shock absorbers. It may therefore be useful in future to focus on the role of credibility and transparency institutions as buffers between income shocks and conflict. We make an additional point here as well. The search for causality may be better served by concentrating on a parsimonious list of suspect conflict determinants (Blattman and Miguel, 2010). The Machine Learning technology we have used provides a validated methodology to cull the number of variables to produce just such a parsimonious list.

But what about Hegre and Sambanis's (2006) identification of the consistent correlates of conflict. How is it that some of their consistent correlates are not predictive? First, recall Blattman and Miguel's (2010) criticism centered on endogeneity. It may be that the correlation is spurious. But it may also be that even if the correlations are not spurious, their causal, and therefore predictive impact, is really small. A mosquito bite might bring about a twitching muscle. That is a causal effect. But it is small. Moreover, this impact reveals nothing about the neurophysiology of muscle movement. Certainly no reasonable person would suggest mosquito bites as a cure for paralysis. It may also be that these less predictive variables operate *through* the more predictive variables. Thus if social trust fails conflict may take an ethnic hue—but the problem here is the lack of credibility and transparency and not the existence of ethnic groups. In any case, our methodological approach succeeds in narrowing the focus of intellectual inquiry more productively. In effect, prediction shorn of theory and correlation shorn of prediction is likely to lead an investigator up a garden path with potentially disastrous consequences for policy effectiveness. Moreover, it's not science.

TAKEAWAYS

In the last couple of chapters, we attempted to choose the most predictive class of theoretical model. In this chapter, we moved our attention toward the most predictive variables. Our goal was to see how these variables affected the likelihood of conflict. Our first finding is that the effect of these most predictive variables on the likelihood of conflict is consistent with the theoretical model strategic models of commitment problems leading to bargaining failure. Both, for example, suggest that transparency and credibility should both reduce conflict and make agents wealthier. Moreover, wealthier agents would choose peaceful bargaining over conflict. The Machine Learning generated PDPs suggest this is indeed true. As a result, we can have some cross-validated faith in our theoretical model choice.

The general pattern of the effect of these most predictive variables on the likelihood of conflict further strengthens our scientific justification for choosing strategic rational choice models of bargaining failure as the way toward a theory of conflict. Recall that the PDPs of the most important predictive variables provide validated evidence of equilibrium *shifts* from peace to war. Unitary agent rational choice models or state capacity models would show more consistent and continuous trends relating variables to the likelihood of conflict. We have PDPs for other variables that are not important predictors. We do not write about them here. Nevertheless, they too show evidence of equilibrium shifts.

Policy makers should be aware of both theoretical models and predictive Machine Learning. That the two approaches justify each other and are validated independently by prediction scores increases the robustness of policy choices based on these variables. Thus, the important predictive variables we suggest could be a basis for practical policy changes because now policy makers know that reducing corruption (a component of the predictive "transparency" factor), for example, is a better theoretically justified predictor and therefore a better policy tool than say merely having more political parties (a component of the not very predictive "democracy" factor). Policy makers might further notice from the PDP's that the most predictive variables affect civil conflict non-linearly. Thus, for example, one should expect a large drop in the likelihood of civil conflict with small improvements in transparency. Nevertheless, there is a region, located around 0 (see Figure 9.3), where even a small increase in transparency decreases conflict a lot. Further increases in transparency have little impact on the likelihood of conflict. Thus, an increase in transparency would reduce conflict only for countries that fall in the "sweet spot" around 0. Civil conflict in other countries with transparency scores outside the sweet spot will not respond as much to a better score in transparency. Alternatively, transparency scores would have to improve a lot for countries with very low transparency scores. In these cases, it may be possible to use some of the other predictors as policy tools if they better match the country. This sort of observation can be made for all the PDP's reported here. The predictive impact of these "important" covariates of conflict depend on where a country figures in the overall range of that covariate. Different countries will fall in different ranges of these important predictors. Thus, the same policy may not be effective for every country.

Variables that do not predict well are unlikely to be sources of causal patterns. Thus, these Machine Learning technologies, while causally agnostic themselves, allow us to narrow our search for causality among the most predictive variables. This, in turn, can fine tune theoretical models and potentially improve predictive accuracy. We therefore suggest that predictive Machine Learning algorithms should be part of an iterative process that gets us closer to a true theory of conflict. In the next chapter, we show a path toward just such a theory.

NOTES

1. Partial dependence plots display the marginal effect of variable *x*k conditional on the observed values of all of the other variables, (x_1, -k, x_2, -k, … x_n, -k) Specifically, it plots the graph of the function below. Here, *s* indexes the classes of the target variable and *C* is the total number of classes. So, if an increase in a given factor, *x*k,

increases the probability of state failure ($s = 1$), then the value of the function plotted by the PDP also increases.

$$\hat{f}(x) = \frac{1}{n}\sum_{i=1}^{n} f(x_k, x_{i,-k}), \text{ where the summand, } f(x_k, x_{i,-k}), \text{ is defined by } f(x) = ln[p_1(x)] - \frac{1}{C}\sum_{s=1}^{C} ln[p_s(x)] \quad (9.1)$$

2. Thus, the vertical axis can have negative numbers.

3. Arguably, a spline regression technique, or adding squared terms in the independent variable space, may capture non-linear relationships between the target and the covariates as well. But then we run into the fundamental endogeneity flaw. Moreover, spline techniques may capture "average" breaks in the fit of a particular regression, but cannot capture non-linear relationships between each variable of interest and the target. Last, deciding on adding a squared term requires a judgment call that we can avoid by automating the relationship divining process in our algorithms. We will proceed to capture these non-linearities and their policy implication for each important variable in the following paragraphs.

Chapter 10

Toward a Predictive Theoretical Model of Conflict

Some Speculation

In earlier chapters, we noted that our top ten most predictive variables support theoretical models that suggest conflict is best predicted by strategic rational choice approaches modeling commitment problems. We did however somewhat ignore the screaming headline—that lagged conflict was the *best* predictor of conflict on average. Even though, as a matter of policy, this finding seems somewhat obvious, it highlights the role of current security in preventing future conflict. The predictive power of lagged conflict also highlights the idea that conflict is path dependent. Given the predictive salience of commitment issues that lead to bargaining failure, a truly predictive theory of conflict should incorporate both this path dependence and the effects of the shadow of the future. What would such a model look like? Here we provide an outline of what a model that incorporates these ideas could look like—a sort of straw man theoretical model.

Collier and Sambanis (2002) formally acknowledge path dependence's role in civil conflict in a symposium collection of articles on civil conflict published in the *Journal of Conflict Resolution*. They note the empirical regularity that the risk of war in countries that have seen war in the past is higher than the risk of war in countries that have not—lagged conflict matters. Why? Perhaps the underlying causes of war may not have improved, or, war may have had lasting consequences on a nation's society and political economy—they leave this unclear. Nevertheless, they suggest that war may encourage the accumulation of perverse types of social capital like hatred, and explicit rebellion-specific capital, like guns and tanks. Further, they suggest that as war continues, the productive economy shrinks and the capture of resource through conflict becomes relatively more attractive. The literature does not model the causal pathways that make conflict linger. It merely acknowledges and explores it as one consequence of perturbations in the opportunity cost of conflict consistent with the rational choice approach.

Murdoch and Sandler (2002) show that conflict reduces economic growth in both the country where the conflict is located, and in neighboring countries, after controlling for the effects of migration, investment, and human capital. Blomberg and Hess (2002) model conflict as a two-way relationship between the likelihood of war and the economy using Markov chain Monte Carlo estimations. They find that the likelihood of recessions and of external conflict combine to increase the likelihood of civil conflict. More to our point, they too find that conflict itself worsens the economy, which in turn increases the likelihood of conflict, potentially sparking a vicious spiral. Given Murdoch and Sandler's (2002) findings, this vicious spiral may engulf neighboring countries as well. They too show, then, that path dependency exists and that conflict once started continues by hurting the economy, which in turn generates more conflict. While this conclusion is inherently plausible, it does not give us any sense of the causal patterns of path dependence: whether there are competing channels, what they may be, or, indeed, how much path dependence matters for conflict relative to other causal patterns. In short, these studies look for data patterns without a clear sense of theory and may be subject to the hoary economist joke: The economist looks for his lost car keys only under the street lamp because "there is no light in the other places!" We need to model some of these other places.

We suggest that there needs to be a sustained investigation into understanding the path dependence of conflict because of the predictive salience of past conflict in predicting future conflict. This investigation should also explore why people may tip in into conflict from peace or vice versa. After all, there are many people in poor countries who are not at war with each other. This suggests that a good theoretical model should not only explain why people may choose conflict, and then stay in conflict, but also have something to say about how the shift in equilibrium from peace to war happens. Moreover, given the predictive salience of schooling, credibility, transparency, GDP per capita, and trade, this theoretical model needs to lay out the connections between institutions and the economy. In fact, the low predictive salience of economic growth (change in GDP per capita) suggests that the long-run level of the GDP may matter more for a predictive theoretical model than short-run growth rates.

The existence of a conflict or a peace equilibrium is often modeled quite simply in game theory (Anderton and Carter, 2009, pp. 53–66) as a simultaneous coordination game where two players have a strategy space for war and peace. More generally, the tension between production and predation lies at the center of public choice. For example, say there are two agents A and B who can specialize in the production of corn and cattle, respectively. Now,

B can trade cattle for corn, but B also has the option to steal A's corn and not give up any cattle in exchange. This sort of scenario is forced to settle in a Hobbesian "natural state" because stealing becomes the dominant strategy for A and B even though trading will make them both better off. This Pareto improvement is only possible with some sort of "constitutional contract" that establishes property rights (Buchanan, 1975). These contracts are costly and are a public good, thus their provision is a matter of conscious choice. In effect, a security system that protects both A and B will only be provided through a mechanism if it is cheaper than private security (Mueller, 2003 pp. 10–13). These models capture our fundamental problem at its basic level—why do people choose war over peace? The answer becomes a matter of transactions costs for providing joint security. These models are structured typically as simultaneous games. Thus, no player has an informational advantage. This modeling approach is therefore consistent with our finding that variables associated with asymmetric information have low predictive salience. Nevertheless, these models do show why agents may not be able to commit to a peace deal as a matter of institutional failure even when the peace dividends of such a deal are obvious.

What do people fight for though? Information structure aside, this is determined within the structure of the game by specifying the nature of the interaction between the players and their payoffs because of this interaction. There is of course a vast multidisciplinary literature that indirectly impinges on this issue. Sandler and Hartley (1995, pp. 308–309) simplify this literature into two major strands.

Rationalists suggest that individuals weigh private benefits and costs before they choose conflict. As we have noted earlier, in this approach, conflict should always be avoided since conflict is costly, particularly since the primary benefit of civil conflict is probably a public good. After all, once a cruel government is overthrown the kind light of the new era should uplift everyone, including those that did not lift a finger to help. Rational folk may not feel the burn to join an insurgency. Of course, if everyone is rational this incentive to free ride prevents the insurgency. Nevertheless, civil conflict evidently happens. Olson (1965) suggests that there are private elements to public goods. These private rents may be sufficient to overcome the free rider problem since nonparticipants can be excluded. Tullock (1974) channels Olson to suggest that revolutionaries get a private benefit—rents from the spoils of war—from participating in a conflict even if a non-excludable public good is an outcome of the conflict. Tullock's innovation solves the free rider problem in the rationalist setting by obliterating the existence of the problem, instead focusing on the methodological individual. In his model, individuals get a private benefit from rents as well as from being part of a crowd. The private benefit from rents is intuitive. The private benefit from other people joining in the "movement," while mathematically well defined in Tullock's objective function, is less intuitive. Why do people get a benefit from joining a crowd?

Civil conflict does require coordinated action. The more people coordinate, the greater the likelihood of victory, and the greater the likelihood of obtaining the private rents that Tullock introduces into the conversation. This likelihood, in turn, drives Tullock's warrior's objective function. Nevertheless, Tullock ignores the individual's tension between joining the rebels or not, even while explicitly modeling his warrior's utility as a function of the size of the group. On this matter, the structuralists suggest that civil conflict happens if enough people hate the state (e.g., Skocpol, 1979). If the proportion of haters is large enough, the group will form as a structural response to the hated state. The structuralist view therefore adds the element missing in Tullock by suggesting that there is something inherent in the structure of the state and in its relationship to citizens that confers a benefit to people if they join the rebels, as long as the rebel population is large enough. In this sense, the structuralist view complements the rationalist view.

We suggest that a theory that can combine the essential elements of the structuralist and the rationalist views can explain path dependence in conflict while acknowledging the salience of the commitment problem in predicting conflict. Evolutionary game theoretic models have the potential to combine both the rationalist and the structuralist views into the payoff structure, and provide a way of understanding path dependence.

In evolutionary game theoretic models, individuals are *culturally* hardwired with certain strategies. This cultural element represents a certain reality. People do not sit around on any given day and then decide to fight. Conflict requires a groundswell that develops over time. We suggest that this groundswell is learned behavior. That is, this groundswell forms part of a cultural "structure." Nevertheless, as individuals in these cultures interact with each other in a population, they get some private benefits. (This is of course pure Tullock.) The likelihood that a particular type of citizen will interact with a particular type of state official depends on the structural distribution of cultures in the population. These interactions have private costs and benefits. A replicator dynamic process then determines equilibria. If a particular culture's expected payoff is higher than another's, that culture is incentivized in the population relative to others. Effectively, more people then *rationally* learn to adopt the successful culture. This changes the mix of cultures in the population. Once a significant section of the population learns to adopt a particular culture, it may benefit others to do the same, placing society on a particular cultural pathway—this is classic path dependence. How this learning happens is also a subject of study, particularly in psychology. However, it is irrelevant to the *process* of cultural change as long as we recognize that people do learn (or mimic) to adopt the culture that is most beneficial to them (Mailath, 1998).

Our predictive models suggest that those variables that are consistent with the commitment-problem approach to bargaining failure are the ones that are most important for predicting conflict. The time-inconsistency problem of commitment can only be modeled if a game is repeated. Thus, repeated interaction between players in these models should be part of the payoff structure. This interaction may continue into the future with some probability δ. A higher δ suggests that the game is likely to continue repeating with a higher probability. Who will expect that a game is more likely to continue into the future? By definition, patient people will. Patience is inherent and a heterogeneous behavioral trait (Wilkinson, 2008, Warner and Pleeter, 2001). Thus, δ captures the psychological idea of patience. Moreover, patience is also a cultural trait (Clark, 2007, pp. 166–175). That is, patient people can learn to be impatient and vice versa depending on their social environment.

In the conflict setting, patience plays an important role in enforcing credible commitment mechanisms. Powell's (2006) model, for example, suggests that a weak state may be willing to make a current side payment to the rebels to buy peace. But this peace may allow the state to become stronger in the future relative to the rebels. Rebels know this, and therefore rather than wait for the future, they go to war now. Patience can change this dynamic. For example, say peace generates a future stream of benefits for both the state and the rebels while conflict generates a large current benefit if the rebels win. Rebels then may be willing to forego the large current gains through conflict only if they are willing to wait for the future stream of peaceful benefits. Patient rebels and states may therefore be more likely to commit to peace, where their impatient counterparts do not, in a direct application of the folk theorem (Fudenberg and Maskin, 1986). Thus, δ, the patience variable, captures the commitment element we suggest should be included explicitly in predictive theories of conflict. In a model of cultural evolution, people may learn to be patient (or impatient).

Patience is also a hallmark of peace. People in conflict-torn societies cannot be certain of their future because institutions do not secure them from a Hobbesian end. Thus, conflict can increase impatience. We suggest therefore that patience can be a conduit for path dependence. Conflict starts and then reduces the patience of participants by increasing future uncertainty. This increase in impatience makes it harder for participants to commit to peace. Conflict continues with further assaults on patience. And so on. The precise pathway for this process can be modeled in evolutionary models.

A fall in patience would also be consistent with a reduction in economic activity. For there to be gains from trade, economic activity requires coordination between economically specialized individuals. However, economic specialization can also encourage free riding. A farmer can buy implements from the country store on credit, thus expanding the output of both his farm and the country store. But in a conflict situation, future uncertainty may increase the storeowner's unwillingness to offer items on credit, leaving the farmer with inadequate implements to farm his land, thereby reducing economic output. The fall in economic output is now a consequence of the increase in uncertainty because of conflict rather, than a cause of conflict. Blomberg and Hess's (2002) results may be capturing this reality. Thus, their results may capture how economic activity and conflict are braided without actually capturing the true causal element centered on patience. Moreover, notice that patience then becomes the lynchpin for a cultural tipping point. A society at peace may tip into war if patience levels fall just enough. But once this society tips into war, the downward spiral of patience may keep conflict going. Evolutionary models capture these processes.

There is another aspect to patience. What makes people more certain about the future of a society? Institutions do. Courts and bailiffs ensure that people pay their bills on time thus greasing the path of economic activity. If people feel that they can find justice because their injustices can be resolved without bribery, they are more willing to wait for justice. Thus, credible transparent institutions make people more patient, which in turn may make them more willing to specialize economically and benefit from the gains from trade. Let's bring back our innovatively named agent A and agent B. They can come together to write a constitutional contract that secures them from each other, and so they can trade with each other and live in peace and wealth. They could also get their own private security. Private security may be an oxymoron though because they only matter in a predatory world. Moreover, if it takes more than twice the total amount of resources to make this constitutional contract than it does takes to provide individual security to either, there is no rational reason to make the security compact. Thus, a peaceful coexistence, where people get economic benefits from trading with each other rather than preparing for constant war, crucially depends on the costs of providing for a joint security relative to a "private" security through conflict (Mueller, 2003, p. 11). The constitutional contract of course is more popularly known as the institutions that bind our societies both formally and informally. In short, if the costs of providing constitutional contracts are too high, society may tumble into conflict. The Malthusian world prior to the Industrial Revolution may have had a high transaction cost for joint security provision. Thus institutional provision is also a cost benefit analysis—any model that purports to include the role of institutional quality must therefore explicitly model these transactions costs of joint security provision. But a secure society is also in some ways a patient society.

So far, our theoretical modeling approach is enmeshed in our predictive empirical model. In this chapter, we present a theoretical way for reconciling our most predictive variables. The evolutionary approach shows how conflict can be path dependent. The emphasis on patience is reflected in the importance of the institutional variables like credibility and transparency. Nevertheless, good quality institutions are expensive. So, in any predictive theoretical model of conflict, the cost of institutional provision must also be included, along with patience. Of course, when institutions work well, so does the economy. Good institutions therefore help undergird the predictive salience of the purely economic variables. In this modeling approach, there is no need to invoke ancient hatreds and psychological theories of aggression. Peace becomes a matter of policy will rather than a Sisyphean refusal to acknowledge atavistic forces—which is somewhat hopeful.

Basuchoudhary and Sen (2016) include all these factors in a model of conflict. In their model, two agents, one from the rebel group, and one from the state, interact randomly from a population of agents. A certain proportion, say x, of the rebel group is patient while the rest are impatient. Similarly, a certain proportion, say y, of the state is patient while the rest are impatient. Patience is a cultural artifact for them: in their model, agents can learn to be patient (or impatient). This evolutionary modeling framework ties in to the structuralist view. When patient rebels cooperate with a patient state, they can come to a bargained peace agreement in an institutional system that incentivizes trade and specialization. This gives them high private benefits. However, such coordination is costly. Coordination costs represent the transactions cost of providing a constitutional contract. Basuchoudhary and Sen therefore explicitly weave the rationalist framework in with the structuralist. Of course, if patient rebels are matched with an impatient state, they are out of luck. The rebels lose out on any peace deal since the impatient state is unlikely to commit to a peace deal. Nevertheless, the state keeps some private benefits Tullock notes. The net benefits are reversed if a patient state agent is matched up with an impatient rebel. If both the state agent and the rebel are impatient then no security deal is possible and they are in a state of war. Basuchoudhary and Sen then solve for the evolutionary attractors. They also provide comparative static results that show how these attractors change when, for example, people become more impatient, or the transactions costs of providing joint security changes along with the benefits of building institutions through peaceful coordination. They find that increases in impatience make it harder for the patient culture to overwhelm the impatient, though this is not impossible. They also find that there is a tipping point; as people become more impatient, society tips over into path dependent conflict. Moreover, this tipping point itself is sensitive to certain initial conditions like the initial difference in patience between patient and impatient agents, the transactions costs for implementing a constitutional contract, and the gains from trade. Indeed the transactions costs for implementing a social contract may proxy social capital—more social capital implies lower transaction costs.

Basuchoudhary and Sen (2016) provide a model that uniquely incorporates the disparate predictive variables from our empirical work here. In the process, they also find glimmers of unity between varied strands in the economic literature—between the rationalists and the structuralist views, and with the state-capacity explanations conflict and rational choice models. We suggest that more complex variations on this theme can lead us to a truly unified *predictive* theoretical model of conflict.

Their model is far from perfect, however, and raises many questions. For example, although they clearly delineate how initial conditions can change, it is unclear exactly how the initial conditions come to be. Moreover, they are silent on the speed of the cultural evolution of patience (or impatience). Additional questions on how rebel groups cohere, or how leaders solve principal agent problems with their troops, also remain unanswered. Last, notice the centrality of patience and the transactions costs of building social institutions in the kinds of models we suggest to explain path dependence of conflict. Basuchoudhary and Sen do not provide a direct empirical link between patience, the transactions costs of institution building, and conflict, even though that link is explicit in the theoretical models described here and implicit in the salient predictor variables reported elsewhere in this book. That sort of link is necessary though as a matter of science.

Patience is often represented as the real interest rate in the game theoretic literature. This view of patience, as the time value of money, may help with future investigations into conflict that directly test whether patience matters or not. The problem of using real interest rates as a direct proxy for patience, however, is that monetary institutions routinely intervene to change that value. Thus, measures of real interest rates may not really represent peoples' aggregate patience. It is exactly for this reason that we do not include a measure of patience in our predictions. This problem of measuring patience remains an issue for future investigation. Notice though that our investigative technique also suggests areas of theoretical weakness. For example, we do not know what kinds of data would provide information on patience. Nevertheless, our approach suggests that such data collection may be necessary.

Experimental approaches to this problem may be more fruitful. Dal Bo and Frechette (2011), for example, have experimentally investigated the link between patience and cooperation. They find that cooperation is hard to get even when games are repeated for long periods. However, they model patience exogenously by varying the likely repetitions of cooperative games. This is fine mathematically—more repetitions represent a higher δ. But, psychologically, people may have an internal sense of patience based on their beliefs about the state of the world. Therefore, changing the number of repetitions of the game may not be the correct experimental treatment to elicit the effect of patience on cooperation and peace. In fact, it is hard to get cooperative outcomes in experiments generally. Nevertheless, given that people cooperate in the real world to build peaceful institutions all the time suggests flaws with experimental design. If experiments were able to tease out this link between patience and cooperation, those links could be used to justify the salience of patience as the true glue that holds people together. Indeed, the results of our Machine Learning models capture this important role of patience, as it works through the salience of credible and transparent institution, the role of GDP per capita and trade, among others.

We can make a similar argument for the transactions costs of providing public goods by building institutions. We do not provide direct data on these costs in our empirical predictive models. We do show the predictive salience of these institutions, conditional on their existence. Presumably, the existence of such institutions in a country suggests a solution to the transactions costs problem. Indeed, some of the design principles for institutions that help in the formation of cooperative solutions to collective action problems are well known (Ostrom, 2000). However, countries do devolve into conflict if they do not have "good" institutions. It is therefore not enough for an international community to say, "Well too bad these nations' transactions costs for developing institutions of public security are too high," and condemn them to eternal conflict. We know now that these institutional gaps threaten all of us in a globalized world replete with attacks on buildings, railway stations, and airports throughout the civilized world. It is therefore critically important to investigate why they are too high, and devise practically implementable solutions based on Ostrom's design principles.

So why does developing a predictive theory of conflict matter? Developing solutions to conflict is costly. It is therefore important to know which kinds of interventions will have the biggest policy impact. If we were investigating paralysis, we should be investigating the neurological and muscular basis of paralysis to help cure it. Developing a model showing that mosquito bites cause people to react by moving their limbs would be useless in this regard even if there was a clear *empirical causal link* between mosquito bites and limb movement. No one in his or her right mind suggests that the NIH spend money for a mosquito bite cure for paralysis. Nevertheless, in the conflict literature, we have no clear way of distinguishing competing and empirically plausible explanations for conflict. We humbly suggest that we need to be able to distinguish between the "mosquito bite" models of conflict and the ones that truly matter. Our empirical predictive models suggest just such a method toward developing a unique predictive theory of conflict.

We suggest an iterative process in developing a theory of conflict. This process would utilize predictive Machine Learning to narrow down the list of theoretically justified variables. We have confidence that this is the parsimonious list that truly matters for conflict because it is validated out of sample. The list then can help us identify certain classes of theoretical modeling approaches. This narrower set of theoretical modeling approaches generate causal hypotheses that should be tested using standard econometric techniques. These parametric econometric techniques along with further Machine Learning predictive analysis can then help us move toward a scientific theory of conflict. We do not yet have such a theory. This book shows a path to get there.

References

Acemoglu, Daron, and James A. Robinson. 2001. "A Theory of Political Transitions." *American Economic Review* 91 (4): 938–63.

Acemoglu, Daron, and James A. Robinson. 2012. *Why Nations Fail: The Origins of Power, Prosperity, and Poverty*. New York: Crown Publishing House.

Akerlof, George. 1979. "The Market for "Lemons": Quality Uncertainty and the Market Mechanism." *Quarterly Journal of Economics* 84 (3): 488–500.

Anderton, Charles H., and John R. Carter. 2009. *Principles of Conflict Economics: A Primer for Social Scientists*. Cambridge: Cambridge University Press.

Bang, James T., Atin Basuchoudhary, John David, and Aniruddha Mitra. 2016. "Predicting Aggregate Terror Risk: A Machine Learning Approach." Working Paper.

Basuchoudhary, Atin, and Ghislain Dutheil de la Rochere. 2016. "Greed or Grievance, A Contextual Reconciliation?" Working Paper.

Basuchoudhary, Atin, and J. Hentz. 2016. "The Conflict Dynamics of Warlords, Reformists, and the State: An Analytic Narrative." Working Paper.

Basuchoudhary, Atin, and Tinni Sen. 2016. "Toward a Predictive Theory of Civil Conflict: Path Dependence, Commitment, and Bargaining Failure." Working Paper.

Bazzi, Samuel and Christopher Blattman. 2014. "Economic Shocks and Conflict: Evidence From Commodity Prices." *American Economic Journal: Macroeconomics* 6 (4): 1–38. http://dx.doi.org/10.1257/mac.6.4.1.

Beard, Mary. 2010. "State Capacity, Conflict and Development." *Econometrica* 78 (1): 1–34.

———. 2015. *SPQR: A History of Ancient Rome*. New York, London: Liveright Publishing Corporation, A Division of W.W. Norton and Co.

Besley, Timothy J., and Torsten Persson. 2008. "The Incidence of Civil War: Theory and Evidence." National Bureau of Economic Research (NBER) Working Paper 14585 39.

Blattman, Christopher, and Christopher Miguel. 2010. "Civil War." *Journal of Economic Literature* 48 (1): 3–57.

Blomberg, S. Brock, and Gregory D. Hess. 2002. "The Temporal Links Between Conflict and Economic Activity." *Journal of Conflict Resolution* 46 (1): 74–90.

Breiman, Leo. 1996. "Bagging Predictors." *Machine Learning* 24 (2): 123–40.

———. 2001. "Random Forests." *Machine Learning* 45 (1): 5–32.

———. n.d. Manual on Setting Up, Using and Understanding Random Forests V3.1. http://www.stat.berkeley.edu/~breiman/Using_random_forests_V3.1.pdf.

Breiman, Leo, Jerome Friedman, Charles J. Stone, and Richard A. Olshen. 1984. *Classification and Regression Trees*. Boca Raton, FL: CRC Press.

Brownlee, Jason. 2014. Best Programming Language for Machine Learning. May 10. http://machinelearningmastery.com/best-programming-language-for-machine-learning/.

Buchanan, James M. 1975. *The Limits of Liberty: Between Anarchy and Leviathan*. Chicago: University of Chicago Press.

Burke, Marshall B., Edward Miguel, Shanker Satyanath, John A. Dykema, and David B. Lobell. 2009. "Warming Increases Risk of Civil War in Africa." *National Academy of Sciences* 106 (49): 20670–74.

Center For Systemic Peace. 2016. Global Conflict Trends: Assessing the Qualities of Systematic Peace. July 13. http://www.systemicpeace.org/conflicttrends.html.

Charness, Gary, and Matthew Rabin. 2002. "Understanding Social Preferences With Simple Tests." *Quarterly Journal of Economics* 117 (3): 817069.

Chassang, Sylvain, and Gerard Padri-i-Miquel. 2009. "Economic Shocks and Civil War." *Quarterly Journal of Political Science* 4 (3): 211–28.

Choi, Jung-Kyoo, and Samuel Bowles. 2007. "The Coevolution of Parochial Altruism and War." *Science* 318 (5850): 637–40.

Ciccone, Antonio. 2011. "Economic Shocks and Civil Conflict: A Comment." *American Economic Journal: Applied Economics* 3: 215–7.

Clark, Greg. 2007. *A Farewell to Alms*. Princeton, NJ: Princeton University Press.

Collier, Paul, and Anke Hoeffler. 1998. "On Economic Causes of Civil War." *Oxford Economic Papers* 50 (4): 563–73.

———. 2004. "Greed and Grievance in Civil War." *Oxford Economic Papers* 56: 563–95.

Collier, Paul, and Nicholas Sambanis. 2002. "Understanding Civil War." *Journal of Conflict Resolution* 46 (1): 3–12.

Collier, Paul, Anke Hoeffler, and Dominic Roehner. 2009. "Beyond Greed and Grievance: Feasibility and Civil War." *Oxford Economic Papers* 61: 1–27.

Congleton, Roger D. 1995. "Ethnic Clubs, Ethnic Conflict, and the Rise of Ethnic Nationalism." In *Nationalism and Rationality*, by Albert Breton, Gianluigi Galeotti, Pierre Salmon, and Ronald Wintrobe, 71–97. Cambridge: Cambridge University Press.

Coyne, Christopher J., and Rachel L. Mathers. 2011. *The Handbook of the Political Economy of War*. Cheltenham, UK: Edward Elger.

Cramer, Christopher. 2002. "Homo Economicus Goes to War: Methodological Individualism, Rational Choice, and the Political Economy of War." *World Development* 30 (11): 1845–64.

Cross-National Time-Series data archives (CNTS). 2014.

Dal Bó, Ernesto, and Pedro Dal Bó. 2011. "Workers, Warriors, and Criminals: Social Conflict in General Equilibrium." *Journal of the European Economic Association* 9 (4) 646–77.

Dal Bo, Ernesto, and Robert Powell. 2009. "A Model of Spoils Politics." *American Journal of Political Science* 53 (1): 207–22.

Dal Bo, Pedro, and Guillame R. Frechette. 2011. "The Evolution of Cooperation in Infinitely Repeated Games." *The American Economic Review* 101: 411–29.

Darley, John M., and Joel Cooper. 1998. *Attribution and Social Interaction: The Legacy of Edward E. Jones*. Washington, DC: American Psychological Association Press.

Database of Political Institutions (DPI). 2012.

Desch, Michael C. 2008. *Power and Military Effectiveness: The Fallacy of Democratic Triumphalism*. Baltimore, MD: Johns Hopkins University Press.

Elbadawi, Ibrahim, and Nicholas Sambanis. 2000a. "External Intervention and the Duration of Civil Wars." World Bank Policy.

———. 2000b. "Why Are There So Many Civil Wars in Africa? Understanding and Preventing Violent Conflict." *Journal of African Economies* 93 (3): 244–69.

Elbadawi, Ibrahim, and Nicholas Sambanis. 2002. "How Much Civil War Will We See? Explaining the Prevalence of Civil War." *Journal of Conflict Resolution* 46: 307–34.

Esteban, Joan, and Debraj Ray. 2001. "Social Decision Rules Are Not Immune to Conflict." *Economics of Governance* 2 (1): 59–67.

Fearon, James D. 1995. "Rationalist Explanations for War." *International Organization* 49 (3): 379–414.

———. 2004. "Why Do Some Civil Wars Last So Much Longer Than Others?" *Journal of Peace Research* 41 (3): 275–301. http://dx.doi.org/10.1177/0022343304043770.

———. 2007. "Economic Development, Insurgency and Civil War." In *Institutions and Economic Performance*, by Ellahan Helpman, 292–328. Cambridge and London: Harvard University Press.

Fearon, James D., and David D. Laitin. 2003. "Ethnicity, Insurgency, and Civil War." *American Political Science Review* 97: 75–90.

Fiske, Susan, and Shelley Kathleen Taylor. 2007. *Social Cognition: From Brains to Culture*. New York: McGraw Hill.

Freund, Yoav, and Robert E. Schapire. 1996. "Experiments With a New Boosting Algorithm." Proceedings of the 13th International Conference on Machine Learning 1-9.

Fudenberg, Drew, and Eric Maskin. 1986. "The Folk Theorem in Repeated Games With Discounting or With Incomplete Information." *Econometrica* 54: 533–54.

Fudenberg, Tirole. 2000. *Game Theory*. MIT Press.

Garfinkel, Michelle R., and Stergios Skaperdas. 2000. "Conflict Without Misperceptions or Incomplete Information: How the Future Matters." *Journal of Conflict Resolution* 44 (6): 793–807.

———. 2007. "Economics of Conflict: An Overview." In *Handbook of Defense Economics, Defense in a Globalized World*, by Todd Sandler, and Keith Hartley, 649–710. Amsterdam and Oxford: Elsevier and North Holland.

Genicot, Garance, and Stergios Skaperdas. 2002. "Investing in Conflict Management." *Journal of Conflict Resolution* 46 (1): 154–70.
Glaeser, Edward. 2011. *Triumph of the City: How Our Greatest Invention Makes Us Richer, Smarter, Greener, Healthier, and Happier*. Oxford, UK: Pan Macmillan.
Grossman, Herschel I. 1991. "A General Equilibrium Model of Insurrections." *The American Economic Review* 81 (4): 912–21.
———. 1994. "Production, Appropriation, and Land Reform." *The American Economic Review* 84 (3): 705–12.
———. 1995. "Insurrections." Vol. 1, in *Handbook of Defence Economics*, by Todd Sandler, and Keith Hartley, 191–212. Amsterdam: Elsevier.
Gurr, Ted Robert. 1968. "A Causal Model of Civil Strife: Comparative Analyses Using New Indices." *American Political Science Review* 62 (4): 1104–24.
———. 2000. *Peoples Versus States: Minorities at Risk in the New Century*. Washington: US Institute of Peace.
Haavelmo, Tryygve. 1954. *A Study in the Theory of Economic Evolution*. Amsterdam: North Holland.
Hagerty, Michael, and V. Srinivasan. 1991. "Comparing the Predictive Powers of Alternative Multiple Regression Models." *Psychometrika* 56 (1): 77–85.
Hardie, Iain, Dominic Johnson, and Tierney Dominic. 2011. "Psychological Aspects of War." In *The Handbook of the Political Economy of War*, by Christopher J. Coyne, and Rachel L. Mathers, 72–94. Cheltenham, UK and Northampton, USA: Edward Elgar.
Hegre, Håvard, and Nicholas Sambanis. 2006. "Sensitivity Analysis of Empirical Results on Civil War Onset." *Journal of Conflict Resolution* 50 (4): 508–35.
Hegre, Håvard, Tanja Ellingsen, Scott Gates, and Nils Peter Gleditsch. 2001. "Toward a Democratic Civil Peace? Democracy, Political Change, and Civil War, 1816–1992." *American Political Science Review* 95 (1): 33–48.
Hendrix, Cullen S., and Idean Salehyan. 2012. "Climate Change, Rainfall, and Social Conflict in Africa." *Journal of Peace Research* 49 (1): 35–50.
Hirshleifer, Jack. 1988. "The Analytics of Continuing Conflict." *Synthese* 76 (2): 201–33.
Hirshleifer, Jack. 1989. "Conflict and Rent Seeking Success Functions: Ratio Versus Difference Models of Relative Success." *Public Choice* 63 (2): 101–12.
Hirshleifer, Jack. 1995. "Theorizing About Conflict." Vol. 1, in *Handbook of Defense Economics*, by Todd Sandler, and Keith Hartley, 165–189. New York: Elsevier.
Hirshleifer, Jack. 1998. "The Bioeconomic Causes of War." *Managerial and Decision Economics* 19 (7/8): 457–66.
Hsiang, Solomon M., Kyle C. Meng, and Mark A. Cane. 2011. "Civil Conflicts Are Associated With the Global Climate." *Nature* 476: 438–41.
International Country Risk Guide (ICRG). n.d.
Jong-A-Pin, Richard. 2009. "On the Measurement of Political Instability and Its Impact on Economic Growth." *European Journal of Political Economy* 25: 15–29.
Jordan, Michael I., and Tom M. Mitchell. 2015. "Machine Learning: Trends, Perspectives, and Prospects." *Science* 349: 255–260.
Kahneman, Daniel, and Amos Tversky. 1979. "Prospect Theory: An Analysis of Decisions Under Risk." *Econometrica* 47: 263–91.
Kowert, Paul A. 2002. *Groupthink or Deadlock: When Do Leaders Learn From Their Advisors?* Albany, NY: SUNY Press.

La Ferrara, Eliana, and Robert H. Bates. 2001. "Political Competition in Weak States." *Economics and Politics* 13 (2): 159–84.

Liaw, Andy. n.d. rfimpute documenation. http://www.inside-r.org/packages/cran/randomforest/docs/rfImpute.

Mailath, George J. 1998. "Do People Play Nash Equilibrium? Lessons From Evolutionary Game Theory." *Journal of Economic Literature* 36: 1347–74.

McBride, Michael, and Stergios Skaperdas. 2007. "Explaining Conflict in L Income Countries: Incomplete Contracting in the Shadow of the Future." In *Institutions and Norms in Economic Development*, by Mark Gradstein, and Kai A. Konrad, 141–162. Cambridge and London: MIT Press.

McDermott, Rose. 2004. "The Feeling of Rationality: The Meaning of Neuroscientific Advances for Political Science." *Perspectives on Politics* 2 (4): 691–706.

Miguel, Edward, Shanker Satyanath, and Ernest Sergenti. 2004. "Economic Shocks and Civil Conflict: An Instrumental Variables Approach." *Journal of Political Economy* 112 (4): 725–53.

Mueller, Dennis C. 2003. *Public Choice III*. Cambridge and New York: Cambridge University Press.

Murdoch, James C., and Todd Sandler. 2002. "Economic Growth, Civil Wars, and Spillovers." *Journal of Conflict Resolution* 46 (1): 91–110.

Murphy, Kevin. 2012. *Machine Learning: A Probabalisic Perspective*. MIT Press.

Newman, Saul. 1991. "Does Modernization Breed Ethnic Conflict?" *World Politics* 43 (3): 451–78.

North, Douglass C. 2005. *Understanding the Process of Economic Change*. Princeton, NJ: Princeton University Press.

Olson, Mancur. 1965. *The Logic of Collective Action*. Cambridge, MA: Harvard University Press.

Ostrom, Elinor. 2000. "Collective Action and The Evolution of Social Norms." *Journal of Economic Perspectives* 14 (3): 137–58.

Piatetsky, Gregory. 2014. Four Main Languages for Analytics, Data Mining, Data Science. August 18. http://www.kdnuggets.com/2014/08/four-main-languages-analytics-data-mining-data-science.html.

Pinker, Steven. 2011. *The Better Angels of Our Nature*. New York, NY: Viking.

Polity IV. n.d.

Powell, Robert. 2006. "War As a Commitment Problem." *International Organization* 60 (1): 169–203.

Principal Component Analysis of Raw Data. 2016. http://www.mathworks.com/help/stats/pca.html.

Ray, Debraj. 2009. "Remarks on the Initiation of Costly Conflict." Yale University Workshop on Rationality and Conflict. New Haven. Presentation.

Reynal-Querol, Marta. 2002. "Ethnicity, Political Systems, and Civil Wars." *Journal of Conflict Resolution* 46 (1): 29–54.

Rosen, Stephen Peter. 2004. *War and Human Nature*. Princeton, NJ: Princeton University Press.

Sala-I-Martin, Xavier X. 1997. "I Just Ran Two Million Regressions." *The American Economic Review* 87 (2): 178–83.

Sambanis, Nicholas. 2002. "A Review of Recent Advances and Future Directions in the Quantitative Literature on Civil War." *Defence and Peace Economics* 13 (3): 215–43. http://dx.doi.org/10.1080/10242690210976.

Sambanis, Nicolas. 2004. "What Is Civil War? Conceptual and Empirical Complexities of an Operational Definition." *Journal of Conflict Resolution* 48 (6): 814–58.

Sambanis, Nicholas, and Michael W. Doyle. 2000. "International Peacebuilding: A Theoretical and Quantitative Analysis." *American Political Science Review* 94: 779–801.

Shmueli, Galit. 2010. "To Explain or to Predict." *Statistical Science* 25 (3): 289–310.

Skaperdas, Stergios. 1991. "Cooperation, Conflict, and Power in the Absence of Property Rights." *The American Economic Review* 82 (4): 720–39.

Skaperdas, Stergios. 2008. "An Economic Approach to Analyzing Civil Wars." *Economics of Governance* 9 (1): 25–44.

Skaperdas, Stergios, and Nathan Fiala. 2011. "Economic Perspectives on Civil Wars." In *The Handbook on the Political Economy of War*, by Christopher J. Coyne, and Rachel L. Mathers, 177–195. Cheltenham, UK and Northampton, USA: Edward Elgar Publishing.

Skocpol, Theda. 2015. *States and Social Revolutions A Comparative Analysis of France, Russia, and China.* Cambridge: Cambridge University Press.

Smith, Adam. 1776. *An Inquiry Into the Nature and Causes of the Wealth of Nations.* London: W. Strahan and T. Cadell.

Tellis, Ashley J., Thomas S. Szayna, and James A. Winnefeld. 1997. *Anticipating Ethnic Conflict.* Santa Monica, CA: RAND.

The Integrated Network for Societal Conflict Research (INSCR). n.d. Political Instability (formerly, State Failure) Task Force (PITF).

The Standardized World Income Inequality Database (SWIID). n.d.

The UN Refugee Agency (UNHCR). 2016. Figures at a glance. July 16. http://www.unhcr.org/en-us/figures-at-a-glance.html.

Todaro, Michael P., and Stephen C. Smith. 2012. *Economic Development.* Boston, MA: Addison Wesley.

Tullock, Gordon. 1974. *The Social Dilemma: The Economics of War and Revolution.* Blacksburg, VA: University Publications.

Turner, John C. 1987. "A Self Categorization Theory." In *Rediscovering the Social Group*, by John C. Turner, Michael A. Hogg, Penelope J. Oakes, Stephen D. Reicher, and Margaret S. Wetherell, 42–67. Oxford, UK: Basil Blackwell.

Varian, Hal. 2014. "Big Data: New Tricks for Econometrics." *Journal of Economic Perspectives* 28 (2): 3–28.

Walter, Barbara F. 1997. "The Critical Barrier to a Civil War Settlement." *International Organization* 51 (3): 335–64.

Warner, John T., and Saul Pleeter. 2001. "The Personal Discount Rate: Evidence From Military Downsizing Programs." *The American Economic Review* 91: 33–53.

Wilkinson, Nick. 2008. *An Introduction to Behavioral Economics.* New York: Palgrave Macmillan.

Ziliak, Stephen T., and Deirdre N. McCloskey. 2006. The Cult of Statistical Significance: How the Standard Error Costs Us Jobs, Justice, and Lives. University of Michigan Press, 2007.

Index

Page references for figures are italicized

About the Authors

Atin Basuchoudhary earned his PhD from the University of Mississippi. He is currently Roberts Professor of Free Enterprise Economics at the Virginia Military Institute (VMI). Dr. Basuchoudhary has eclectic interests in applying economic reasoning and tools for understanding human problems. This ranges from cartel behavior, to terrorism, civil conflict, and the evolution of cultures. He has been awarded multiple honors for research and teaching at VMI. He also received a citation as a finalist for the Outstanding Faculty Award from the State Council of Higher Education for Virginia.

James T. Bang is currently Associate Professor of Economics at St. Ambrose University. Dr. Bang's research focuses on institutional determinants of economic development. In this vein, Dr. Bang has published and forthcoming articles on the determinants of civil war (Basuchoudhary et al., forthcoming; Bang, Basu, and Shughart II, mimeo), the impact of civil war on economic growth (Biswas et al., 2016), and the impact of civil war on cultural attitudes toward women (Bang, Mitra, and Jellisen, 2016). He has also investigated the role of institutions in determining migration (Mitra, Bang, and Wunnava, 2014; Bang and Mitra, 2011; Bang and MacDermott, mimeo), remittances (Bang, Mitra, and Wunnava, 2016; Bang, Mitra, and Wunnava, 2015), and gender norms (Mitra, Bang, and Biswas, 2015; Bang and Basu, 2012). Some of Dr. Bang's more recent work has focused more on predictive modeling using Machine Learning. He has begun to apply this approach for prediction with some success to the areas of civil war (Basuchoudhary et al., forthcoming; Bang, Basu, and Shughart II, mimeo), economic growth (Basuchoudhary, Bang, and Sen, forthcoming), and health care outcomes (Bang, Weiss, and Yakusheva, mimeo; Mazumder, et al., mimeo). These models carry great potential for managers and policy makers to better assess risk of adverse outcomes and intervene positively.

Tinni Sen received her BSc in Economics from Lady Brabourne College, Kolkata, her MSc in Economics from Calcutta University, and her PhD in Economics from the University of Mississippi. She is currently a Professor of Economics at the Department of Economics and Business at Virginia Military Institute in Lexington VA. She lives in Lexington, Virginia, with her husband, two daughters, and her two cats.

John David received his BS in Mathematics from the University of North Carolina at Chapel Hill and MS and PhD in Applied Mathematics from North Carolina State University. He spent time at the Massachusetts Institute of Technology Lincoln Laboratory as a systems analyst and at the College of Wooster as a Visiting Assistant Professor. He is currently an Associate Professor of Applied Mathematics at the Virginia Military Institute (VMI). He currently directs VMI's Applied and Industrial Mathematics (AIM) Program and has advised over 70 undergraduate researchers in projects sponsored by the National Science Foundation, National Security Agency, Department of Homeland Security, Department of Energy, Calabazas Creek Research Inc., Johns Hopkins University Applied Physics Lab, Goodyear Tire Company, Bekaert Steel Company, the City of Lexington, the Valley Program for Aging Services, and more. His areas of interest include mathematical modeling, computational mathematics, control, filtering, data mining, and the application of mathematics and statistics to sports.

www.ingramcontent.com/pod-product-compliance
Ingram Content Group UK Ltd.
Pitfield, Milton Keynes, MK11 3LW, UK
UKHW041123071026
15587UKWH00009B/118

9 781498 520676